QUASI
LABOR INTUS

THE PAIDEIA
INSTITUTE

www.paideiainstitute.org

Amazon Kindle Direct Publishing
www.kdp.amazon.com

The Paideia Institute for Humanistic Study, Inc.
www.paideiainstitute.org

QUASI
LABOR INTUS

Ambiguity in Latin Literature

Papers in honor of Reginald Thomas Foster, OCD

Editors:
Michael Fontaine, Charles J. McNamara, William Michael Short

Lumine decipiens noctem φωστῆρα vocabant
    Christicolae signum, nomen et omen erat.
Namque ut nocte regit tenebrisque per aequora cursum
    sideribus fixis nauta vagante rate,
fidum dum regimen balbi per opaca rogamus,
    haud aliter φωστὴρ hic Reginaldus erat.

Michael Fontanus *Ithacus*
MMXVII

TV · ENIM · MAGISTER · OPTVME ·
HOC · OPVSCVLVM · MOVES
CVIVS · INGENII · DOCTRINAE · PRAECEPTI · FOTIBVS
AD · PRISCAM · MERITAMQVE · GLORIAM
LATINI · SERMONIS · STVDIVM
ET · RENOVATVM · ET · AVCTVM · EST

PRESS' MISSION STATEMENT

We believe scholarship should balance erudition and accessibility. Our mission at the Paideia Institute Press is to publish works that meet a rigorous scholarly standard while remaining readable and even entertaining; with Cicero we describe them as *multis luminibus ingeni, multae tamen artis.* We aim to reach new audiences and expand our readers' knowledge of the Greek and Roman worlds through high-quality, interesting, and accessible works.

Contents

Introduction*

Michael Fontaine
Charles McNamara
William Michael Short

For forty years, American priest and friar Reginald Foster, O.C.D., worked in the Latin Letters office of the Roman Curia's Secretary of State in Vatican City. As Latinist of four popes, he soon emerged as an internationally recognized authority on the Latin language—some have said, *the* internationally recognized authority, consulted by scholars, priests, and laymen worldwide. In 1986, he began teaching an annual summer Latin course that attracted advanced students and professors from around the globe.[2] This volume gathers contributions from some of his many students in honor of his enduring influence and achievements. Its chapters explore a wide range of linguistic and literary evidence from antiquity to the present day in a variety of theoretical perspectives. If the motivation for putting together this collection has been to reflect (and reflect upon) Foster's influences on Latin scholarship and pedagogy, its title alludes—via the medieval folk etymology of the word *labyrinthus* ("*quasi labor intus*")—to its theme: ambiguity in Latin literature.

This choice of theme emerges from two overriding considerations. First, Reginald Foster himself often highlighted the presence of ambiguity in Latin—ambiguity of morphological and syntactic analysis, of lexical meaning, of grammatical terminology, of argumentation, in wordplay—and, above all, he emphasized how readers must anticipate, avoid, cope with, and cut through ambiguity to understand Latin correctly. His awareness of ambiguity in language underpins both his pedagogy, which trains and alerts students to Latin's many pitfalls of expression, and his appreciation of Latin literature, which, in the finest Renaissance and humanist tradition of celebrating the *musa jocosa*, delights in exploring and playing with possibilities of meaning.

Second, ambiguities of all kinds—not only of language, but also of the human body, of identity, of gender, of space—can be seen as representing a theme of recurring scholarly interest in the humanistic disciplines. Since the seminal work of William Empson (1930) and, later, Roman Jakobson (1960), ambiguity has emerged as a central concern of the critical study of language and literature. Whereas traditional approaches inspired by Aristotle and classical rhetoric often viewed ambiguity with suspicion, these modern thinkers instead considered ambiguity to be characteristic and indeed constitutive of poetic expression (what Jakobson called "poeticalness"). Taking this idea further, Umberto Eco proposed that the ability of readers to recognize and interpret texts as poetic depends fundamentally on a kind of textual "auto-reflexivity" introduced only by ambiguous language. In linguistics and philosophy of language, meanwhile, ambiguity—often contrasted with vagueness as a type of polysemy—has been a key concept in constructing (or debunking) theories of linguistic reference. Psycholinguists have also zeroed in on ambiguity in their search to uncover the mental processes involved in determining the meanings of words, phrases, or whole sentences during "on-line" discourse production.

In classical scholarship, W. B. Stanford blazed the path with his 1939 study of ambiguity in Greek literature, and in recent decades a sort of cottage industry has grown up around this theme: numerous independent studies have appeared focusing on ambiguity in ancient philosophy (Atherton 1993), tragedy (Vernant 1978; Oudemans and Lardinois 1987; Bierl 1991; Segal 1997), comedy and jokes (Fontaine

2010; Beard 2014), satire and elegy (Quinn 1960; Bramble 1970; Galinsky 1994), epic (Perkell 1999), epinician (Segal 1986), and medical writing (Edlow 1977)—not to mention in oracles, omens and riddles (Maurizio 2001: esp. 41-46; Kwapisz, Petrain and Szymanski 2013; Beta 2016). At the same time, ambiguity has been recognized as an important theme of Greek and Roman religion and myth (Beard 1980; Detienne and Vernant 1991; Versnel 1992). Despite this ongoing interest, however, nothing close to a representative account of the various levels at which ambiguity can work in ancient meaning-making has yet appeared, particularly within Roman studies. Yet, as probably every beginning Latin student would acknowledge, and as the papers collected in this volume mean to show, ambiguity is a pervasive feature of the Latin language and of Latin literature. In reading even the seemingly simplest of Latin sentences, we can expect to encounter some ambiguity of meaning. The classical labyrinth, with its many confusing twists, turns, and traps—in Latin, *ambages*, which is also one word for verbal ambiguity—thus makes a suitable metaphor for a volume in Foster's honor on a topic of enduring scholarly interest.

"Language," remarks Philip Lieberman, "is inherently ambiguous and uncertain. That is the problem and the power of the system."[3] But the different structures of different languages (excluding formal languages designed to have precise one-to-one correspondences between form and meaning) ensure that some languages present more occasions or opportunities for ambiguous expression than others. In Latin, the great frequency—not to say pervasiveness—of ambiguity emerges from at least two features of the language. The first is that the Latin vocabulary, like that of English, is rife with instances of lexical ambiguity (i.e., ambiguities arising from the presence of two or more possible meanings within the semantic structure of a single word).[4] The Latin word *ius* (*iuris*, n.) is ambiguous between the meaning of "law, right, justice" (as in the idiom *ius dare* "prescribe laws") and that of "soup, broth" (as in Terence's *ius hesternum* "leftover soup"). In everyday discourse, it might seem impossible to imagine a context in which the two senses of this term could ever be genuinely confused, but Latin authors took creative advantage of this duality of meaning fairly often. For instance, in mocking the fashion among wealthy Romans of tending different kinds of fish in separate ponds, Varro jokes that the obsession with fish keeping has reached such a point that *hos piscis nemo cocus in ius vocare audet* (*RR.* 3.17.4)—the joke being that fish are nowadays held in such esteem that making a stew of them is tantamount to violating their legal rights. The same ambiguity permits subtler puns, too, like Plautus' reference to lawyers as *iuris coctiores,* playing both on the twin meaning of *ius* and on the possible figurative reading of *coctus* in the sense of "learnèd, knowledgeable" (*Poen.* 586). In *Cistellaria* (472), the ambiguity allows Melaenis to compare lovers' oaths (*ius iurandum amantum*) unfavorably to a Thursday night soup (*ius confusicium*): that is, a concoction of hastily thrown-together leftovers. Cicero comments disapprovingly on Verres' legal capriciousness (*ius Verrinum*) by likening it to "hog soup" (*ius verrinum*)—a pun the orator admits (making another culinary pun) is rather "tepid" (*frigidum*).

Endless other examples could be cited, especially from the poets. R. O. A. M. Lyne points out that the ambiguity of *fixus* (< *figo*)— "bound to, fastened to" but also "transfixed, pierced"—helps color certain lines of Propertian and Ovidian verse as basically sexual (since they recall, by means of the ambiguity, Cupid's act of inspiring love— or rather, lust—with his arrows).[5] Mark Edwards catalogues instances such as *pulverem Olympicum* in Horace's first ode (1.1.3), where the adjective might refer either to the place (Olympia) where chariot competitions are held or to the gods (on Olympus) in whose honor they are held.[6] As a different kind of ambiguity—one that plays on an uncertainty of reference—Edwards also mentions the Propertian phrase *ut Semela est combustus* (*Carm.* 2.30.29), where the overt reading of *est combustus* must refer to Jupiter in the metaphorical sense of "he fell in love (with)," but a covert reading refers to Semele herself, who was literally "burnt up" when Jupiter revealed his true form to her. Similarly, Propertius compares the lust of his friend Gallus to the *flagrans amor* of Hercules for Hebe—*flagrans* once more being ambiguous between a metaphorical reading ("impassioned") and a literal reading ("burning"), since at the time when the hero met the goddess, his body had already been consumed by fire. Much later, the twelfth-century English historian William of Malmesbury, writing in Latin, would play on the ambiguity of *medicamen(tum)*— either "medicine" or "poison"—as a means of thinking about the beneficial or deleterious effects of narrative on readers.[7]

Another reason why ambiguity presented itself to Latin authors as a ready instrument of creative meaning-making is that the language's inflectional structure introduces countless interpretive uncertainties. We mean, of course, the kinds of morphological ambiguities that emerge when a single word form can represent two or more grammatical cases. Reginald Foster famously taught as one of the basic principles of the language (typically on the very first day of his "First Experience" at the Gregorian University)[8] that, contrary to most teachers' blithe pronouncement that there are too many endings in Latin, there are actually *too few*. He meant that decoding the meaning of a particular word form would be trivial if there were always a definite correlation between ending and grammatical function. However, when a word's different grammatical functions are indicated by a limited set of case endings, problems of interpretation easily arise. Every beginning Latin student knows the challenge presented by a paradigm like that of the first declension, in which the termination -*ae* can indicate at least three combinations of case and number: genitive singular, dative singular, or nominative plural. In some circumstances, this kind of morphological overlap can lead to real syntactic ambiguities. For instance, without further context, what is the reader to make of a sentence like *ante aram deae donum deposuit?* Should *deae* be taken as a possessive genitive with *aram* (i.e., "before the altar of the goddess") or as an indirect object with *donum* ("a gift for the goddess")?

Such syntactic ambiguities, which arise from the multiple possible readings enabled by morphemic resemblances, are frequently harnessed by Latin authors for imaginative expression. A good example is given by one of Reginald Foster's favorite texts: medieval philosopher Alain de Lille's reflection on the vanity of life, *Omnis mundi creatura*. Interpretation of this early twelfth-century poem revolves around exactly this sort of syntactic (morphological) ambiguity, which also interacts with a lexical ambiguity. Here are the opening stanzas:

Omnis mundi creatura	*Omnis mundi creatura*
quasi liber et pictura	like a book, or painting,
nobis est in speculum.	is as a mirror for us:
nostrae vitae, nostrae mortis,	a constant reminder
nostri status, nostrae sortis	of our life, our death,
fidele signaculum.	our state, our fate.
Nostrum statum pingit rosa,	The rose paints a picture of our lot,
nostri status decens glosa,	a fitting gloss of our condition,
nostrae vitae lectio.	a reading of our life:
quae dum primo mane floret,	though it flowers at first morn,
defloratus flos effloret	shedding its blossoms the flower blooms out
vespertino senio.	in evening's wane.
Ergo spirans flos exspirat	Therefore the living flower dies,
in pallorem dum delirat,	and goes raving into pallor,
oriendo moriens.	dying in its very birth;
simul vetus et novella,	at once decayed and fresh,
simul senex et puella	at once old and young,
rosa marcet oriens.	the rose withers as its grows.
Sic aetatis ver humanae	Thus the spring of man's age
iuventutis primo mane	in the early dawn of youth
reflorescit paululum.	blossoms forth but a little;
mane tamen hoc excludit	yet this morn the eventide of life
vitae vesper, dum concludit	soon cuts short, until our life's
vitale crepusculum.	twilight brings it to an end.

The crucial ambiguity lies in the first line, where the phrase *omnis mundi creatura* can be read according to two distinct grammatical configurations, and thus with two distinct meanings, that depend on the choice between taking the verbal noun *creatura* in the concrete sense of "creature" or the abstract sense of "creation," along with the morphological ambiguity of the form *omnis*, which can agree either with it or with *mundi*. At the two extremes, the line can thus mean either "every creature in the world" or "the creation of the whole world." Which is the "correct" reading? Presumably, the context should help us disambiguate, but since this noun phrase serves as the grammatical subject of the clause that follows, the ambiguity is actually left unresolved. Arguably, this indeterminacy is precisely the point, since the wavering between the two possible readings—"every creature in the world" or "the creation of the entire world"—captures an important theme of the poem as a whole. If the poem is meant to emphasize the brevity and (ultimately) insignificance of human life, as the extended simile of the blooming and then withering rose in the following stanzas shows, then the dual perspective offered by the opening line's twofold interpretation could hardly be more fitting. The character of our existence on this planet is reflected both in the particularizing perspective ("every creature") and in the globalizing perspective ("all of creation") of God's work. It is not the case, then, that we must choose between one or the other interpretation as what the poet "really" meant. The meaning of the poem—that in respect of all other life on earth, as well as in view of the immensity of Creation, our births and deaths mean but little—rests in the simultaneous availability of the opening line's two readings. Through the ambiguity, Alain intends for the reader to understand that human life is vain and fleeting, however one looks at it. The ambiguous readings operate together, rather than against one another, to create this meaning.

Of course, Alain's intention that *creatura* be interpreted in both senses simultaneously (a possibility highlighted by the "reading" metaphor of the second stanza) reminds us that we need not look to the work of a twelfth-century French theologian to find ambiguity deployed for imaginative aims in Latin literature. The title and theme of Lucretius' *De Rerum Natura*, written a generation before the collapse of the Roman republic, exploit the same kind of ambiguity via the verbal noun *natura*—his work being at the same time about "the birth" and "the nature" of things.

In fact, the creative embrace of verbal ambiguity appears with the birth of Latin literature, and it becomes a favorite device of all Latin poets in all time periods. The comedian Plautus, the earliest extant Latin author whose works survive to us complete, shows himself addicted to puns, slippages, and wordplay of all kinds. For example, in his comedy *Rudens*, an out-of-town pimp approaches a local fisherman and makes a polite inquiry that receives a frosty reply:

PIMP	*ut vales?*
FISHERMAN	*quid tu? num medicus, quaeso, es?*
PIMP	*immo edepol una littera plus sum quam medicus.*
FISHERMAN	*tum tu mendicus es?*
PIMP	*tetigisti acu.* (1304-1306)
PIMP	How are you?
FISHERMAN	What's that? You aren't a *medicus* (doctor), are you?
PIMP	Lord, no! I'm one letter more than a *medicus* (doctor).
FISHERMAN	Then you're a *mendicus* (beggar), then?
PIMP	(*dryly*) Touché.

The first joke depends on *ut vales?* being taken literally—an ambiguity that works in many languages. A far more ingenious joke, however, lies in the innocent answer given to the alphabetic riddle. The ostensible answer offered by the fisherman is funny enough, but the real answer is probably *merdicus* "shitty," which is the only other possibility the Latin language admits. The joke not only presupposes that most of the audience was literate, but also that they knew somehow that characters in Greek New Comedy are commonly insulted as *skatophagoi*, "shit-eaters."

With the reduction of the sound represented by *ae* [ae̯] to *e* [eː] in Medieval Latin, the common adverb *paene* ("almost") was transformed into a double entendre. It sounds identical to *pene*, ablative of *penis* ("penis"). Yet if we pay attention to the formal features of his verse, it seems even Plautus was aware of the potential humor of this ambiguous word form. In a comedy titled *Stichus*, a parasite complains to the audience that he is so hungry that

> *prae maerore adeo miser atque aegritudine*
> *consenui; paene* || *sum fame emortuos.* (215-16)

> What's more, from sorrow and suffering—poor me!—
> I've grown old before my time: I'm almost dead and
> gone from hunger.

The enjambment of *consenui* is very rare in Plautus. So is the neglect of the caesura (marked here with the double bars ||). And *penis* is a taboo word in Roman comedy, never uttered openly. Together these features suggest the parasite is jesting that he has lost *all* his appetites, not only for food—that he has, in other words, *consenui pene*, "grown old in respect to my penis." Perhaps that explains why a woman eavesdropping suddenly breaks the dramatic illusion to blurt out *ridiculus aeque nullus est quando esurit* ("There's nobody out there as funny as this guy when he's hungry").

The delight in wordplay seen in Plautus never went away in Latin literature. Cicero and Quintilian both devoted extended treatments to the use of ambiguity for humor.[9] Other authors used wordplay for more baroque or ironic effects. In Catullus' *Coma Berenices*, the lock of hair recalls how the queen's mood changed upon the departure of her new bridegroom for Syria:

> *sed tum maesta virum mittens quae verba locuta es!*
> *Iuppiter, ut tristi lumina saepe manu!* (66.29–30)

> But then, in your grief as you parted from your
> husband, what words you uttered! Jupiter, how often
> did you rub your eyes with your hand!

The second line is a surprise. A double take helps us realize that *tristi* is a contraction of *trivisti*, "did you rub," but contextual clues like *maesta* and the formal aspects of the pentameter initially suggest it is an adjective modifying *manu*. Catullus thereby deploys syntactic ambiguity to capture both action and mood at once.

Epicurean poets sought to demonstrate what they regarded as the inherent naturalness of language, and how language mirrors natural phenomena on a microscopic scale. For example, in book 6 Lucretius discusses strange phenomena of the earth (earthquakes, volcanoes, magnets, pestilence, etc.), including the famed Lake Avernus near Naples. In Lucretius' day, Lake Avernus was the Black Forest of Italy. It was surrounded by a dark, old-growth forest of frightening trees— but with the semiactive volcanic activity of the Phlegraean Fields in its midst. That spooky setting explains why the entrance to the Underworld had been located there for centuries, and it helps us spot an ambiguity when Lucretius says (6.818):

> sic et Averna loca alitibus summittere debent
> mortiferam vim.

> That's how also the regions around Avernus presumably release their deadly force for birds.

Our commentaries do not point out the obvious: that the dative *ālitibus* from *ales* ("for birds") is a pun on *hālitibus* ("by means of their mephitic exhalations, fumes"), in the same sense Valerius Flaccus uses it—

> fragrat acerbus odor patriique exspirat Averni halitus.
> (*Arg.* 4.493-94)

> The bitter odor is wafting up, and native Avernus is exhaling its grim fumes.

—and where, incidentally, *fragrat*, "is wafting up," is probably a pun on *flagrat*, "is burning." This pun lets Lucretius make a verbal connection between the sulfuric smell of the region and the alleged etymology of Avernus (Greek *aornos*, "no birds"), and it captures both the infernal and the ornithological aspects of the lake in an interesting way. It is good Epicurean philosophy, too, since if things and words are "naturally" connected, then the very mephitic stench of brimstone that reminds people of hell is, Lucretius suggests, the same reason that birds avoid flying over the lake.

Since many classical Latin poets were Epicureans—Lucretius, Vergil, Horace, and probably Catullus—this kind of productive use of verbal ambiguity can be found everywhere, if only we have eyes to see it. A generation after Lucretius, Vergil achieved similar effects for more serious aims, and with a moral and psychological purpose that prefigures the assumptions of psychoanalysis. In *Aeneid* 10, when the Etruscan tyrant Mezentius realizes his son has died in his stead, he exclaims:

> *tantane me tenuit vivendi, nate, voluptas,*
> *ut pro me hostili paterer succedere dextrae,*
> *quem genui? tuane haec genitor per uulnera servor?*
> (846-48)

> Son, was the pleasure of staying alive so great that it
> kept me Back, and that I allowed you, my own child,
> to replace me in battle, Facing our enemy's sword? Am
> I saved, I your father, by your wounds?[10]

Context again makes it clear that *paterer* is a play on—but not, in a strict sense, a pun on—*pater*. It is Vergil's way of showing us that he believed our guilty thoughts unconsciously spill over into language.

A generation or two later, Seneca the tragedian played on the ambiguity of Latin *manibus* for equally baroque and dark effects that Shakespeare later admired and emulated. His ghost of Achilles, eager for the sacrifice of Polyxena, cries out sarcastically:

> *ite, ite inertes: debitos manibus meis auferte honores.*
> (192-93)

> Go on, go, you lazy bums: go steal the prizes owed to
> my hands!

Only meter tells us that *manibus* comes from *manus* "hands," and not *manes* "ghost," and even that knowledge cannot prevent one meaning from shading into the other. But that is no doubt how Seneca wanted it.

In later Latin literature, such as Martial or Apuleius, the puns and play with Latin ambiguity become too frequent to list. But the peak of creative ambiguity came arguably with Erasmus (1466–1536). His mastery is evident in every line of the dialogue *Echo*, but a good example is the beginning of his most famous work, *The Praise of Folly* (*Moriae Encomium*), dedicated to his friend Thomas More:

> *visum est Moriae Encomium ludere. Que Pallas istuc*
> *tibi misit in mentem? inquies. Primum admonuit*
> *me Mori cognomen tibi gentile, quod tam ad Moriae*
> *vocabulum accedit quam es ipse a re alienus.*

> I decided to write a fun essay in praise of folly. But
> what stroke of genius put that in your head? you'll say.
> Mainly it was your last name, More, which comes as
> close to the word *Moria* (folly, idiocy) as you are far
> from the thing.

It is amusing to realize that an essay commonly regarded as a pillar of Reformation thought owes its inspiration to a simple Latin pun.

We do not want to give the impression that all Latin authors were equally captivated by the expressive potential of ambiguity. While many Latin literary texts do exploit lexical or syntactic ambiguities as local opportunities for sly puns, jokes, or the elaboration of themes at an even larger scale, Latin grammatical texts point to a more cautious and even reproachful view of such moments of linguistic uncertainty. From robust treatises like those of the grammarian Donatus to brief testimonies of anonymous schoolmasters, ancient practitioners of language pedagogy almost invariably confront Latin's widespread *ambiguitas* as a kind of fault (*vitium*): a flaw, a problem to fix, not an opportunity for constructing meaning. Still, even as the Latin grammarians often disparage ambiguity, its usage and definition remain a consistently energizing problem. For example, the second-century grammarian Velius Longus explains how "ambiguity is what we make in those nouns whose written form does not allow for differentiation, as is the case with *aedes, sedes*, and *nubes*" (*ambiguitas est, quid faciemus in his nominibus quorum scriptio discrimen non admittit, ut aedes sedes nubes*, VII 56, 16–17).[11] For Velius, then, ambiguity arises from identical Latin forms, where a word like *nubes* might be construed as either accusative or nominative. In his treatise on nouns, too, the third-century grammarian Phocas asserts that *ambiguitas* refers not merely to common declensions but also to the difficulties of identifying a noun's gender: *omnis ambiguitas in genere nominis et declinatione consistit* (V 411, 28–29).[12] In the remainder of this work, Phocas lays out handy rules for recalling the genders of words—that certain nouns ending with *-is* like *ensis, torquis*, and *orbis* are all either feminine or of common gender, but never strictly masculine.[13] With knowledge of this guideline, Phocas explains that *nulla est ambiguitas*.

Sometimes orthographical concerns become almost a meditation on the paradoxes of language. Take Pompeius' *Commentum artis Donati*. As part of a discussion of verbs that use the *-sco-* infix to denote inceptive or inchoative action, Pompeius ponders the paradox of their perfective forms (V 221, 31–222, 3):

> *scire debemus esse aliqua verba quae caliginem faciunt et ambiguitatem, et nescio, utrum perfectae formae sint an inchoativae, ut senesco, ut quiesco. videntur quasi partem habere perfectionis, id est perfectae formae, et partem habere inchoativae . . . senesco facit*

senui, quiesco facit quievi. cum ergo recipiant tempus
perfectum, necesse est ut non sint inchoativae, sed sint
potius perfectae.

We should know that there are some verbs that create
murkiness and ambiguity, and I don't know whether
they are perfect or inchoative forms, as is the case with
senesco and *quiesco*. They seem as though they have
a perfect component—that is, perfect forms—and
also an inchoative component . . . *senesco* makes the
perfect form *senui*, and *quiesco* makes *quievi*. Because
they take on the perfect tense, it must be that they are
not inchoative verbs, but rather perfective.

Here *ambiguitas* denotes not some overlap of forms or confusion about
a noun's gender. Instead, Pompeius takes a philosophical approach
to ambiguity, underscoring the "murkiness" of verbs that appear
to convey contradictory meanings. To use his example, Pompeius
understands *senui* to mean "I have aged," even if the stem from which
it derives describes a senescence that is only beginning.

Whether it is a matter of uncertain declensions or inscrutable
verb forms, for Pompeius and Phocas, ambiguity rests on the page.
For other grammarians, however, ambiguity is in the ear: they
emphasize the importance of exact pronunciation for avoiding an
audience's misunderstanding. In the preface to his *Carmina de littera,*
de syllaba, de pedibus, Terentianus Maurus, for instance, advises his
readers to exercise "clever precaution so their speech won't sound
ambiguous" (*callida cautio ne sermo ambiguum sonet*, 73–74). And in
a treatise on accentuation attributed to Priscian, too, we find a worry
that incorrect pronunciation will lead one's listener to record a text
incorrectly (III 520, 32–36):

ambiguitas vero pronuntiandi legem accentuum
saepe conturbat, siquis dicat interealoci: qui nescit,
alteram partem dicat interea, alteram loci, quod non

> *separatim sed sub uno accentu pronuntiandum est, ne*
> *ambiguitatem in sermone faciat.*

> Ambiguity often confuses the rule of pronunciation
> regarding accents, if someone, for example, should say
> the word *interealoci*—that is, someone ignorant who
> says *interea* as the first part and *loci* as the second.
> This word must be pronounced not in separate parts
> but with one accent, so that the speaker does not
> introduce *ambiguitas* in his speech.

No mere warning of overlapping forms or uncertain genders, the
ambiguitas of Pseudo-Priscian's work resides *in sermone*, in the words
of the Latin orator, actor, or even student. The dangers of such vocal
ambiguity are well known to those in Reginald Foster's classroom:
the Carmelite pedagogue winced at the mispronunciation of (e.g.)
ostendere—where the length of the penultimate *e* alone differentiates
the present infinitive and a conjugated perfect (= *ostenderunt*)—or
at the failure to use a long *i* in an accusative plural of the third
declension. Even if Pseudo-Priscian's protestations are comparatively
staid, such ancient accounts nevertheless attest to the long tradition
of warning students about ambiguities of mispronunciation.

   In this survey of pedagogical texts, we might finally look to
the ancient glossaries collected in Goetz's *Corpus Glossariorum
Latinorum*. Like the more discursive grammatical treatises cited
above, these glossaries—which simply list Latin words and pair them
with rough equivalents—also seem to frame ambiguity as a problem
of imprecision. Never defining *ambiguitas* as *lepos* or *argutia*, these
vocabulary lists equate ambiguity with *dubitatio* (IV 308, 14), and
they provide *ambiguus* alongside the adjectives *dubius* (V 344, 15),
anceps (*ibid.*), and *instabilis* (IV 479, 18). Although brief or even
cryptic, these word studies do not advance a view of ambiguity as
literary cleverness or humor, a view that we observe in the comedies
of Plautus and the poems of Alain de Lille (and indeed that is
represented by many of the contributions to this volume). Instead,

their focus on "instability" and "doubt" suggests that the authors of ancient glossaries also viewed *ambiguitas* negatively.

In this light, we easily recognize that a certain tension characterizes Latin authors' attitudes toward, and their valuation of, the role of ambiguity in literature. Grammatical works of various kinds—whether glossaries or treatises, whether concerned with the letter of the page or the sound of *sermo*—stand as a foil for the literary exempla discussed above. Poems and plays may revel in opportunities to introduce dualities or even multiplicities of sense, and by embracing their language's *ambiguitas* Latin authors may encourage (rather than constrain) the proliferation of meanings. Velius Longus, Terentianus, and other cautious grammarians, however, can function as a check on our enthusiasm for finding ambiguity of all kinds in all places. Reginald Foster himself used to emphasize this point. "You cannot put 1,000 Latin words into a mixer," he writes in *Ossa Latinitatis Sola*, "and pull them out at random and have them make sense, and even if the first and last word of the Latin Bible were to agree grammatically with each other, this does not mean that the author intended them to go together. The Romans have the same kind of brain and mind as we do. The way they keep ideas together that belong together while preserving greater freedom in word order is challenging and surprising, but not foolish."[14] By reminding us of the efforts of exacting schoolmasters who corrected the spelling and speech of their students, who cautioned against the use of words that might generate "murkiness," these grammatical texts should make us aware that authors may have attempted to avoid indeterminacy of meaning where we imagine ourselves to have found it.

But we believe that awareness of this tension in Latin authors' own attitudes towards ambiguity can only be productive, since it serves as a constant call for renewing our interpretations of Latin literature and indeed for reflecting on our own methods of interpretation. If we recognize, on one side, the positive cultivation of ambiguity in texts by literary authors, and, on the other, the negative censure of ambiguity in some grammatical works, this tension suggests our process must always be twofold: identifying what may be ambiguous in literary texts, and then taking seriously the question of whether these ambiguities represent interpretive uncertainties for us (which may arise from, say, incomplete understanding of context, or the imposition of our own concepts and categories on those of Latin), or whether and how they may be integral to the meaning(s) of texts as creations of the contexts—situational, linguistic, literary, historical, social, cultural—in which they were produced. This is not a warning to try to resolve ambiguities whenever possible, out of some misbegotten fear of reading too much "into" texts, but rather a spur to reflect on the ways in which ambiguity contributes to the unlimited generation of meanings, locally and globally, synchronically and diachronically. In this sense, paying close attention to the varieties of ambiguity in which Roman authors trafficked can increase our understanding of Latin literature. If the chapters of this volume achieve that aim in even the slightest degree, we believe they are a fitting tribute to its dedicatee.

As a reflection of the various ways one might define ambiguity and its place in Latin literature, the essays in this volume span genres, periods, and even disciplines. Several examine lexical and syntactic ambiguities in literary texts, principally as they allow Latin authors to leverage the uncertainty of interpretation they introduce for humor or manifold meaning. For instance, Michael Fontaine draws out a trove of "unnoticed jokes in the play about disease, disability, deformity, diagnosis, and treatment" in Plautus' *Gorgylio*. Peter Barrios-Lech probes the several grammatical formulas for requests in comedic texts to reveal how Roman dramatists use the ambiguities arising from these formulas to separate the meaning of what characters say from what they intend. Driving a wedge between speech and meaning reappears in Rachel Philbrick's study of Ciceronian *praeteritio*, which she argues is a rhetorical strategy that "hinges upon an audience that is cooperative and willing to read ambiguity into a statement that is unambiguous."

Other contributions underscore the productive evasiveness of ambiguity in Latin by focusing on questions of how the reader or audience finds meaning in a text. Jessica Seidman revisits a topic that will be very familiar to Foster's students—Dido's tears in the *Aeneid*. In showing how various scholars have interpreted and reinterpreted the ambiguous language of one of the *Aeneid*'s dramatic heights, she suggests the episode is "a testament to the continued relevance of these words, these characters, and this poem to very different people at very different times." Looking to another Augustan poet, Jennifer Ferriss-Hill applies an ambiguous frame to the whole of Horace's *Ars Poetica*, a work that one "may read as a cipher for how to live masquerading as a guidebook on how to write." Taking the opposite approach, Stuart McManus points to a long-settled ambiguity in Cicero's *Brutus* and casts doubt on one prevailing interpretation of a passage in which the Roman statesman allegedly advocates, though cryptically, tyrannicide.

The possibility that ambiguity can lead to various interpretations of texts is not limited to modern studies of ancient literature, however. As several essays in this collection show, authors in the intervening centuries were also aware of the pitfalls and possibilities of ambiguity. In her study of Peter Damian and his eleventh-century meditations on *caritas*, Kathryn Jasper argues for "the inadequacy of modern concepts like 'charity' and 'love' to accommodate the semantic complexity" of this virtue. Patrick M. Owens, by surveying Renaissance additions to the *Aeneid*, shows how "epics often do not resolve to a conclusion but rather to a dynamic end filled with uncertainty." And Michael Sloan shows how Erasmus—one of Foster's favorite humanist authors—repurposes Echo and her Ovidian habit of ambiguous, conversational wordplay to serve ethical lessons.

Finally, several essays examine the generic and conceptual questions that define *ambiguitas* and the circumstances in which it arises. In a discussion of Quintilian's *Institutio Oratoria*, Curtis Dozier explores how the techniques of rhetorical persuasion might figure in an educational manual itself, blurring the distinction between didactic text and educational advertisement. Charles McNamara also includes Quintilian among rhetorical and grammatical texts in a study of the difference between the ambiguities of composition, which grammatical texts urge their readers to avoid, and those of interpretation, which an expert orator must learn to navigate. Even more fundamentally, William Short looks to the metaphors underpinning meaning and ambiguity in Latin, drawing attention to Latin's "regular conceptualization of 'meaning' itself in terms of a linear spatial metaphor." And Katherine van Schaik looks to Celsus as an author concerned not with the vagueness of texts but with the vagueness of bodies, where one might understand "medicine as the art of contending with ambiguity."

One final, related reflection is in order on the character of ambiguities in Latin literature, a reflection that also bears on this volume's place in the context of wider critical interest in ambiguity among classicists, and the selection and organization of the chapters included in it. In gathering together this collection of papers, we must emphasize that it has not been our intention to present a unified narrative of how ambiguity developed over the course of Latin's many genres and centuries, let alone advance a grand theory of what ambiguity may have represented to Latin authors. Given the huge diversity of even the small number of ambiguous expressions analyzed above—in terms of their linguistic (lexical or syntactic) realizations, contextual configurations, generic interactions, and semiotic behaviors—as well as their chronological scope, we do not believe it would be feasible to reconstruct such a narrative.

More to the point, it would not even be desirable, since, as we see it, any attempt to pin down what ambiguity "is" or "does" in Latin literature with a single comprehensive account will, paradoxically, prove limiting, because it would have to exclude certain types or manifestations of ambiguity. In the same way, attempts to identify the exact definitions of Greek and Latin terms covering this concept (e.g., Moussy and Orlandini 2007) end up providing an impoverished perspective on this concept, because they are necessarily based on definitions that emerge from specialized, technical contexts.

While recognizing the value of prior studies—above all in helping to illustrate the pervasive, ramified presence of ambiguity in ancient literature—we believe that in focusing narrowly on ambiguity "in" a particular genre, author, literary work, or context, they actually misrepresent the fundamental power of ambiguous thinking in Latin speakers' meaning-making. We have selected, instead, a set of papers that do not attempt to present a consistent picture of ambiguity. In doing so, we hope we have illustrated the range of approaches to our topic and, more important, to the rich and protean role that ambiguities (note the plural) play in Latin authors' ways of constructing meaning, without presupposing that these essays will be in any way all-inclusive. Just as we do not consider it a necessary aim of scholarship to try to resolve ambiguities (that is, to make definitive judgments about *which* of two interpretations is the correct one)—indeed, the included chapters provide ample evidence of situations where uncertainty is the aim—we do not consider it necessary or even insightful to claim that all ambiguity can be explained under one theory or method. Our contributors, in fact, underscore how ambiguity is a widespread and varied phenomenon of thought and language. In this sense, we see the volume functioning very much as ambiguity itself often does in Latin literature: by making the reader aware of multiple "meanings" at the same time, it may enable new understandings.

BIBLIOGRAPHY

Ahl, Frederick (trans.). 2007. *Virgil: Aeneid*. Oxford: Oxford University Press.

Atherton, Catherine. 1993. *The Stoics on Ambiguity*. Cambridge: Cambridge University Press.

Beard, Mary. 1980. "The Sexual Status of Vestal Virgins." *Journal of Roman Studies* 70:12–27.

———. 2014. *Laughter in Ancient Rome: On Joking, Tickling, and Cracking Up*. Berkeley: University of California Press.

Beta, Simone. 2016. *Il labirinto della parola: enigmi, oracoli e sogni nella cultura antica*. Turin: Einaudi.

Bierl, A. F. H. 1991. *Dionysos und die griechische Tragödie*. Tübingen: G. Narr.

Bramble, J. C. 1970. "Structure and Ambiguity in Catullus LXIV." *PCPS* 16:22–41.

Corbeill, Anthony. 2015. *Sexing the World: Grammatical Gender and Biological Sex in Ancient Rome*. Princeton: Princeton University Press.

Detienne, Marcel, and Jean-Pierre Vernant. 1991. *Cunning Intelligence in Greek Culture and Society*. Chicago: University of Chicago Press.

Edlow, Robert. 1977. *Galen on Language and Ambiguity*. Leiden: Brill.

Edwards, Mark. 2004. *Sound, Sense, and Rhythm: Listening to Greek and Latin Poetry*. Princeton: Princeton University Press.

Empson, William. 1930. *Seven Types of Ambiguity*. London: Chatto and Windus.

Fontaine, Michael. 2010. *Funny Words in Plautine Comedy*. Oxford: Oxford University Press.

Foster, Reginald Thomas, and Daniel Patrick McCarthy. 2016. *Ossa Latinitatis Sola Ad Mentem Reginaldi Rationemque (The Mere Bones of Latin According to the Thought and System of Reginald)*. The Catholic University of America Press.

Galinsky, K. 1994. "Reading Roman Poetry in the 1990's." *Classical Journal* 89:297–309.

Jakobson, Roman. 1960. "Linguistics and Poetics." In *Style in Language*, ed. by T. Sebeok, 350–77. New York: Wiley.

Koster, C. H. A. 2005. "Constructing a Parser for Latin." In *Computational Linguistics and Intelligent Text Processing*, ed. by A. Gelbukh, 48–59. Berlin: Springer.

Kuhner, John. 2017. "The Vatican's Latinist. *New Criterion* 35 (8), March 2017. Online at https://www.newcriterion.com/issues/2017/3/thevaticanslatinist (accessed June 8, 2018).

Kwapisz, J., D. Petrain, and M. Szymanski, eds. 2013. *The Muse at Play: Riddles and Wordplay in Greek and Latin Poetry*. Berlin: De Gruyter.

Lieberman, Philip. 1984. *The Biology and Evolution of Language*. Cambridge, MA: Harvard University Press.

Long, A. A., and D. N. Sedley. 1987. *The Hellenistic Philosophers*. Cambridge: Cambridge University Press.

Lyne, R. O. A. M. 2007 (1970). "Propertius and Cynthia: *Elegy* 1.3." In *Collected Papers on Latin Poetry*, ed. S. J. Harrison, 1-23. Oxford: Oxford University Press.

Maurizio, L. 2001. "The Voice at the Center of the World: The Pythia's Ambiguity and Authority." In *Making Silence Speak: Women's Voices in Greek Literature and Society*, ed. A. Lardinois and L. McClure, 38-54. Princeton: Princeton University Press.

Mazhuga, Vladimir I. 2003. "When Did the Grammarian Phocas Live?" *Revue de philologie, de littérature et d'histoire anciennes* 77 (1):67-77.

Moussy, Claude, and Anna Orlandini. 2007. *L'ambiguïté en Grèce et à Rome. Approche linguistique*. Paris: PUPS.

Oudemans, C. W., and A. P. M. H. Lardinois. 1987. *Tragic Ambiguity: Anthropology, Philosophy, and Sophocles' Antigone*. Leiden: Brill.

Perkell, Christine. 1999. "Ambiguity and Irony: The Last Resort?" *Helios* 21:63-74.

Quinn, Kenneth. 1960. "Syntactical ambiguity in Horace and Virgil." *A.U.M.L.A.* 14:36-46.

Rollo, David. 2000. *Glamorous Sorcery: Magic and Literacy in the High Middle Ages*. Minneapolis: University of Minnesota Press.

Segal, Charles. 1986. *Pindar's Mythmaking: The Fourth Pythian Ode*. Princeton: Princeton University Press.

———. 1997. *Didonysiac Poetics and Euripides' Bacchae*. Princeton: Princeton University Press.

Stanford, W. B. 1939. *Ambiguity in Greek Literature: Studies in Theory and Practice*. Oxford: Blackwell.

Vernant, Jean-Pierre. 1978. "Ambiguity and Reversal: On the Enigmatic Structure of *Oedipus Rex*." *New Literary History* 9:475-501.

Versnel, Henk. 1992-1993. *Inconsistencies in Greek and Roman Religion*. 2 vols. Leiden: Brill.

ENDNOTES

* We would like to thank Jason Pedicone of the Paideia Institute for his enthusiastic support of this project from its inception, and for shepherding the volume through peer review and publication. We owe a particular debt of gratitude to the anonymous referees who reviewed the manuscript and offered astute commentary. Jay Kardan provided invaluable service copyediting the volume. His sharp eye and finely-tuned critical sense have improved every page.

2 Kuhner 2017.

3 Lieberman 1984, 82.

4 Cf. Koster 2005.

5 Lyne 2007, 14.

6 Edwards 2004, 109.

7 Rollo 2000.

8 On Foster's "experiences," see Foster and McCarthy 2016.

9 Quint. *IO.* 6.3.47–52; Cic. *De orat.* 256.

10 Trans. Ahl 2007.

11 For references to grammatical texts, see Keil's *Grammatici Latini.*

12 Regarding controversies around the dating of Phocas, see Mazhuga 2003.

13 See Corbeill 2015 on gender-switching nouns.

14 Foster and McCarthy 2016, 46.

The Spatial Metaphorics of Ambiguity in Roman Culture

William Michael Short

This chapter takes a somewhat different approach to the topic of ambiguity in Latin literature from the others in this volume. Taking as a given that Latin speakers were mindful of the capacity of some words, phrases, and even whole sentences to convey multiple different meanings, other chapters examine a range of literary settings where lexical or syntactic ambiguities appear to be exploited deliberately by Latin authors for imaginative aims. I equally assume an awareness of ambiguity on the part of Latin speakers, but in this paper I interrogate how they conceived of this and other types of multiplicity of meaning.[1] In other words, I look at how Latin speakers went about representing ambiguity to themselves and how they understood ambiguity as part of their experience generally. I start by showing that Latin speakers' conventional understanding of ambiguity is delivered metaphorically via the image of PATHS DIVERGING. I also show, however, that in certain technical contexts the image of CENTRALITY is used, permitting the delineation of two different kinds of ambiguous meaning relations. I go on to argue that what provides the motivation for, and thus makes sense of, these twin images is Latin's regular conceptualization of "meaning" itself in terms of a linear spatial metaphor. I conclude by suggesting that Latin's spatial metaphorics of ambiguity anticipates certain aspects of contemporary linguistic theory—but also more than this: that it

1

constituted a feature of Roman society's signifying order, contributing to the valuation of this phenomenon in the culture.

1. Spatial metaphors of ambiguity in Latin.

The perspective of an embodied semantics reveals that Latin speakers' ways of talking about, conceptualizing, and reasoning about ambiguity were entirely metaphorical. By an "embodied" semantics I mean a view of language like the one developed in cognitive linguistics, which posits that much of people's ability to make sense of, and communicate about, their experience depends on the nature of human bodily interaction with the world. Rather than treating the meanings of words as mental lists of "necessary and sufficient" features expressed in the form of propositions similar to dictionary definitions, cognitive linguists propose that many words are instead understood "image schematically," that is, in terms of recurrent patterns of sensory and motor experience. In this theory, an image schema is an imagistic (i.e., vision-like) mental representation that captures aspects of how we experience our own bodies in relation to locations, objects, and other living things. Because image schemas are derived from sensorimotor experience and thus subject to visual and spatial modifications "in the mind's eye" (such as superimposition, rotation, scanning, or viewpoint shifts), they are seen as actually constituting the inferential mechanism by which linguistic meaning is normally extended. Image schemas are additionally said to be open to figurative interpretation, as a means of understanding abstract concepts in terms of more concrete—and so more readily comprehensible—physical domains.[2]

Evidence suggests that Latin speakers' conceptualization of ambiguity, as a kind of multiplicity of meaning (especially, but not exclusively, of words), was built up on just this kind of image-schematic basis. As Claude Moussy has shown, Latin's most conventionalized way of conveying this concept was given by forms derived from the stem *ambag-* or (with regular weakening of *a* → *i*) *ambig-*: namely, because it can mean "praise (= *laudo*)" or "foresee (= *divino*)" or "sing (= *canto*)" (in *Aen.* 1.1); *agmen,* because it can mean either an "attack (= *impetus*)" or a "crowd (= *multitudo*)" (1.82); and *subigo,* either "sharpen (= *acuere*)" or "compel (= *compellere*)" (6.302). *Ambiguus* then covers situations of interpretive uncertainty arising, instead, from competing considerations of an expression's grammatical role in context. So, for example, commenting on Vergil's description of Venus taking Vulcan into her lap—*coniugis infusus gremio per membra soporem* (*Aen.* 8.406)—Servius writes that "*per membra* can seem ambiguous (*ambiguum*), whether Vulcan's or Venus's." Similarly, on *uidit ab aduerso uenientis aggere Turnus* (12.446) he remarks that "Some see an ambiguity (*ambiguitatem*), whether Turnus himself is 'on the mound' or they are coming 'from a mound,'" and on *Turnusque feratur / per medios insignis equis* (10.20–21) that "It is ambiguous (*ambiguum*) whether 'famous for his chariot' or 'carried by chariot.'" In this usage, *ambiguus* characterizes *contexts* defined by a word or phrase whose denotation actually remains the same— *per membra* always refers to "limbs," *ab . . . aggere* to a "mound," *equis* to "horses"—but whose precise grammatical referent cannot be determined absolutely between two contextual alternatives.

Understood as a kind of interpretive uncertainty arising from overall contextual effects (rather than one owing to the multiple meanings inhering in any one word), *ambiguus* can be compared to another, also metaphorical means by which Servius characterizes multiplicity of meaning: the adjective *medius* (literally, "in the middle") or, using the fixed-form expression in Greek, (τῶν) μέσων (always in the genitive, again describing a word as, literally, "of those (words) in the middle"). The following passages illustrate this usage:

(8) LOCA FETA *sciendum est autem "fetam" dici et gravidam et partu liberatam . . . ergo quia 'feta' medius sermo est, bene hoc loco epitheto discrevit, dicens "graves fetas,"* "We must realize that a pregnant woman as well as one who has just given birth can be called *fetam . . .* Therefore, since *feta* is a word

'in the middle,' in this case he nicely distinguished by means of an adjective, saying 'heavily pregnant'" (Serv. in *Aen.* 1.51);

(9) NOVAS ARTES *ars τῶν μέσων est, unde sine epitheto male ponitur. veteres autem artes pro dolis ponebant,* "*Ars* is one of the 'in-the-middle (words),' for which reason its usage without an adjective is inappropriate. The ancients in fact used *artes* in the sense of 'tricks'" (1.657; cf. 2.106, 2.152);

(10) PIABUNT *expiabunt: et τῶν μέσων est; nam plerumque et impiare significat,* "'They will ritually purify'; *piare* is one of the 'middle (words),' since often it can even mean 'defile'" (2.140);

(11) MONSTRA DEUM *et modo mala; nam medium est, quia interdum dicuntur et bona,* "In this case, they are bad; for the word is 'in the middle,' because sometimes omens can also be good" (3.59);

(12) RAUCI *rauci autem τῶν μέσων est: nam modo canoros significat, alias vocis pessimae,* "*Rauci* is one of the 'middle (words),' since sometimes it means 'melodious,' and sometimes 'of the worst voice'" (11.458);

As may be seen, *medius*—like *ambiguus*—defines a class of words that can be interpreted in (at least) two different senses. Yet the kinds of words described by this term suggests this category represents a somewhat different semantic phenomenon. The category of *medius* includes, first, words that refer to either an earlier or a later stage of some state's chronological development (e.g., *fetus* means either "pregnant" or "recently delivered"). Second, words signifying either "good" or "bad" versions of the same object, action, or quality (*monstrum, raucus;* also *facinus,* meaning either "feat" or "crime"; *venenum,* either "liquid" or "poison"; and *odor,* "smell" or "stench"). And, third, words which can be used in reference to some activity that occurs in two or more sociocultural contexts appearing somehow incompatible (i.e., *piare* can be an act either of religious purification or of pollution; elsewhere, *ululare* is described in this way because it can be understood as an expression either of joy at a wedding or of grief at a funeral). Generalizing over these subtypes, *medium* appears to represent the category of words whose meanings are ambiguous only when considered apart from any particular case of usage. That is, these are words whose meanings are in some way neutral between two possible interpretations, only one of which, however, is likely to be activated within a given context.[6]

The semantic category of *medius* is manifestly also—again like *ambiguus*—understood metaphorically by virtue of a spatial metaphor. Whereas *ambiguus* represents an understanding of ambiguity through the metaphorical image of PATHS DIVERGING (AROUND), though, in *medius* the operative image is that of CENTRALITY (BETWEEN). This image can be illustrated graphically as in Figure 2. Represented in this way, the images underpinning Latin's metaphorical conceptualization of *ambiguus* and *medius* as types of ambiguous meaning relations actually appear to be structurally corresponsive: they both depict a central element or point surrounded on two sides by dynamic trajectories. Where they differ is in the relative conceptual foregrounding or backgrounding of the elements comprising their shared imagistic basis. In the image underlying *ambiguus* (the class of *per membra, ab . . . aggere* and so on), it is the two paths that receive focus: hence the linguistic label, "leading (around) on two sides." Conversely, in *medius* (the category including *raucus, facinus, venenum*, etc.), the central element is foregrounded, while the two paths recede from view: hence, "in the middle." This kind of conceptual "highlighting" can be likened to depth-of-field effects in photography, though the differences here involve shifts not in relative visual clarity but in relative cognitive prominence.[7]

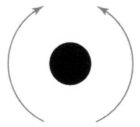

Figure 2: Metaphorical conceptualization of ambiguity in terms of CENTRALITY (BETWEEN) = *medius*

2. Latin's "linear" metaphor of meaning.

What motivates the use of spatial imagery in Latin speakers'
metaphorical understanding of these semantic categories, as well as
the specific figurative meanings of PATHS DIVERGING and CENTRALITY
vis-à-vis "ambiguity"? An answer to these questions rests, I believe, in
the fact that "meaning" itself was conceptualized in Latin in terms of
a metaphor of linear motion. This metaphor is easily made out in the
etymological derivation of the two words that most regularly convey
this concept at all periods of the language: *sententia* and *sensus*.[8] Both
sententia and *sensus* derive uncontroversially from *sentio*, which in
turn can be traced to PIE *s(e)nt-.[9] Now, while reflexes of this root in
some daughter languages do have meanings that mirror the abstract
intellectual sense of Latin *sentio* (e.g., Lithuanian *siñti*, "think";
Old Church Slavonic *sęštъ*, "wise"; Italian *sentire*), cognate words
from several others exhibit spatial meanings that represent what is
very likely its literal sense: in particular, Old Irish *sét* "road"; Proto-
Germanic *sandjan-*, "send," *sinþa-*, "road; way," and *sindō-*, "travel";
and Old Armenian *ənt'anam*, "go; walk." The co-occurrence of these
senses in attested outcomes of *s(e)nt-* suggests that "meaning"—
at least when captured by means of *sententia* and *sensus*—was
conceived of by Latin speakers as a kind of motion along a path,
as when travelling on a journey (other means were also available:
see below). The development of Dutch *zinnen*, "think; consider," as
well as German *sinnen*, "contemplate," and especially *Sinn*, "sense;
meaning," from earlier *sinnan-* (*sént-ne-*), "head for (a place)," in fact
points to a regular pathway of figurative meaning extension in the
Indo-European family of languages that goes something like: "path"
> "thought" > "meaning (of an expression)."[10]

But what, more precisely, do I mean when I say that *sententia*
and *sensus* capture an understanding of "meaning" in terms of a
linear spatial metaphor? After all, neither of these words exhibits
any spatial semantics whatsoever. Their denotations in fact
remain exclusively within the realm of sensation, perception, and
intellection.[11] (By the same token, other words equally belonging to

Latin's "path" vocabulary—*via, limes, callis, semita,* and so forth—though routinely susceptible of figurative interpretation, do not tend to lend themselves to metaphorizing "meaning.") In essence, my claim is that these words deliver Latin speakers' concept of "meaning" by way of a verbal root whose concrete literal denotation has to do centrally with directed motion along a path. Very specifically, I am proposing that this concept is understood via what cognitive linguists call the PATH schema—an image schema that, in Mark Johnson's description, emerges from our primary experience of learning to focus on and track objects moving through our visual field, as well as from repeated bodily activities, beginning in infancy, that involve intentional movement from one location to another (reaching for a toy, crawling, walking, or running toward a caregiver, or indeed traversing space to reach any desired destination).[12] As a cognitive representation that subsumes these and myriad similar activities, the PATH schema organizes and makes sense of experience by affording a certain conceptual structure or "topology" to perceptions, images, and events. Figure 3 illustrates this structure, which consists of a moving entity or "trajector" (TR) that traces a linear path from a source-point to a fixed end-point.[13]

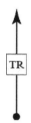

Figure 3: The PATH schema (after Lakoff and Johnson 1999, 33)

Like other image schemas, the PATH schema is easily adapted for abstract understanding through metaphorical interpretation. English speakers, for instance, conceive of purposes as paths when we talk about working *toward* and *reaching goals,* becoming *sidetracked,* changing *course,* or having a *long way to go.* All these expressions refer literally to motion along a path, but they are normally interpreted as having to do with purposes, because our conceptual system includes the metaphor 'ACHIEVING A PURPOSE IS MOTION ALONG A PATH.'[14] (Note that the metaphor structures meaning systematically: the figurative sense does not belong to the semantic structure of a particular word, but represents an avenue of interpretation for almost any talk about paths). Careers are also very often conceptualized as paths in English: we can speak directly of someone's *career path*—a metaphor Latin shares in the concept of the *cursus honorum* and in expressions like *magistratum consequi*, literally "arrive at a magistracy" (cf. Cic. *Planc.* 24).[15] Moreover, in being projected metaphorically to *abstracta*, the PATH schema—with its particular topological arrangement—brings with it a kind of "metaphysics" in the form of an inferential structure that corresponds to the logic of movement in physical space. More substantially, then, my claim is that when Latin speakers conceptualize "meaning" in terms of a linear metaphor (viz., "MEANING IS A PATH"), they are actually taking advantage of their full knowledge about motion along a path to reason about meaning as an abstract domain.

Of course, as Andreas Zanker has shown, this was by no means the only way in which Latin speakers conceptualized "meaning." Idiomatic expressions with *sibi vult*, for instance, suggest a kind of personification that allows words to be given human-like intentions—so that what a word "wills" or "wants (for itself)" is metaphorically understood as its meaning.[16] Plautus's *ut litterarum ego harum sermonem audio* (*Ps.* 98), where Pseudolus likens understanding the message of a letter he has just read aloud to hearing its "speech," suggests that meaning could sometimes also be construed in terms of vocal utterance.[17] Otherwise, meaning could be understood as the "(state of) mind" (*mens*) a word conveys (as in, e.g., Rut. Lup. *Fig.* 1.5, *non in eam mentem quae intellegitur, sed in aliam aut contrariam accipitur*),[18] or as a kind of "force" (*vis*, and later *potestas*) residing in words (in formulations like Cic. *Fam.* 6.2.3, *quae uis insit in his paucis uerbis* and *Fin.* 2.2.6, *quae uis subiecta sit uocibus*, or Gell. *NA.* 10.29.1, *particula quasdam potestates habet*).[19] In a letter to Tiro (*Fam.* 16.17.1), Cicero once refers to the meaning of a word as its "house" (*domicilium*). At the same time, *significatio*, the preferred jargon term of the Latin grammarians—commonly in Varro and Quintilian, and in the titles of lexical treatises by Aelius Gallus, Verrius Flaccus, and Pompeius Festus—employs the image of "marking" or "stamping" (< *signum*, "sign, mark" + *facio*, "make").[20] The overall set of metaphors converging on Latin speakers' conceptualization of MEANING can therefore be represented as in Figure 4.

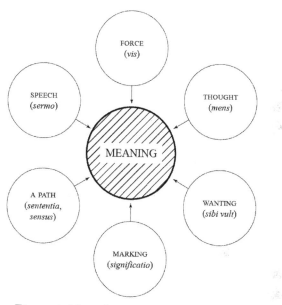

Figure 4: Metaphors converging on Latin
speakers' conceptualization of meaning

Still, it is probably fair to say that the PATH metaphor represents Latin speakers' most entrenched and most systematic conceptualization of "meaning." This interpretation appears to be confirmed by the construction Latin speakers employ when talking about understanding a word's meaning. As illustrated by (2) above, to understand an expression is literally to "take" or "accept" it: *sententiam accipere*.[21] Very often this construction will include an adverb specifying the manner of interpretation: so, for example, *non recte accipis*, "You're misconstruing it" (Ter. *Andr.* 367) and *generaliter enim et specialiter accipitur*, "It (sc. the word *tempus*) can be taken in a general or a specific sense" (Quint. *IO.* 5.10.42). Alternatively, a prepositional phrase consisting of *in* + *sententiam* or *mentem* or *partem* may be used, as, for instance, in Plautus's *equidem pol in eam partem accipioque et volo*, "For my own part I am quite willing to accept it in that sense" (*Eun.* 867). Quintilian uses the expression *ad eundum intellectum* to mean "in the same sense" (*IO.* 8.3.39 and 10.1.11). What is telling about this alternate form of the construction is that when Latin speakers want to stipulate the particular sense in which a word is interpreted, they turn reflexively to a spatial construal that once more represents "meaning" as linear motion.

Additional confirmation comes from Latin speakers' use of *intendo* to mean "mean"—where the etymological sense of the verb and the meaning of the preposition are clearly spatial, "head for (a place)"[22]—as well as from the concept of an "interpreter" or "translator," *interpres*.[23] If, on the one hand, this word's formation from **pret-* indicates that meaning could be understood metaphorically in terms of commercial "value," on the other hand *inter-* "between" again appears to evoke the image of meaning as a path.[24] More elaborate expressions like *licet eo trahere significationem scripti quo expediat* and *a verbis . . . sententiam scriptoris abducere* (Cic. *Part.* 108), where the spatial image is encoded in the semantics of *trahere* (*quo*) and *abducere* (*ab*), imply that the metaphor formed part of Latin speakers' unconscious, automatic, "everyday" representation of this domain.

Given what I have suggested is the systematic nature of Latin's PATH metaphor of meaning—that it structures meaning pervasively across levels of linguistic encoding (etymology, idiomatic expression, phrasal constructions)—Servius's elaboration of a typology of "ambiguity" through the images of PATHS DIVERGING (*ambiguum*) and CENTRALITY (*medium*) now appears fully motivated. The particular kind of ambiguity described by each category in fact follows naturally from the underlying spatial imagery, in the sense that the structural configuration of each image determines what is inferred about the relation of meaning(s) to context. PATHS DIVERGING (AROUND) thus provides a fitting metaphor for understanding the kind of contextual ambiguity in which words characterized as *ambiguus* are involved—where their denotations remain always the same, but their grammatical referents are indeterminate between two contextual alternatives—because, in the underlying image, conceptual focus falls on the "paths," while the central point (understood as the stable element of meaning) provides a sort of background. In *ambiguus*, in other words, what is conceptually salient is the "divergence" between possible meanings-in-context. CENTRALITY (BETWEEN), meanwhile, can be seen as a fitting metaphor for the category of words described as *medius*—whose decontextualized meanings are in some way neutral between two possible interpretations—because, in this image, focus falls on the aspect of meaning that is independent of any context. In *medius*, that is, what is salient is the meaning "in the middle" of different possible contextually determined senses of a word. Tellingly, in articulating concepts of other kinds of multiplicity of meaning, Latin authors make use of very different metaphors: for instance, in characterizing the class of contronyms (words with two contradictory meanings), Gellius (*NA.* 12.9.1-2) employs the image of "two-headedness" (*anceps*).[25]

3. A "cultural" metaphor of ambiguity.

Looking closely at the ways in which Latin speakers conceptualized ambiguity has revealed that—in certain technical situations, at any rate—they distinguished two types of ambiguous meaning relations on the basis of a single linear metaphor. The first type, captured through the metaphorical image of PATHS DIVERGING (AROUND) (*ambiguum*), represents the category of words whose ability to be interpreted in more than one sense emerges primarily as a function of their contextual embeddedness. Indeed, some of the words categorized in this way are ambiguous only to the extent that they appear in contexts where the compression characteristic of Latin poetry does not permit grammatical dependencies to be made out precisely. The second, captured through a related image of CENTRALITY (BETWEEN) (*medium*), represents the category of words that are instead open to interpretation in multiple senses only when considered independently of any specifying context in which just one sense could be plausibly activated. Roman interest in the role of context in the relationship between a word's senses thus appears surprisingly modern. In contemporary linguistic semantics, consideration of the different ways in which context appears able to interact with a words' different senses has led to a distinction between "ambiguous" and "vague" meaning.[26] Basically, the idea is that in cases of ambiguity, context causes one of a word's meanings to be selected or activated, while in cases of vagueness, context provides information not already specified by a word's meaning, helping to determine its sense in a given instance—in an almost exact one-to-one mapping with the Latin categories.[27] Similarly, to the extent that *ambiguum* and *medium* share a common underlying imagistic structure, the Latin categories also appear to anticipate a view that has recently emerged in cognitive linguistics, according to which ambiguity and vagueness are closely related phenomena whose difference hinges largely on the distance between a word's different senses and some covering category.[28]

But in my view the significance of Latin's spatial metaphorics of ambiguity goes well beyond constituting (yet) another way in which ancient linguistic thought appears to presage modern theory, since it can in fact be seen as a distinctive feature of Roman culture.[29] As the title of this book suggests, spatiality was in fact part and parcel of how Roman culture imagined ambiguity—as thematized repeatedly by Latin authors, and especially by Catullus in his image of the labyrinth (*Carm.* 64.112-15), which emblematizes a whole series of thematic ambiguities.[30] Comparison with metaphors from other languages and cultures is telling in this regard. To begin with, Latin differs from most other languages in conceptualizing ambiguity primarily through spatial imagery (naturally, its direct descendants tend to follow suit: cf. It. *ambiguo*, Sp. *ambiguo*, Fr. *ambigu*). Probably the commonest metaphor for this concept across even typologically distinct languages is a perceptual one that draws on images of "darkness." Thus in English ambiguity is often referred to as the "haziness," "murkiness," or "opacity" of meaning, and the sense of an ambiguous word can be said to be "muddy," "clouded," "tenebrous," or simply "unclear." Similarly, in Mandarin Chinese what is ambiguous is "obscure" (含糊, *hán hú*) or "shady" (暧昧, *ài mèi*). In Arabic, it is "opaque, cloudy" (غامِض, *ghāmid*) or "hazy, dark" (مُبْهَم, *mubham*). Turkish *belirsiz*, "ambiguous" literally means "shadowy" or "nebulous." Speakers of Chicheŵa, a Bantu language spoken in parts of Malawi, say *osamvekera bwino*, "not clear." German, alongside *doppel-* or *zweideutig*, in which ambiguity is figured in numerical terms, says *unklar*. Though such images certainly presented themselves for figurative utilization by Latin authors, they tend to characterize unintelligibility or forgetfulness rather than ambiguity.[31]

What's more, Latin stands out even from languages with seemingly analogous metaphors of ambiguity in the precise details of its mappings. Take ancient Greek's vocabulary of ambiguity, which, like Latin's, relies partly on spatial imagery. In ἀμφιβολία (ἀμφιβολητικός), ἀμφίγλωσσος, and ἐπαμφότερος, for example, and likewise in διχόγνωμος, it is in fact chiefly the prepositions ἀμφί and δίχα whose spatial meanings of "around; on two sides" deliver the figurative sense.[32] Greek's metaphorical construal of ambiguity may thus appear to coincide with Latin's. On further reflection, however, the meaning engendered by these forms turns out to be quite unlike the image of PATHS DIVERGING underlying the Latin metaphor. The literal sense of ἀμφί seems to have to do above all with notions of containment and even concealment: think, for instance, of Hom. *Il.* 13.439, ῥῆξεν δέ οἱ ἀμφὶ χιτῶνα, or *Od.* 6.292, ἐν δὲ κρήνη νάει, ἀμφὶ δὲ λειμών, where adverbial ἀμφί includes the notion of "(completely) surrounding (so as to protect)." Similarly, δίχα seems to refer prototypically to static position (rather than to linear motion) "on two sides," as in Thuc. *Hist.* 4.100.2, κεραίαν μεγάλην δίχα πρίσαντες, and Xen. *Anab.* 6.4.11, δίχα τὸ στράτευμα ποιεῖν. The image of Greek's metaphor is therefore probably closer to that of ENCLOSURE. Indeed, in figurative usage of (ἐπ)αμφιβάλλω and ἀμφιβολία, ambiguity is straightforwardly likened to a kind of garment or net.[33] In this light,

Greek's metaphors of ambiguity can be called "spatial" only in a very limited sense.

But the difference between the Latin and Greek metaphors amounts to more than a difference in imagery. Because, in a cognitive-linguistic view, metaphors like these involve the transfer of whole systems of concepts from concrete to abstract, each society's way of figuratively conceptualizing ambiguity (reflected in their languages) can often bear significantly on the sorts of inferences its members will tend to make about multiplicity of meaning.[34] Consider the logical consequences of each metaphorical image. In the Greek, ambiguity is an ENCLOSURE that surrounds or encloses or conceals another object. As such, ambiguity renders its "object" (temporarily) inaccessible, and, being something placed on top of and "(completely) around" and "on both sides" of its object, it will also require additional effort to be removed in order to uncover whatever lies beneath. The image thus implies a specific "theory" of linguistic meaning. First, it implies that any expression has both an "outer" meaning, which is in some way contingent, and an "inner" meaning, which represents the true sense of the expression. Second, it implies that ambiguity belongs squarely to the level of "outer" meaning and is, as something obstructing access to "inner" meaning, detrimental to truth. This conception explains why, in the Greek world, as Catherine Atherton writes, "Ambiguity was . . . regarded . . . as a difficulty or defect, something to be coped with, not courted, and eliminated if possible."[35]

By contrast, in the image of the Latin metaphor, ambiguity is a kind of detour from an expression's meaning-path, presenting the availability of alternate meaning-paths "around" or "on both sides of" but nevertheless still towards its true meaning-destination. Understood according to this image, ambiguity does not actually seem to preclude the discovery of true meaning at all, as implied by the Greek image. In fact, just as a detour on a journey can eventually bring a traveler back to his or her initial path, or provide simply different—but no less achievable—ways of reaching the originally intended destination, under this metaphor ambiguity constitutes merely a different, even if somehow indirect and unforeseen, means of discovering an expression's true meaning. In fact, like a fork in the road, ambiguity emerges not as an obstruction on the way to true meaning that must be avoided at all costs, but rather as a naturally occurring and perhaps even essential part of any meaning-journey: indeed, unlike a garment or other covering, ambiguity in this sense cannot be considered separate from true meaning at all. Ambiguity would thus turn out to be a mode of truth-finding that is as equally feasible as—or at any rate no less acceptable than—what may otherwise have seemed the most direct route. There may even be something appealing and worthwhile about ambiguity, just as stepping off the beaten path can often bring unexpected rewards.

What makes this metaphor a cultural metaphor (and more than just a linguistic curiosity) is that the "theory" of ambiguity implied by the image of PATHS DIVERGING—that ambiguity is in no way preclusive of true meaning—appears to mark Roman society's default ways of valuing ambiguity across different areas of social life. We know that Roman authors, far from avoiding this kind of interpretive uncertainty, frequently employed ambiguity as a part of their imaginative literary expression. As Karl Galinsky has written, "The Romans' concept of *ambiguitas* . . . is more akin to a polysemy which is deployed quite intentionally, and not just by the poets."[36] But ambiguity was also an essential element of Roman religious thought. Maurizio Bettini has suggested that ambiguity in fact typified much of Roman belief about the nature of divinity—and even had its own patron saint, so to speak, in the figure of the god Vertumnus.[37] At the same time, a god could be represented as singular or plural, male or female—a linguistic ambiguity pointing up the fact that the gods escape humanly defined categories.[38] Ambiguity also characterizes certain distinctly Roman ritual formulas like *sive deus sive dea* and *sive quo alio nomine fas est nominare*, or *sive mas sive femina*, which function as hedges against human fallibility or ignorance in the performance of sacred (or juridical) texts. In circumstances where a single mistake in the performance of religious and legalistic acts was believed to render them invalid, introducing ambiguity ("whether a god or a goddess," "or by whatever other name it is lawful to name," "whether male or female") helped guarantee the efficacy of an utterance by opening simultaneously multiple possible understandings of a truth—the divinity's identity—that lies outside the speaker's own interpretive competence. Far from obscuring an utterance's "true" meaning, the ambiguity enables its ritual efficacy. We also know that Roman society introduced ambiguities of identity between "master" and "slave" and "public" and "private" in festival contexts—especially in the role-inversions of the Saturnalia and Compitalia—as well as in imagining spaces like the luxury garden.[39] Such welcoming of ambiguity in so many and so different circumstances indicates that Roman culture appreciated multiplicity of meaning as a feature of its symbolic world generally, viewing it as not only not inconsistent with, but also in fact determinative of, a kind of truth.

BIBLIOGRAPHY

Atherton, C. 1993. *The Stoics on Ambiguity.* Cambridge: Cambridge University Press.

Beta, S. 2014. "Enigmi." In *Con i Romani: Un'antropologia della cultura antica,* ed. M. Bettini and W. M. Short, 287-302. Bologna: Il Mulino.

Bettini, M. 2012. *Vertere: Un'antropologia della traduzione nella cultura antica.* Turin: Einaudi.

Bramble, J. 1970. "Structure and Ambiguity in Catullus LXIV." *PCPhS* 16:22-41.

Christol, A. 2007. "Du latin *ambiguus* à l'ambiguïté des linguistes." In *L'ambiguïté en Grèce et à Rome: approche linguistique,* ed. C. Moussy and A. Orlandini, 9-22. Paris: Presses de l'université Paris-Sorbonne.

Copilowish, I. 1939. "Borderline Cases, Vagueness, and Ambiguity." *Philosophy of Science* 6 (2):181-95.

Corbeill, A. 2015. *Sexing the World: Grammatical Gender and Biological Sex in Ancient Rome.* Princeton: Princeton University Press.

Doob. P. 1990. *The Idea of the Labyrinth from Classical Antiquity to the Middle Ages*. Ithaca: Cornell University Press.

Ernout, A. and A. Meillet. *Dictionnaire Etymologique de la Langue Latine*. Paris: Klincksieck.

Evans, H. B. 1978. "Horace, *Satires* 2.7: Saturnalia and Satire." *Classical Journal* 73 (4):307-12.

Galinsky, K. 1994. "Reading Roman Poetry in the 1990's." *Classical Journal* 89:297-309.

Gaisser, J. 1995. "Threads in the Labyrinth: Competing Views and Voices in Catullus 64." *AJP* 116:579-616.

Inkson, K. 2002. "Thinking Creatively about Careers: The Use of Metaphor." In *Career Creativity*, ed. M. Peiperl, M. B. Arthur, and N. Anand, 15-34. Oxford: Oxford University Press.

Johnson, M. 1987. *The Body in the Mind*. Chicago: University of Chicago Press.

———. 1993. *Moral Imagination*. Chicago: University of Chicago Press.

Katz, A. and T. Taylor. 2008. "The Journeys of Life: Examining a Conceptual Metaphor with Semantic and Episodic Memory Recall." *Metaphor and Symbol* 23:148-73.

Kövecses, Z. 2005. *Metaphor in Culture: Universality and Variation*. Cambridge: Cambridge University Press.

Lakoff, G. and M. Johnson. 1980. *Metaphors We Live By*. Chicago: University of Chicago Press.

———. and M. Johnson. 1993. *Philosophy in the Flesh*. New York: Basic Books.

———. and M. Turner. 1989. *More than Cool Reason*. Chicago: University of Chicago Press.

Langacker, R. 2008. *Cognitive Grammar*. Oxford: Oxford University Press.

Lucy, J. 1992. *Grammatical Categories and Cognition: A Case Study of the Linguistic Relativity Hypothesis*. Cambridge: Cambridge University Press.

Manetti, G. 1993. *Theories of the Sign in Classical Antiquity*. Bloomington, Ind.: Indiana University Press.

Moussy, C. 2007. *"Ambiguus, ambiguitas, anceps, utroqueversus* dans le vocabulaire de l'ambiguïté." In *L'ambiguïté en Grèce et à Rome: approche linguistique*, ed. C. Moussy and A. Orlandini, 57-64. Paris: Presses de l'université Paris-Sorbonne.

Palmer, G. 1996. *Toward a Theory of Cultural Linguistics*, Austin, University of Texas Press.

Pucci, J. 2014. "Order, Ambiguity and Authority in Venantius Fortunatus, *Carm.* 3.26." In *Fakes and Forgers of Classical Literature*, ed. J. Martinez, 219-30. Leiden: Brill.

Ritchie, D. 2008. "X is a journey: Embodied simulation in metaphor interpretation." *Metaphor and Symbol* 23:174-99.

Roller, M. 2001. *Constructing Autocracy*. Princeton: Princeton University Press.

Russell, A. 2015. *The Politics of Public Space in Republican Rome*. Cambridge: Cambridge University Press.

Short, W. M. 2012. "A Roman Folk Model of the Mind." *Arethusa* 45 (1):109-47.

Sluiter, I. 1990. *Ancient Grammar in Context*. Amsterdam: VU University Press.

Sluiter, I. 1997. "The Greek Tradition." In *The Emergence of Semantics in Four Linguistic Traditions*, ed. W. J. van Bekkum, J. Houben, I. Sluiter, and K. Versteegh, 147-224. Amsterdam: John Benjamins Publishing Company.

Spencer, D. 2010. *Roman Landscape: Culture and Identity*. Cambridge: Cambridge University Press.

Spencer, D. 2011. "Movement and the Linguistic Turn." In *Rome, Ostia, Pompeii: Movement and Space*, ed. R. Laurence and D. J. Newsome, 57-80. Oxford: Oxford University Press.

Stanford, W. B. 1939. *Ambiguity in Greek Literature. Studies in Theory and Practice*. Oxford: Oxford University Press.

Talmy, L. 2003. *Toward a Cognitive Semantics*. Cambridge, Mass.: MIT Press.

Tuggy, D. 1993. "Ambiguity, Polysemy and Vagueness." *Cognitive Linguistics* 4 (3):273-90.

Turner, M. 1996. *The Literary Mind*. Oxford: Oxford University Press.

De Vaan, M. 2008. *Etymological Dictionary of Latin and the Other Italic Languages.* Leiden: Brill.

Versnel, H. 1992. *Inconsistencies in Greek and Roman Religion.* Leiden: Brill.

Wallace-Hadrill, A. 1993. "*Horti* and Hellenization." In *Horti Romani*, ed. M. Cima and E. La Rocca, 1-12. Rome: L'Erma di Bretschneider.

Williamson, T. 2002. *Vagueness.* London: Routledge.

Zanker, A. 2016. *Greek and Latin Expressions of Meaning.* Munich: Beck.

ENDNOTES

[1] I do not mean that Latin speakers were necessarily always conscious of an expression's ambiguity. If this were true, Q. Petillius Spurinus, consul in 176 BCE, probably would not have uttered the words *hodie ego Letum utique capiam*, reportedly spoken before the battle at the Campi Macri, in which he was killed—since the name of the town also means "death" in Latin (see Liv. *AUC.* 14.18.7 and Val. Max. *Mem.* 1.5.9). Likewise, as Cicero recounts (*De div.* 2.84), Marcus Crassus would not have embarked on his military campaign after hearing the fig-seller shouting *cauneas, cauneas!*—since in addition to the name of a certain kind of fruit, this phrase could also be interpreted (but was not by the Roman general) as *cave ne eas*, i.e., "Beware of going." Omens generally work on this principle: see Beta 2014, 301.

[2] See esp. Lakoff and 1980; Johnson 1987 and 1989; Lakoff 1993; Kövecses 2005.

[3] See Moussy 2007; *ambiguus* had a wider extension than *ambiguitas*, which was mainly reserved for cases of linguistic polysemy. Cf. also Christol 2007.

[4] Cf. Moussy 2007, 57-58.

[5] Ernout and Meillet 1939, 17, 24, s.v. *ago, ambages*. We cannot, I think, accept any analysis like that of Pucci 2014, 220, n. 6, "bearing on both sides," which presupposes a derivation from *ambo + gerere*. For two reasons: Phonologically, *ambiguus* cannot represent the verbal stem *ger-*, since in compounds this never reduces to *-ig-*, whereas

this is exactly the outcome we expect for *ago*: cf. *exiguus* < *ex-ago-*. Semantically, *gerere* would also be completely unmotivated, since Latin does not normally speak of "having" or "bearing" or "carrying" meaning, whereas *agere* neatly fits the linear spatial metaphor. Though expressions like *quot significationes capiat* (Gell. *NA.* 18.7.1) do occur, this "possession" metaphor is not at all conventional in Latin.

6 For a similar set of words that lend themselves to syntactic ambiguity, like *ignarus* ("not knowing" vs. "unknown"), Gellius sometimes uses the label *utroquoversus* "turning both ways," employing an again linear spatial image (e.g., *NA.* 9.12.13, 16, 20); cf. Moussy 2007, 60–61.

7 On conceptual highlighting, see Talmy 2003.

8 For this meaning of *sententia*, cf., e.g., Lucr. *RN.* 4.561-62, *ergo fit sonitum ut possis sentire, neque illam / internoscere, verborum sententiam quae sit*, "Thus it happens that you can hear the sound, but you cannot make out the meaning of the words"; Cic. *Caec.* 57, *cognita sententia interdicti, verba subtiliter exquiri noluerunt*, "When the meaning of the interdict was ascertained, they did not think it necessary to scrutinize the wording too carefully." *Sensus* occurs in this sense especially in the Latin of the empire: e.g., Phaedr. *Fab.* 4.5.19, *nec testamenti potuit sensus colligi*, "The meaning of the will could not be gathered"; Quint. *IO.* 1.9.2, *salvo modo poetae sensu*, "without losing the poet's meaning."

9 For the etymology, see De Vaan 2008, 554. Zanker 2016, 52, still calls the etymology "unclear."

10 Though manifesting the somewhat different surface image of an arrow's "path," the metaphor underpinning the semantic development of Sanskrit *artha* and *lakṣya* "target" > "meaning (of a word)" also suggests it was inherited. The figurative sense of English *drift*, as in "I don't catch your drift" seems to be based on a similar metaphor.

11 Except, perhaps, in the fixed formula *sensim et pedetemptim*. Since in other semantic pairings of this kind the second term typically glosses and also specifies the meaning of the first term, *sensim* may here exhibit some trace of its root's literal meaning: cf. *gradatim et pedetemptim*.

12 Johnson 1987, 113-14; see also Johnson 1993, esp. 166 and Turner 1996. Katz and Taylor 2008 and Ritchie 2008 provide experimental evidence for the psychological reality of this schema.

13 For the formal description of image-schematic structure, see esp. Langacker 2008.

[14] Johnson 1987, 114-17, gives the details of this metaphor, along with ample evidence of its linguistic expression in English.

[15] Inkson 2002 discusses the metaphor in English, with copious examples; for *cursus honorum*, see Spencer 2011, 64.

[16] Zanker 2016, 31-35. *Quid hoc sibi vult?* and similar expressions used in reference to verbal utterances are very likely an extension of personal constructions like *quid igitur sibi volt pater?* (Ter. *Andr.* 375).

[17] Through the regular metonymy "(SPOKEN) WORDS STAND FOR THE CONCEPTS THEY EXPRESS": see Lakoff and Turner 1989, 108.

[18] Via the same metonymy "A CONTAINER STANDS FOR ITS CONTENTS" that is operative in English *meaning* < **men-* "mind." Cf. Zanker 2016, 45.

[19] Perhaps by influence of Greek (esp. Platonic) models: e.g., Plat. *Crat.* 394b, ἐν ἄλλοις παντάπασιν γράμμασίν ἐστιν ἡ τοῦ ὀνόματος δύναμις; cf. *Crit.* 113a. For the Greek vocabulary of "meaning," see Sluiter 1997, 151–55. Cf. Zanker 2016, 41-42.

[20] Again probably reflecting Greek usage, where σημεῖον, literally, "a sign, marker," had the sense of "meaning": see Manetti 1993. See Zanker 2016, 84-86, which suggests the metaphor instead emerges through a transference from animate silent communication to inanimate phenomena (including abstractions like words).

[21] In Latin, mental apprehension is normally construed in terms of a haptic metaphor (i.e., "UNDERSTANDING IS GRASPING"): for the mapping, see Short 2012. Sweetser 1990 has shown that this metaphor in fact operates in a large number of Indo-European languages.

[22] Zanker 2016, 54-56, analyzes the metaphor as one of mental intention, but as mental activity was often conceptualized in terms of spatial motion (see Short 2012), this begs the question.

[23] E.g., Plaut. *Curc.* 434, *quod te praesente isti egi, teque interprete;* Cic. *Fam.* 10.11.3, *utor in hac re adiutoribus interpretibusque fratre meo et Laterense et Eurnio nostro.* Cf. Ernout and Meillet 1965, 320.

[24] See Bettini 2012, ch. 5, for discussion of the "commercial" dimension of *interpres.* Cf. Zanker 2016, 64.

[25] On this term, see esp. Moussy 2007, 59-60.

[26] On the "rehabilitation" of vagueness in philosophy of language, see Williamson 2002, 70-95. The mainline view begins perhaps with Copilowish 1939.

27   So, for example, Latin *ius* would be considered a case of ambiguity, since there is probably no context in which both its meanings of "law; right; justice" and "soup, broth" could reasonably be activated (except perhaps a humorous one: cf. Plaut. *Poen.* 584, *iuris coctiores*, "better versed in law" or, punningly, "more cooked in (?) broth"). By contrast, *sermo* would be considered vague, since it is context that determines whether this word is interpreted as "oration," "conversation," "language," "word," or in any of its other numerous possible senses.

28   See Tuggy 1993 for ambiguity and vagueness in cognitive linguistics. On this account, ambiguity is the perception that arises when there is no salient concept covering a word's multiple senses: e.g., English *bank* is ambiguous because the closest category including both its senses of "financial institution" and "land at river's edge" is probably "thing." Vagueness is the perception that arises when, instead, a highly salient concept exists: so *uncle* is vague because in a society with a bilateral kinship system "parent's brother" is a more relevant concept than either "father's brother" or "mother's brother."

29   On ancient linguistic (especially Stoic) thought in relation to modern semantic theory, see Long 2005 and Sluiter 1990.

30   See Bramble 1970 and Gaisser 1995; cf. Doob 1990.

31   As shown by Short 2012, 118-19. In some late medieval Latin texts, however, the "darkness" metaphor appears to be making inroads: cf., e.g., Petrarch, *De viris illustribus* pr. 1, *omnem historie sue textum nebulosis ambagibus . . . involverunt.*

32   In δίφατος, δίληπτος, δίλημμα there is a metaphor from verbal utterance, ambiguity being conceived as what "speaks" two things at once; in λοξότης and ἀμφίλοξος the image is of "slantedness" or "crookedness." Greek also utilizes a weaponry image, conceptualizing ambiguity as "two edged": e.g., ἀμφιδέξιος, ἀμφήκης.

33   A similar "enclosing" or "covering" metaphor is detectable in Arabic in the semantic structure of *labs* "garment" > "ambiguity" and *multabis* "clothed" > "ambiguous."

34   In this sense, cognitive linguistics entails a weak version of the so-called Sapir-Whorf ("linguistic relativity") hypothesis, or the idea that the structure of a language, including its metaphorical structure, determines—in the sense of "limits"—its speakers' possible pathways of thought. Insofar as a language's expressions reflect its speakers' conceptualizations, the categories in terms of which they habitually

speak about some domain will tend to bias thought, all other things being equal: see esp. Lucy 1992.

[35] Atherton 2007, 24; see also Stanford 1939, 12-24.

[36] Galinksy 1994, 305.

[37] Bettini 2014.

[38] Cf. Corbeill 2015, 104-42.

[39] On role ambiguity in festival contexts, see Roller 2001, 269; Versnel 1992, esp. 150-57; and Evans 1978. On the spatial ambiguities of the luxury garden, see Wallace-Hadrill 1998 as well as Spencer 2010, especially 10-30. For monumental spaces like the Forum and Comitium, see Russell 2015.

A Cute Illness in Epidaurus:
Eight Sick Jokes in Plautus'
Gorgylio (Curculio)

Michael Fontaine

For Reginald Foster, who knows that
a *torpedo* is both torpor and a fish,
and who once told me so with a grin;
and who knows a thing or two about
doctors in Italy. *aVfVgIat MoMVs!*

P lautus' *Gorgylio* is set in Epidaurus, a city famed in antiquity
for the great sanctuary of Asclepius (Aesculapius) that
attracted pilgrims and patients from around the Greek world.
The sanctuary, called the Asclepieion,[1] was a holistic health center. It
consisted of temples, a theater, a stadium, a gymnasium, and a library.
This setting provides the backdrop for many unnoticed jokes about
disease, disability, deformity, diagnosis, and treatment, most of which
involve ambiguities. The following eight are either hiding in plain
sight or have defied previous attempts at explanation. Taken together,
they reveal some surprises about Roman attitudes toward illness and
healing in the time of Plautus (*fl.* 210–184 BCE), as well as several new
connections between Roman and Greek Comedy.

1.

Plautus' play was written for performance in the Roman forum; the manager's speech of lines 462–86 points out its monuments, including the *comitium* (470) and fish market (474).[2] This performance context explains a curious interruption in the action when, late in the play, the parasite Gorgylio returns to the stage, disguised as a war veteran. His disguise includes a patch or bandage over one eye. He refers to it only by the neuter pronoun *hoc*, but that pronoun suggests the word he has in mind is *splenium* (Greek σπληνίον), the usual name in Latin and Greek for a bandage, linen pad, or compress placed on a wound. As he crosses the stage, the "veteran" is approached by a banker named Lyco, who sizes up his appearance and greets him rudely:

LYCO   *unocule, salve.*

GORGYLIO   *quaeso, **deridesne me?** . . .*
catapulta hoc ictum est mihi / apud Sicyonem . . .
. . . adulescens, ob rem publicam — hoc — intus mihi
*quod insigne habeo, **quaeso ne me incomities.***
(392, 394–5, 399–400)

LYCO   Greetings, One-Orb.

GORGYLIO   I'm sorry, are you **making fun of me?** . . . This (*indicating his eye patch*) got hit by a spear in Sicyon[3] . . . Young man, it was in defense of my country that I won the honorable wound beneath this (*tapping the bandage*). **Please don't be mean to me.**

As I have pointed out elsewhere, *incōmities* (pronounced *incŏmĭchēs*), "be mean to," is a synonym of *derides*, "make fun of." It comes from *incōmis*, "impolite."[4] Despite the request, however, Lyco twists the word to continue making jokes at the disabled man's expense:

LYCO   *licetne inforare, si **incŏmitĭare** non licet?* (401)

LYCO   Can I **inforare** (bugger) you, if I can't **incomitiare** you?

Pretending that *incōmitiare* comes not from *incōmis* but *in* + *cŏmitium*, the public meeting place in the Roman forum, Lyco makes up the word *incŏmitĭare* to pun on *inforare*, "perforate, bugger," a word that itself puns on *forum*. Gorgylio's response makes the basis of the coinage clear (402–3): *non inforabis me quidem, nec mihi placet / tuom profecto nec forum nec comitium!* "You won't be buggering *me*, and I certainly don't like / your forum or your *comitium!*" Any gesture at the Roman forum around him, and at the *comitium* in particular, would make the joke obvious.

My interest here is not in the philology or delivery of Lyco's pun, however, but in the remarkable attitude toward disability and disfigurement it reveals. Far from being viewed as a token of heroic self-sacrifice or a cause for pity, Gorgylio's maiming instead presents an occasion for drumming up good laughs. It gives us a glimpse of the kind of humor favored in this comedy: that is, *sick* humor.

Technically, a "sick" joke is an offensive joke. In practice, a sick joke is often a joke about a sick person. According to the *American Heritage Dictionary*, a sick joke is "an anecdote intended to be humorous but actually in very bad taste, as in *His stories turn out to be sick jokes about people who are handicapped in some way.*" The ancients would have agreed with this example. Cicero calls a joke about a one-eyed man "tasteless" (*scurrile*, "buffoonish, clownish"), and elsewhere Plautus, Persius, and Antigonus the One-Eyed make it clear that jokes about one-eyed people crossed the lines of social decency.[5] As we shall see, however, the casual embrace of tasteless jokes that mock disease or deformity actually pervades Plautus' play. Let me begin with an obvious example.

29

2.

Early in the play (216–50), we meet a brothel keeper, named Cappadox, who is in great pain. His stomach is distended, his eyes pale, his complexion off, and his spleen so enlarged he's afraid that he will, in his words, "split in two" (*ne medius disrumpar*). He has failed in his attempt to heal these ailments by ritual incubation, a faith-healing procedure that entailed spending a night in the Asclepieion:

> *valetudo decrescit, adcrescit labor;*
> *nam iam quasi zona liene cinctus ambulo,*
> *geminos in ventre habere videor filios.*
> *nil metuo nisi ne medius disrumpar miser.* (219–22)

> My strength is decreasing, and my pangs are increasing. I'm already walking around with my spleen wound around me like a girdle; I feel like I've got (my) twins in my stomach! I'm seriously worried my abdomen is going to explode—arrgh!

Line 221 conceals a joke probably no ancient audience would have missed. Ostensibly, the pimp means he feels pregnant with twins, as if he were the male equivalent of Alcumena in Plautus' *Amphitryo*. Actually, since "twins" (*gemini*, δίδυμοι) commonly denotes the testicles, the pimp is "ambiguously" complaining of ascending testicles, or the sensation that "my testicles are in my stomach." His is only one of several jokes about testicles in this play (cf. *intestabilis*, 30–1; *intestatus*, 621, 695?).

Whatever the reason for those jokes, Cappadox's chief complaint of abdominal pain, and about his spleen in particular, is no laughing matter. According to the *Aphorisms* of Hippocrates (c. 400 BCE), an enlarged spleen can be fatal. Aphorism 6.48 states that "For those suffering from an enlarged spleen, it is a good sign when dysentery comes on" (τοῖσι σπληνώδεσι δυσεντερίη ἐπιγενομένη, ἀγαθόν), but another adds that dysentery (bloody diarrhea) sometimes heralds certain death:

Ὁκόσοι σπληνώδεες ὑπὸ δυσεντερίης ἁλίσκονται,
τουτέοισιν, ἐπιγενομένης μακρῆς τῆς δυσεντερίης,
ὕδρωψ ἐπιγίνεται, ἢ λειεντερίη, καὶ ἀπόλλυνται. (6.45)

If dysentery seizes people suffering from an enlarged spleen and becomes chronic, then edema or lientery [*diarrhea*] invariably supervenes, and they die.

From this perspective, it may be surprising to find people laughing at poor Cappadox's symptoms. But that is precisely what everyone else goes on to do.

3.

As Cappadox continues moaning and groaning, a slave named Palinurus approaches and asks him what is wrong. The pimp explains:

CAPPADOX | *lien enecat, renes dolent,*
| *pulmones distrahuntur, cruciatur iecur,*
| *radices cordis pereunt, hirae omnes dolent.*
PALINURUS | *tum te igitur **morbus** agitat **hepatiarius**.*
CAPPADOX | *facile est miserum inridere.* (236–240)

CAPPADOX | My spleen's killing me, my kidneys hurt, my lungs are splitting, my liver's in agony, the roots of my heart are dying,[6] all my intestines hurt.
PALINURUS | In that case, then, you must be suffering from ***hepatiarius*** (liver?) illness.
CAPPADOX | It's easy to make fun of a man when he's in bad shape.

Cappadox's complaints are real symptoms of liver disease,[7] but Palinurus is not offering a real diagnosis: his reply echoes Gorgylio's to Lyco in 392 (*inridere ~ deridesne*, § 1). Suspicious, too, is the fact that *hepatiarius* is a *hapax legomenon*, whereas the regular term for liver disease in Greek and Latin medical writers is ἡπατικός (*hepaticus*). But what is the joke? No one knows, and nothing in the context favors the best guess—namely, that *hepatiarius* comes not from ἧπαρ, "liver," but from ἡπάτιον, "pâté," and that Cappadox has a stomachache from eating too much of it.[8]

I would like to suggest that we have here a clear case in which only the fragments of lost Greek comedy (rather than, say, parallels from elsewhere in Latin literature) can shed light on a passage of Plautus. In so doing, those fragments tell us a great deal about the audiences in Rome that came to watch Plautus' comedies—and, in particular, what those audiences knew about Greek proverbs and Greek humoral medicine.

In my view, *hepatiarius* is a made-up word. It comes not from ἧπαρ, "liver," but from ἧπατος, "the hepatus fish." According to Aristotle, the hepatus (in later Latin, *hepar*) lacks the pyloric ceca, or digestive innards, that fish typically have:

> A peculiar feature of fishes and most birds is that they have ceca . . . Fish have them high up, around their stomach, and some have many of them . . . But some fish, such as the hepatus, possess these appendages only in small numbers.[9]

In those days of humoral medicine, the absence of ceca left people wondering how the hepatus could produce χολή, the gall or bile thought to be essential for sustaining mood and energy. The mystery was sufficiently popular that Eubulus, the poet of Middle Comedy (*fl.* 4th c. BCE), could make it the basis of a simile. In a fragment of his comedy *Spartans* or *Leda*, a character blusters,

*οὐκ ᾤου <σύ> με / χολὴν ἔχειν, ὡς δ᾿ ἡπάτῳ μοι
διελέγου; ἐγὼ δέ γ᾿ εἰμὶ τῶν μελαμπύγων ἔτι.* (fr. 61)

Did you think I've got no gall? Like I'm some hepatus
you're talking to? Pfft! I'm still a badass!

Literally, χολή refers to gall or bile (Latin *fel* or *bilis*). Metaphorically,
it refers to the associated temperament (= χόλος, wrath or passion).
A man who lacks it is ἄχολος, listless, impassive, a pushover—or,
as the Renaissance zoologist Conrad Gesner put it, a Micio rather
than a Demea.[10] In the Renaissance, Eubulus' jest became standard
lore about the fish's physiology and behavior. For Hadrianus Junius
(1558, 811) the hepatus was a *"piscis felle carens,"* for Conrad Gesner
(1604, 413) it was *"fellis prorsus expers,"* and for Joannes Jonston
(1650, 48) it was *"moribus . . . insulsis, et parum ad vindictam pronus."*
With the emergence of modern ichthyology, that nugget of ancient
popular wisdom dropped down the memory hole. We have forgotten
all about it.

Nevertheless, in Plautus' *Gorgylio*, Palinurus is making the
same point—Cappadox does not have hepatitis, he has hepatusitis.
It is like diagnosing a depressed man today with "mussel fatigue,"
but better, because the humor of the joke is tied to the humor of
the body.[11] And that is not all. The joke fits squarely with the fact
that pimps in Plautine comedy are routinely compared to fish. In
Rudens and *Poenulus*, they are named Labrax and Lycus respectively.
Both words mean "bass," a notorious predator fish for the Greeks
and Romans, much as "shark" or "piranha" is for us. In *Pseudylus*,
Phallio means "whale" (Greek φάλλαινα, Latin *ballaena*).[12] These
"fishy" connotations, remarked A. S. Gratwick, "presumably imply
something unpleasantly ichthyoid about the physiognomy of your
standard Plautine *leno*-mask."[13] He is probably right. According to
Aristotle, the hepatus "is solitary, carnivorous, and jagged-toothed;
black in color; and has disproportionately large eyes and a white,
triangular heart."[14] That seems an apt description for surviving
specimens of the pimp's mask, such as this one.

Comic mask traditionally identified as a Pornoboskos. 1st half
of the 2nd c. BC. Bpk Bildagentur/Antikensammlung, Staatliche
Museen zu Berlin—Preussischer Kulturbesitz TC 8568/Johannes
Laurentius/Art Resource, NY. Reproduced by permission.

Incidentally, it is worth emphasizing that Plautus' wordplay on
ἧπαρ (liver) and ἥπατος (hepatus) is a true pun, not an etymological
figure. According to D'Arcy Thompson (1947, 76), ἥπατος is "one
of the Greek fish-names for which I suspect an Egyptian origin;

34

to wit, *abtu*, a word for a fish occurring in the Book of the Dead." Pronunciation may have made the pun obvious.[15]

All that remains is a detail of philology. Recent editions all print *hepatiarius*, with an unexpected *i* before the suffix.[16] If Plautus did write that, then the base of the word must be ἡπάτιον, "(little) hepatus fish," though that meaning is attested only by a pun in Eubulus fr. 23 (*Deucalion*), ἡπάτια, νῆστις, πλεύμονες, μήτρα ("livers, intestine, lungs, womb" or "(little) hepatus, mullet, jellyfish, paunch"). Otherwise the word must be segmented not *hepati-arius* but *hepat-iarius*, built on the rare suffix *-iarius* (= French *-ière*; a dozen examples in Zimmermann 1902). Since neither is likely, Plautus probably wrote *hepatarius*, and future editions ought to print it that way.

4.

It is no surprise that unpleasant bowel odors often accompany abdominal pain. This fact suggests Palinurus is not offering a real remedy, but making another sick joke when, in the sequel, he advises Cappadox to hang in there for a few days:

PALINURUS   *quin tu aliquot dies /* **perdura***, dum intestina exputescunt tibi.* (240–1)

PALINURUS   Why don't you **tough it out** a few days, while your intestines are rotting out?

Perdura is more than just a rare variant of *dura* or *obdura*. It is an unnoticed pun on Greek πέρδου (ἄ)ρά, "then keep up the farting, fart on!" A pedant might object that the *a* of *perdura* is long, while the first alpha of the enclitic ἄρά is short; if so, then the pun is limited to *perdu* and πέρδου. Either way, the words *aliquot dies* seem to reinforce the continuous aspect of the Greek imperative, which is in the present rather than aorist tense.

"The humor of crepitation," observes Jeffrey Henderson, "is extremely frequent in [sc. Greek Old] comedy."[17] Karion releases a bit of intestinal gas in front of the Asclepieion in *Wealth* (696). And fart jokes are not rare in Plautine comedy; Gorgylio himself threatens to knock a *crepitum polentarium*, a "pungent fart," out of any Greek philosopher that gets in his way (*Gorgylio* 295). The pun can therefore hardly be accidental here—and a toot from the *tibicen*, as well as a "Greek" accent, would make the double entendre obvious.[18]

In this connection, moreover, it is worth emphasizing the salvific link established in the Hippocratic aphorism between dysentery and an enlarged spleen (§ 2 above). It suggests that from a Hippocratic point of view, Palinurus' advice is both medically sound as well as funny. In § 6 we will see another example of this kind of humor.

5.

When Palinurus proceeds to elaborate on his recommendation—

> *quin tu aliquot dies / perdura (πέρδου ῥά), dum*
> *intestina exputescunt tibi. nunc dum salsura sat bonast*
> *si id feceris, venire poteris intestinis vilius.* (240–3)

—the lines look like an obvious joke, but no one knows what they mean. I would like to suggest, however, this this is another case in which the fragments of Greek Comedy clarify matters, and that Palinurus means:

> Why don't you (*tough it out* / *fart on*) a few days,
> while your intestines are rotting out? If you do it now,
> while the brine sauce is pretty good, you'll be a better
> bargain than gray mullets!

This is another sick joke. Palinurus is developing his jest that Cappadox is a hepatus, but with a different metaphor. His *morbus hepatarius* joke casts the pimp as a fish-as-animal. These lines cast the pimp as a fish-as-food, a distinction that was made more sharply in the Greek and Latin of Plautus' time than it is in English today.

In a 1997 book, James Davidson, of whose work I shall say more in § 8, remarked:

> *Opson* together with its diminutive *opsarion* [ὀψ-άριον] . . . corresponded to *ichthus* as pork does to pig, referring to fish as food. In fact it is from *opsarion*, and not *ichthus*, that the modern Greeks get their own word for fish, *psari*. (27)

This distinction is reflected in the comedies of Plautus, who regularly uses *obsonium* (= ὀψ-ώνιον) of fish purchased as food. Indeed, it is one reason I suspect the cook silently watching the banter between Cappadox and Palinurus, rather than the slave himself, was meant to speak lines 242–3.[19] Be that as it may, the distinction between *icthus* and *opson* helps us understand what the Latin means.

The key is to realize that in 243, *intestinis* is a calque, or loan translation, of νῆστις. As we saw in § 3 above, the latter word is ambiguous: it can mean an intestine (*intestinum*, as in 241) or a grey mullet (*mugil*), one the great luxury fishes in Greek antiquity. Athenaeus tells us a great deal about their preparation and price, and quotes Archestratus to show they were best prepared when roasted whole in a brine sauce (ἄλμη).[20] But the flavor and quality of such sauces could vary, which is why a comedy of Philemon specifies an ἀγαθὴ ἄλμη, a "*good* brine sauce."[21] That is the phrase that must lie behind Plautus' *salsura sat bona*. It shows that Plautus is not alluding to garum, the fish sauce made from the fermented entrails of fish, but to the sauce that fish were cooked in—and which, therefore, could easily mask the stench of expired fish. That is the point of "waiting a few days" in 240. Ancient fishmongers knowingly sold expired fish, or so characters in ancient comedy liked to allege. Plautus makes this point himself in *Captivi* 813 (*piscatores, qui praebent populo pisces foetidos*, "fishermen that offer to sell people rotten fish"), and it is common in Greek comedy.[22] Aware of those shady practices, Palinurus "advises" Cappadox to turn those circumstances to his advantage: By "waiting a few days," the sickly pimp will turn into a *more affordable* fish to eat—because though "he will rot," "a nice brine sauce" can cover up his disgusting smell, and thus enable him to "be sold cheaper than mullets."

Plautus apparently found this sick joke in his Greek model and sought to replicate it in *Gorgylio*. His choice of *intestinis* to translate νῆστις may seem strained, but it is easily paralleled. He supplies an exact parallel himself to the calque, if not the pun, in *Persa* 60, where he renders ἀνὴρ κεστρεύς, "mullet man" (a facetious nickname for hungry parasites) as *vir capito*, because the comedian knew that yet another name in Greek for the mullet is κέφαλος.[23] And because σκιά means shadow, his contemporary Ennius chose *umbra marina*, "sea shadow," to render σκίαινα in his adaptation of Archestratus' *Hedyphagetica*.[24]

6.

Ignoring this "advice," in the next verse Cappadox clutches his chest and moans *lien dierectust*, "My spleen is wrecked!" Palinurus replies (244), *ambula, id lieni optumumst*, ("Go for a walk, that's the best thing for a spleen!"). These words show that Palinurus is once more offering real Hippocratic advice while making a joke at the ailing pimp's expense. In the *Epidemics* and the *Internal Affections*, patients suffering from an enlarged or painful spleen are advised to go for walks (περιπατεῖν).[25] At the same time, because *ambula*, "Go for a walk," can mean *abi!* "Get lost!" it seems Palinurus has merely brought in the Hippocratic recommendation to cover the joke. In reality, he means, "Take a hike! That's (*as if quoting an adage*) 'the best thing for a spleen.'"

Unaware of the connection with Hippocratic medicine, in a 2005 paper, J. Welsh deemed this ambiguity insufficiently funny. Welsh felt that such medical advice "does not have widespread appeal and depends rather too much on technical knowledge" for Plautus' audience.[26] He therefore wanted to see in this line a pun on *lieni* and *lenoni*, "pimp," but that kind of looseness with the sounds is closer to a psychoanalytic explanation than an elucidation of what Plautus' characters actually say. In reality, the problem lies solely with Welsh's assumption about the audience. If anything, the jokes in *Gorgylio* reveal a great interest among the audience in medicine— and Hippocratic medicine in particular. I would suggest, therefore, that we simply reverse Welsh's assumption and acknowledge that Plautus' audience in Rome must somehow have known a great deal more about Greek humoral medicine than we might assume they did. That must be true even if Romans regarded the humoral theory as merely "a Greek thing," like Plautus' characters themselves. I shall come back to this point in a moment, but let us finish with a brief look at a joke that brings everything full circle.

7.

Later in the play, Cappadox meets Gorgylio himself. The ruse is underway, so the parasite is still in his disguise as a one-eyed war veteran (§ 1). When Cappadox goes to hand a courtesan over to him for safe delivery to the soldier, he asks the alleged veteran to take good care of her (*ut cures*, 517). The request prompts Gorgylio to retort:

GORGYLIO	*ecquid das qui bene sit?*
CAPPADOX	*malum.*
GORGYLIO	*opust **hoc** qui te procures.* (521)

GORGYLIO	Are you giving me anything to make sure things go well for her?
CAPPADOX	A thrashing!
GORGYLIO	You need ***hoc*** to take care of yourself.

What is *hoc*? Unsure of the answer, some editors want to delete it. If the text is sound, however, I suggest it can only be Gorgylio's eye patch; and the understood referent of that is, as I have pointed out (§ 1), σπληνίον in Greek and *splenium* in Latin. In receiving an offer of a "little spleen," the poor brothel keeper has, it seems, at last found a fitting treatment (*procures*) for his condition! Just as in *Rudens* 576, where a saucy slave sarcastically offers a different ailing pimp a "raincoat" (actually a roof tile) to warm up in, the word that creates the punch line, *splenium*, is never used. As with other sight gags, Plautus—and probably, too, the Greek comedian whose play he adapted as *Gorgylio*—trusted his audience to come up it with for themselves.[27]

8.

Omnes videmur nobis esse belli, festivi, remarked Varro, *saperdae cum simus* σαπροί: "We're sure we're cute, we're fun (we think)— though really we're sardines: we stink."[28] The great polymath of republican Rome thereby plays on the connections among *sāperda* (sardine), σαπρός (rotten, putrid) and πέρδεσθαι (to fart). In tying together many of the points raised in this paper, his contention prompts us to reflect on what we can learn from these seven sick jokes in Plautus' *Gorgylio*. I suggest five conclusions:

1) Greater attention to the fragments of Greek comedy will continue to throw light on the murky parts of Plautus. I have made this point elsewhere.[29]

2) Plautus' comic genius lay at least as much in inspired translation as in "originality" (free invention). I have also made this point elsewhere.[30]

3) Plautus expected his audiences in Rome to know as much about the price, preparation, and quality of the hepatus fish as a food (*opsarion/obsonium*) as Greek comedians expected their audiences to know about those matters. How is that possible? Perhaps Romans knew Greek comedy, or perhaps they simply heard Greeks while shopping in the fish market in Rome pointed out in v. 474 (§ 1).[31]

4) Plautus expected his audiences in Rome to know as much about the humoral theory of medicine as Eubulus expected his audiences in Greece to know about it.

5) Plautus expected his audiences in Rome to know as much lore about the hepatus' alleged animal behavior (*ichthus*) as Eubulus expected his audiences in Greece to know about it.

The fifth point is quite a surprise, but it ought not be. Drug and alcohol addiction is a mental or social illness today; just so, as James Davidson brilliantly showed in his 1997 book *Courtesans and Fishcakes*, fish addiction was a bona-fide mental or social illness in ancient Greece. Davidson grasped a fundamental point about Greek society, and since his book has made no discernible impact on the study of Roman Comedy, his insight deserves to be reasserted.

Because Greeks consumed fish as their luxury par excellence, Davidson explained, fish became their basic metaphor of alluring sensuality and seduction. Later Greek comedy is shot through with endless, mouth-watering lists of different kinds of fish; book seven of Athenaeus' *Deipnosophistae* is a massive catalogue of examples, most of them drawn from Greek comedy. This is the background against which fossils of such lists in Roman comedy, such as Plautus' *Captivi* 850–1, should be viewed and understood.[32] It is also the context in which we can make sense of the courtesans and other sexy women in ancient comedy, many of whom have "fishcake" names: Bacchis in *Bacchides* and *Hecyra* (mullet), Delphium in *Mostellaria* (dolphin), Pardalisca in *Casina* (leopard fish), and Phrynesium in *Truculentus* (toad).[33] As Davidson remarks (2011, 10):

> [T]he practice of comparing women to mouth-watering fish and fish to women seems to have been rather more general in Athenian society [sc. *than just in comic discourse*]. Apart from the anchovy sisters mentioned above, we find flute-girls and hetaeras given nicknames like 'Sand-smelt,' 'Red Mullet' and 'Cuttlefish.'"

41

The peak of this trend is reached in Antiphanes fr. 27 (*Fisherwoman*), in which a speaker instructs her servant about selling fish at the market, and we cannot tell whether the varieties she names are real fish or the nicknames of Athenian courtesans. This is fitting background for both the comparison of courtesans to salted fish (*muriatica*) in Plautus' *Poenulus* 240–4 and the pun at *Bacchides* 371, commonly misunderstood as an etymological figure, *Bacchides non bacchides* (mullets) *sed bacchae* (bacchants) *sunt accerrumae*.[34]

This last example brings up an obvious point. Another reason fish are so popular in Greek and Roman comedy is that fish names tend to be inherently ambiguous, and hence potentially always funny. They are regularly drawn from other and more familiar domains, especially domestic or bodily: bird names, plant names, body parts, and so on. That makes them ripe for generating puns or clever associations.[35] I have already mentioned the names of Plautus' pimps, Labrax, Lycus, and Phallio, but a similar example is Tranio in *Mostellaria*—or rather, Thranio, as I suggest we spell the name. That clever slave alludes to the etymology of his name, "swordfish" (θρανίς), at several points.[36] Very similar is Palinurus' pun on the hepatus, which is especially interesting is that it presupposes not only widespread familiarity among the audience with lore about Greek fish, but also with ancient Greek humoral theory. That too may surprise us. Should it? A few other pieces of evidence for knowledge of the humoral theory have been scraped together before, but most of them are debatable or ambiguous.[37] By contrast, the pun on *hepat(i)arius* presupposes an unmistakable link between physiology, health, and behavior.

Taken together, these sick jokes reveal some surprising attitudes among ancient Romans toward illness and healing in Plautus' time, bespeaking an indulgence of disease and disfigurement that may seem shocking to the traditional morality of any time and place, but particularly in ancient Rome.

A final example makes this clear. *Gorgylio* begins with Palinurus and Phaedromus outside the brothel run by Cappadox, home to Phaedromus' ladylove, Planesium. The fact that it stands next door to the Asclepieion (v. 14) seems to explain a strange joke. Phaedromus greets the door as if it were a person, calling it *ostium oculissumum*, "most adorable door," and asks how it has been. Hearing this, his slave seizes on the literal meaning of that question to tease his lovesick master:

> PALINURUS   *ostium occlusissumum, / caruitne febris te heri vel nudiustertius / et heri cenavistine?*
>
> PHAEDROMUS *deridesne me?* (16–8)

> PALINURUS   Most durable door! Did the fever spare you yesterday or the day before, and did you manage to eat yesterday?
>
> PHAEDROMUS Are you making fun of me?

Apart from the obvious pun (*oculissumum* ~ *occlusissumum*), I would like to suggest the slave is making a second pun we have all missed, viz.:

> PALINURUS   *caruitne **febris** te **eri**—vel nudiustertius?*

> PALINURUS   Did **my master's fever** spare you—er, or did the day before?

That is, the slave says *eri*, "my master's," but quickly "corrects" himself to *heri*, "yesterday," and brings in the rest of the line for plausible deniability. The first point is that Phaedromus' presence in the household is noxious, unwanted—an annoyance, as Plautus uses the metaphor at *Pseudylus* 643; while the slave's "correction" suggests that the door—etymologically, a "mouth" (*ostium* from *os*)— has caught a fever from its proximity to the patients in the Asclepieion. There is a close parallel to this kind of subversive wordplay at the start of Plautus' *Persa*, where a slave puns on the *aerumnas* (*H*)*erculi* and *eri culi*, the "labors of Hercules" or "of the master's asshole."[38] It is surely no accident that this joke appears in *Gorgylio*. Like every other example in this paper, it is a doubly sick joke—that is, a joke that is both about a sick person and that is likely to offend many people.

Why, then, are these jokes there? Since most of their humor centers on the pimp, an inherently unsympathetic character, perhaps we should not be shocked. Young masters in Roman comedy are also typically the butt of humor, and they too are unsympathetic at the start of a play. With the one-eyed war veteran, however, something else seems to be at work. I would suggest that the jokes reveal a quiet but unmistakable skepticism toward the efficacy of faith healing—that is, the very kind of treatment offered by the cult of Asclepius.

Plautus' play never says why the disguised Gorgylio is wearing an eye patch, but two sources of evidence suggest two reasons. Ostensibly, the "veteran" has come to Epidaurus to deliver a letter. Ancient audiences would assume that he also hopes to have his sight restored. In Aristophanes' *Wealth*, the titular character is cured of blindness in the Asclepieion, and pair of steles found in Epidaurus, contemporary with the lost Greek model of *Gorgylio* (second half of the fourth c. BCE), lists the "Cures of Apollo and Asclepius." The inscriptions prove that the god of Epidaurus was mighty indeed, for he twice healed wounds exactly like the "veteran's" own:

> **Anticrates of Cnidos, eyes**. In a battle he had been hit by a spear in both eyes and had become blind; and the spear point he carried with him, sticking in his face. While sleeping he saw a vision. It seemed to him that the god pulled out the missile and then fitted the so-called pupils into his eyelids again. When day came, he walked out sound.

> **Timon**...wounded by a spear under his eye. While sleeping in the Temple he saw a dream. It seemed to him that the god rubbed down an herb and poured it into his eye. And he became well.

Elsewhere the inscriptions record miracles still greater than this, such as Asclepius' restoration of sight to a man who had no eyeballs![39]

These testimonia bring to mind Émile Zola's quip about the efficacy of faith healing: "The road to Lourdes is littered with crutches, but not one wooden leg." I would suggest that by way of Gorgylio's eye patch, Plautus is making a similarly wry observation about the efficacy of Asclepian faith healing, a growing fashion in the Rome of his time. The mighty god had been "evoked" from Epidaurus to Rome not a century earlier, in 291 BCE, and installed in a temple on Tiber Island. But he soon faced competition. Traditional household remedies extended back in Rome to time immemorial, but in Plautus' era, a powerful new alternative appeared on the scene:[40] the medicine offered by the Hippocratic doctors, whose practice was rooted in science and the humoral theory. The first such doctor, Archagathus of Sparta, had arrived in Rome only two generations after Asclepius, in 219 BCE: within a generation of Plautus' play.[41]

Not everyone in Rome welcomed Hippocratic revelation, however. Plautus' skepticism toward faith healing squares with the attitude of Cato the Elder (234–149 BCE), his younger contemporary, who feigned shock that priests did not burst out laughing when they spotted each other in public. He assumed they were all charlatans, *tout court*.[42] But this does not mean he welcomed the humoral theory, either. It is sobering to realize that the same Cato regarded the Hippocratic oath as a Greek version of the *Protocols of the Elders of Zion*. As he warned his son in a letter, the Hippocratic doctors "have sworn an oath to one another to kill all the *goyim* with their medicine."[43] Plutarch, who read Cato's letter, contextualizes this remark:

> He [Cato] was also suspicious of Greeks who practiced medicine at Rome. He had heard, it would seem, of Hippocrates' reply when the Great King of Persia consulted him, with the promise of a fee of many talents, namely, that he [Hippocrates] would never put his skill at the service of barbarians that were enemies of Greece. He [Cato] said all Greek physicians had

45

taken a similar oath, and urged his son to beware of them all.[44]

Cato had a point. The Hippocratic oath does seem a bit weird. Why not codify medical ethics in a contract, enforceable in a court of law, rather than in an "oath" sworn by physicians?

At any rate, these attitudes reveal that the status and credibility of medicine in the time of Plautus' *Gorgylio* was anything but a settled question. The resistance to acupuncture in western medicine suggests something of Roman attitudes toward these Greek novelties. The cult of Asclepius had been in Rome for nearly a century, enough time for thinking Romans to realize its cures were nothing but placebos. Their skepticism points the way to understanding all the sick jokes in Plautus' *Gorgylio*. Romans did not laugh at diseases, disabilities, and deformities themselves. They laughed because the characters turn their eyes in vain to the snakes of Epidaurus, or Tiber Island, to save them.

Carving of the Snake—Prow of Tiber Island.

The good news is that time passed, and with it, the customs. If you go to Tiber Island today, you will still see the snake of Asclepius, and you will still find a hospital—but, as Reginald Foster can attest, that hospital today is a wonder of modern medicine and compassionate care. I dedicate this essay to him in fond affection and eternal gratitude.

BIBLIOGRAPHY

Ammer, Christine. 2003. *The American Heritage Dictionary of Idioms*. New York: Houghton Mifflin.

Baier, Joannes Jacobus. 1717. *Adagiorum medicalium sylloge*. Altdorf bei Nürnberg.

Conrad, C. 1918. "The Rôle of the Cook in Plautus' 'Curculio.'" *Classical Philology* 13:389–400.

De Comitibus, Natale, tr. *Athenaei Dipnosophistarum sive coenae sapientum libri* XV. Venice: Andreas Arrivabenus.

Davidson, James. 2011. *Courtesans and Fishcakes. The Consuming Passions of Classical Athens*. Chicago: University of Chicago Press. [Original edition 1997.]

De Camp, L. Sprague. 1963. *The Ancient Engineers*. New York: Doubleday.

———. 1965. *The Arrows of Hercules*. New York: Doubleday.

De Melo, Wolfgang, tr. 2011. *Plautus. Casina; The Casket Comedy; Curculio; Epidicus; The Two Menaechmuses*. Loeb edition. Cambridge, Mass.: Harvard University Press.

Dickey, Eleanor. 2016. *Learning Latin the Ancient Way*. Cambridge: Cambridge University Press.

Edelstein, Ludwig and Emma Edelstein. 1998. *Asclepius: Collection and Interpretation of the Testimonies*. Baltimore: Johns Hopkins University Press. [Original edition 1945.]

Fenkel, Jonathan. 2015. "A Chronic Illness in Epidaurus?" Personal communication of August 13, 2015.

Fontaine, Michael. 2010. *Funny Words in Plautine Comedy*. New York and Oxford: Oxford University Press.

———. 2014. "Between Two Paradigms: Plautus." In *The Oxford Handbook of Greek and Roman Comedy*, ed. Michael Fontaine and Adele Scafuro, 516–537. Oxford: Oxford University Press.

————. 2016. "Reconsidering Some Plautine Elements in Plautus (*Amphitryo* 302–7, *Captivi* 80–4)." *Classical Journal* 111:417–427.

Gesner, Conrad. 1558. *Historiae animalium liber IIII qui est de piscium & aquatilium animantium natura.* Zürich.

Gratwick, A. S. 1990. "What's in a Name? The 'Diniarchus' of Plautus' *Truculentus*." In *Owls to Athens: Essays Presented to K. J. Dover*, ed. E. M. Craik, 305–309. Oxford: Clarendon Press.

Hanses, Mathias. Forthcoming. "Men among Monuments: Roman Topography and Roman Memory in Plautus's Curculio." Classical Philology.

Henderson, Jeffrey. 1991. *The Maculate Muse: Obscene Language in Attic Comedy.* Second edition. Oxford: Oxford University Press.

Hunter, Richard. 1983. *Eubulus: The Fragments.* Cambridge, UK: Cambridge University Press.

Jonston, Joannes. 1650. *Historiae naturalis de piscibus et cetis libri V.* Frankfurt.

Junius, Hadrianus. 1558. *Adagiorum Centuriae VIII.* Basel: Froben.

Kassel, Rudolf, and Colin Austin, eds. 1983–2001. *Poetae Comici Graeci.* Berlin: de Gruyter. 8 vols.

Mazzini, I. 1988. "La medicina nella letteratura latina. I. Plauto: conoscenze mediche, situazione e instituzioni sanitarie, proposte esegetiche." In *Civiltà materiale e letteratura nel mondo antico*, ed. I. Mazzini, 67–113. Macerata: Università degli Studi di Macerata.

Pieczonka, Joanna. 2016. "The Names of Fish in the Plautine *Captives* (vv. 850–851) – An Attempt at Conjecture." *Philologus* 160:366-371.

Rusten, Jeffrey S., ed. 2011. *The Birth of Comedy: Texts, Documents, and Art from Athenian Comic Competitions, 486–280.* Baltimore: Johns Hopkins University Press.

Thierfelder, Andreas. 1955. "De morbo hepatiario." *Rheinisches Museum* 98:190–2.

Thompson, D'Arcy Wentworth. 1947. *A Glossary of Greek Fishes.* Oxford.

Tylawsky, E. I. 2002. *Saturio's Inheritance: The Greek Ancestry of the Roman Comic Parasite.* New York: Peter Lang.

Ussing, J. L., ed. 1875. *T. Macci Plauti Comoediae*. Copenhagen.

Vienne-Guerrin, Nathalie. 2016. *Shakespeare's Insults: A Pragmatic Dictionary*. New York: Bloomsbury.

von Bradshaw, A. T. S. 1973. "Sceparnio's 'Raincoat' in Plautus, *Rudens* 576." *Classical Quarterly* 23:275–278.

Welsh, Jarrett. 2005. "The Splenetic *Leno*: Plautus, *Curculio* 216–45." *Classical Quarterly* 55:306–309.

Woytek, Erich. 1973. "*Viri Capitones*." *Wiener Studien* 86:65–74.

Zimmermann, A. 1902. "Zur Etymologie des frz. Nominalsuffixes *-ier*." *Zeitschrift für romanische Philologie* 26:591–2.

ENDNOTES

[1] Plautus calls it the *Aesculapi fanum*, the sanctuary of Asclepius. In Fontaine 2010 I explain my preference for Gorgylio (Greek Γοργυλίων, "Furioso") over Curculio (Latin, "Mr. Weevil"); since the book contains an *index jocorum*, I do not cite page numbers. Except as noted, the Latin text, punctuation, translations, and stage directions that follow are my own. Fragments of Greek comedy are cited from Kassel and Austin 1983–2001.

[2] Hanses forthcoming.

[3] Hellenistic catapults fired spears or arrows, not rocks (De Camp 1963, 1965). In Plautus, *catapulta* denotes the missile, not the contraption.

[4] Fontaine 2010.

[5] Cicero *De Oratore* 2.246; Plautus *Miles Gloriosus* 322–3, 1306–7; Persius *Satire* 1.128, Plutarch *Moralia* 633c (*On the Education of Children*).

[6] Perhaps Cappadox is supposed to be complaining about the "pit of his stomach." In his account of the Athenian plague, Thucydides calls an orifice in the stomach καρδία, a word that Lucretius naturally mistranslated *cor*, "heart" (*De Rerum Natura* 6.1152 ~ Thucydides 2.49.3). The odd phrase *radices cordis*, "roots of the heart," suggests Plautus fell prey to the same ambiguity.

[7] Celsus 4.15.1–4; Galen, *De compositione medicamentorum* 8.8 (12.197K); Mazzini 1992. Fenkel 2015 suggests Cappadox is suffering from either familial Mediterranean fever or end-stage liver disease—both chronic conditions. On Celsus, see van Schaik in this volume.

8   Thierfelder 1955.

9   *Historia Animalium* 508b19:Ἴδιον δὲ τῶν ἰχθύων ἐστὶ καὶ τῶν ὀρνίθων τῶν πλείστων τὸ ἔχειν ἀποφυάδας . . . οἱ δ' ἰχθύες ἄνωθεν περὶ τὴν κοιλίαν, καὶ ἔνιοι πολλάς . . . Ἔνιοι δ' ἔχουσι μὲν ὀλίγας δέ, οἷον ἥπατος.

10   Gesner 1568, 490: "Quasi diceret, Mitionem me putabas, qui adhuc sum Demea."

11   The play on *truculentus* (truculent, melampygus) ~ *truncum lentum* (a phlegmatic, apathetic blockhead) at *Truculentus* 265–6 looks like another attempt to capture a similar joke in Greek. In this connection, it is probably relevant that in the *Eudemian Ethics*, Aristotle defined composure as the balance between apathy and irritability.

12   I explain my preference for the spellings "Pseudylus" and "Phallio" in Fontaine 2010.

13   Gratwick 1990, 306; amplified in Fontaine 2010.

14   Fr. 202 = Athenaeus *Deipnosophistae* 7.301c (tr. Olson).

15   According to Athenaeus (107f), the first letter of ἧπαρ (liver) was no longer aspirated in his own time (late 2nd–early 3rd c. CE). According to the MSS of Athenaeus 301c, by contrast, in the mid-4th c. BCE Archestratus spelled the accusative of ἥπατος as χῆπατον, which suggests the name of the fish was aspirated (fr. 28 Olson-Sens).

16   Manuscript B (the oldest and best) has *epatiarius*. *Hepatiarius* appears in J. P. Valla's 1499 commentary on Plautus, from a late MS correction (E³), while Camerarius' 1545 edition of Plautus prints *hepatarius* (the late manuscripts F and Z have *epatarius*).

17   Henderson 1991, 195; some examples on 195–9, many more in Rusten 2011 (157, 179, 233, 522, 571, 681, 693, and 696).

18   Henderson 1991, 433: "Garry Wills suggests ways in which αὐλοί [= *tibiae*] could produce elaborate sound effects to accompany crepitation in comedy. There can be no doubt that such sound effects were employed." In Fontaine 2010 I discuss similar bilingual puns in Plautus, such as *pascite*/πάσχετε in *Mostellaria* 23.

19   Ussing 1875 thinks the cook enters from the forum at v. 223, laden with provisions, and "is a silent spectator of their colloquy until vs. 251" (Conrad 1918, 394–5, summarizing but rejecting the view).

20   Athenaeus 7.306d–308b. Athenaeus 7.311 quotes Archestratus fr. 46 Olson-Sens. Antiphanes fr. 216 and Apicius 424 and 425 also give advice on salting and brining mullets.

21   Philemon fr. 42.

22   Athenaeus 6.225e–6.226a; in Antiphanes fr. 217, note σαπροὺς κομιδῇ, "completely rotten." In Antiphanes fr. 159, note Athenaeus' word σεσηπότας, "rotten," and Antiphanes' σήπονθ᾽, ἕωλοι κείμενοι δύ᾽ ἡμέρας ἢ τρεῖς, "rot, lying there going bad for two or three days." He goes on to comment on the (bad) smell.

23   Woytek 1973; Fontaine 2010; compare Athenaeus 7.307d.

24   Quoted in Apuleius, *Apologia* 39.

25   *Internal Affections* 246: περιπατείτω δι᾽ ἡμέρης, "Let him take walks all throughout the day." *Epidemics* 7, 464: περιπατεῖν συχνά, "Go for frequent walks." Similarly, Celsus *De Medicina* 4.16 recommends exercise (*exercitatio*).

26   Welsh 2005, 308.

27   On the ironic "raincoat," see Von Bradshaw 1973; for other jokes that require Plautus' audience to generate the missing word themselves, see Fontaine 2010, chapter 4.

28   Fr. 312 Astbury (*Modius*).

29   Fontaine 2014.

30   Fontaine 2016.

31   A papyrus fragment of the 1st or 2nd c. CE preserves a section of a Greek-Latin glossary of fish names (P.Oxy 23.2660). As Dickey 2016, 124–5, says: "The words in this glossary would not be high on the priority list of any Latin learner today . . . The ancient attitude to such words was clearly different, for both vegetable names and fish names are common among surviving bilingual glossary materials."

32   Pieczonka 2016.

33   I explain my preference for Phrynesium over Phronesium in Fontaine 2010.

34   By a remarkable coincidence—since it seems to be no more than that—in Shakespeare's time, the term "fishmonger" was allegedly slang for a pimp or procurer (*Hamlet* 2.2.174, Vienne-Guerrin 2016).

35   Examples include Diphilus fr. 64 (ἀνθηρός/splendid, ἀνθίας/a fish) and Plautus' *Casina* 493–8: *hordeias* (~ *triticeias*), *soleas* (~ *sculponeas*), and *lingulacas* (~ *linguas*).

36   (1) 1115 (*elixus esse quam assus soleo suavior*, where Plautus has translated a Greek jingle on ἐφθά and ὀπτά, "boiled" and "roasted" (Fontaine 2010, 59; the pun on *assum* ~ *elixus sis* in *Poenulus* 279–80 seems to imply that Milphio is a fish, too.) (2) 362 (*Adest, adest opsonium: eccum Tranio a portu redit.*) *Opsonium* (*obsonium*) means

"fish" and *obsonari* means "to buy *fish*" (§5 above). (3) 1070 (*non ego illi* [= Tranio] *extemplo hamum ostendam, sensim mittam lineam*).

[37] Mazzini 1992, 68–72 finds a few alleged allusions to humoral views of blood (*Pseudylus* 1215, *Mostellaria* 508–9), yellow bile (*Bacchides* 537–8, *Frivolaria* fr. 2), black bile (*Amphitryo* 727–8, *Captivi* 594–601, *Casina* 413–6), and phlegm (*Mostellaria* 1109–10). Except for the black bile, however, all his interpretations seem debatable or forced.

[38] *Persa* 1–2; Fontaine 2010.

[39] Stele II, 32 and 40; stele I, 9; Edelstein and Edelstein 1998, 235, 237, and 231.

[40] Greece too had its traditional remedies, and not just in the remote past. Pyrrhus of Epirus (319–272 BCE) "was believed to have the power to cure diseases of the spleen. He would sacrifice a white cock, and then, while the patient lay flat on his back, he would gently press upon the region of the spleen with his right foot. There was nobody so poor or obscure that Pyrrhus would refuse him this healing touch, if he were asked for it. He would accept the cock as a reward after he had sacrificed it, and was always very pleased with this gift" (Plutarch, *Life of Pyrrhus* 3).

[41] Pliny, *Historia Naturalis* 29.12–13.

[42] Cicero, *De Divinatione* 24: *Vetus autem illud Catonis admodum scitum est, qui mirari se aiebat quod non rideret haruspex haruspicem cum vidisset.*

[43] Pliny, *Naturalis Historia* 29.7.14: *iurarunt inter se barbaros necare omnis medicina.*

[44] *Cato*, 23.

Indirect and Off-Record Speech in Roman Comedy: The Case of the Conditional Request

Peter Barrios-Lech

1. Introduction.

The reader is invited to work out the principle that orders the following requests. All involve the speaker asking the addressee to pay attention.

(1)　Simo's slave Davos speaks, aside. Simo listens in but cannot quite make out what he hears.

SIMO	*carnufex quae loquitur?*
DAVOS	*erus est neque provideram.*
SIMO	*Dave.*
DAVOS	*hem quid est?*
SIMO	**eho dum ad me.** (*An.* 183–84)

SIMO	What is the knave saying?
DAVOS	It's master and I hadn't noticed before.
SIMO	Davus.
DAVOS	(*pretending to hear a noise from somewhere*) Oh! What is it?
SIMO	**Hey, you! Here!**

(2) Nicobulus tries to get his slave to listen.

CHRYSALUS *iustumst <ut> tuos tibi servos tuo arbitratu serviat.*

NICOBULUS **hoc age sis nunciam.**

CHRYSALUS *ubi lubet, recita: aurium operam tibi dico. (Bac. 995–996)*

CHRYSALUS It's right for *your* slave to serve *you* to *your* liking.

NICOBULUS Come now, pay attention.

CHRYSALUS Read whenever you like: Unto you do I vouchsafe the tendance of mine ears.

(3) The prologue speaker of Terence's *Phormio* asks for a fair hearing of the play.

PROLOGUS *adporto novam Epidicazomenon quam vocant comoediam Graeci, Latini Phormionem nominant quia primas partis qui aget is erit Phormio parasitus,* **per quem res geretur maxume voluntas vostra si ad poetam accesserit.** *(Ph. 24–29)*

PROLOGUS I bring to you a newly minted comedy: one the Greeks call *The Claim He Made*; Latin speakers call it *Phormio*, since Phormio's the one who'll play the leading role—that of the parasite. **By him especially will the action be carried out If your own will is in agreement with the poet's.**

(4) Demipho, an old, married man, is in love with a slave girl, but he's diffident about revealing this illicit love to his friend Lysimachus.

DEMIPHO *Lysimache, salve.*

LYSIMACHUS *euge, Demipho, salveto. quid agis? quid fit?*

DEMIPHO *quod miserrumus.*

LYSIMACHUS *di melius faxint.*

DEMIPHO *di hoc quidem faciunt.*

LYSIMACHUS	*quid est?*
DEMIPHO	***dicam, si videam tibi esse operam aut otium.*** *(Mer.* 283–86)

DEMIPHO	Hi Lysimachus.
LYSIMACHUS	Demipho! Hello! What's going on? What are you doing?
DEMIPHO	Whatever the worst of all wretches does.
LYSIMACHUS	Gods make it better!
DEMIPHO	That's precisely what they *are* doing.
LYSIMACHUS	What do you mean?
DEMIPHO	**I'd tell you, if I saw that you had attention or time to give.**

If you guessed that the ordering proceeds along the principle of more to less direct request, you are correct. The first two utterances, (1) and (2), are phrased in a direct manner, while the last two passages, (3) and (4), exemplify the subject of this essay: they are "indirect," and thus potentially ambiguous requests. Let me now clarify what I mean by these terms, "direct," "indirect," and "ambiguous."

2. Indirect and off-record requests.

If direct speech involves conveying a speech act—for instance, a request—using the conventional means (e.g., an imperative), then indirection in language is conveying that same speech act (A), conventionally phrased with an imperative (e.g., "Pass the salt.") by means of a different speech act (B), for instance, as a question (e.g., "Is the saltcellar around anywhere?").[1]

In the right context, the latter, "indirect" speech act would trigger, however reflexively, a chain of inference by which the addressee gets from B ("Is the saltcellar around anywhere?") to A ("Pass the salt."). Thus, imagine that I have the saltcellar at my elbow; that it is well out of my dinner companion's reach, and she and I both know it. I now hear her ask, "Is the saltcellar around anywhere?" Hers is not an (otiose) question about the whereabouts of a table condiment. Instead, there is a "point" to this question, namely, to have the salt passed. This inference (viz., "my companion wants the salt passed") squares well with our shared situation (we are at dinner, and my companion can't reach the salt) and with the common-sense assumption that my companion would not purposely utter an irrelevance.

To return to passages (1) and (2), then, a master orders a slave in a remarkably direct way; in both, function follows form, in a one-to-one relationship, with the utterance (*eho* or *hoc age sis*) correlated, by conventions of usage, to the meaning *animadverte huc*.[2] Incidentally, we should note, alongside their directness, the utterances' syntactic minimalism. Both these features—directness and minimalism—are typical of "master's talk," where "unmodified imperatives, direct expression of will (in forms like *volo* and *nolo* + infinitive), and little to no politeness are typical."[3] By contrast, linguistic elaboration was, for the Romans, a sign of respect.[4]

And linguistic elaboration is precisely what we get in the third passage, where the roles are reversed from those in passages (1) and (2). For a Terentian prologue speaker appeals to his superiors—the audience—for their attention: *per quem* [sc. *Phormionem*] *res geretur maxume / voluntas vostra si ad poetam accesserit* ("By him especially will the action be carried out / If your own will is in agreement with the poet."). Function does not follow form in this case, since the "speaker meaning," or actual intent behind the words, cannot be straightforwardly "read off" from the meaning of the words, the "sentence meaning."[5] Particularly ambiguous is *voluntas vostra*, "your inclination"—to do what is left unclear. The audience must infer from the context, in addition to other cues, what is meant: their inclination (*voluntas*) to give a fair hearing.

Given the relevant contextual cues, the prologue speaker's intent is clear enough. True, the *prologus* could have just come out and asked the audience to give their undivided attention, but his more indirect way of putting that idea, while risking obscurity, gains in politeness (and, dare one say, elegance).[6]

Similarly indirect, but more ambiguous, is the fourth passage, uttered by Demipho to his friend Lysimachus: *dicam, si videam tibi esse operam aut otium* ("I'd tell you, if I saw that you had attention or time to give."). Here the "speaker meaning" is ambiguous. On the one hand, Lysimachus could understand from the line that his friend Demipho does not want to impose. This is certainly one plausible intent behind the words of passage (4). But if Lysimachus, the addressee, adopted this interpretation, and answered something like, "You're right, I don't have the time," he would come off as rude. Thus, Lysimachus is pushed—manipulated—towards the other possible intent behind the words, specifically, that the line "I'd tell you, if I saw that you had attention or time to give" is really a request for attention. Demipho's motive for conveying such a manipulative request to his friend is to test the relationship: if Lysimachus agrees to listen, that confirms the friendship, for friends, as a rule, are supposed to set aside time and attention for friends.[7]

Why might a Latin speaker have chosen one of these more-or-less ambiguous formulations? For an answer, we can turn to some ideas from Brown and Levinson's work on linguistic politeness.[8] Suppose we want to persuade our interlocutor of something, to tell him or her what to do, to criticize. In so imposing our point of view, commanding, or critiquing the listener, we may imply that we do not value his or her public image, or "face." To avoid that unwelcome implication, we could decline to carry out the imposition, the "face-threatening act." But if we find that we must impose, we could compensate for the imposition by showing we *do still* value the listener's "face." For instance, Thais, courtesan of Terence's *Eunuch*, counterbalances criticism, a "face-threatening" act, with praise of the other and depreciation of herself.

(5) Thais confronts the *adulescens* Chaerea, suspected of violating the young woman who had been in Thais' custody.

THAIS   *missa haec faciamu'. non te dignum, Chaerea,*
                 fecisti; nam si ego digna hac contumelia sum

> *maxume, at tu indignu' qui faceres tamen.* (*Eu.*
> 864–866)

THAIS   Let's dismiss this charade [sc. of Chaerea pretending to be a eunuch]. You have done something that does not befit you, Chaerea; for even if *I* deserve this outrage by all means, *you* at any rate, were not equal to committing it.

Thais mitigates her criticism (that Chaerea has committed outrage, *contumelia*), a speech act which would potentially inflict a wound on Chaerea's face, precisely by acknowledging her awareness of both her and Chaerea's relative positions in society. Someone of Thais's station may deserve to be treated as Chaerea has treated her, but Chaerea has acted in a manner that does not befit his position in society. Donatus notes precisely this counterbalancing of "face-threatening act" and the compensatory "polite" strategies when he says Thais' is "a marvelous accusation blending praise and politeness": *mira accusatio mixta laudi et blandimento.*[9]

Note, however, that, although compensating for it, Thais still goes "on-record" with her criticism: *non te dignum, Chaerea, / fecisti.* Yet a speaker might believe the "face-threatening act" was so potentially injurious that she or he had best not go on record with it at all. In that case, the speaker has the option to use a less direct means, as the prologue does, above, in passage (3). The "face-threatening" intent would still be unambiguously conveyed, but the utterance would gain in politeness, precisely by being expressed in a more roundabout way.

Now, some of these indirect utterances are so often used that they become standard polite ways of handling routine matters, like asking for salt at the dinner table. Thus, "Can you please pass the salt?" far from being a question about your ability to hand over a saltcellar, functions as a request. This standard formula, every bit as direct as "Pass the salt," is nevertheless more polite; it is a "whimperative," to use Steven Pinker's apt term.[10] We might expect that Latin had its share of such standardized indirect requests, and it does. In

Roman comedy, we find such "pre-fab" indirect requests as *potin' ut istuc facias?*; *quin facis?*; and *dasne?* or *dan'?* Conventional, also, are statements like *aequom est* (*te facere*). Surprisingly, however, few such "pre-fab" requests are polite in the Latin of Plautus and Terence.[11]

So far, then, we have three options for conveying a request: (1) convey it directly; (2) compensate for it by adding polite elements, like praise, words for "please," and the like; (3) use an indirect means. A fourth (4) means is simply to go off-record with the request, as in passage (4), above: an utterance that could pass, ambiguously, either as a refusal to impose or a request. Brown and Levinson report that one secretary in an office, who wants her employer to pass a stapler, instead asks another secretary for it, even though the boss stands right next to the device. In this way, "[h]is face is not threatened, and he *can* choose to do it himself as a bonus 'free gift.'"[12] Or consider the following:

(6)   A suggestion that violent means be used against a rival candidate.

Hillary wants to abolish, essentially abolish, the Second Amendment. By the way, and if she gets to pick her judges, nothing you can do, folks. *Although the Second Amendment people, maybe there is, I don't know.* But I'll tell you what, that will be a horrible day (emphasis added).

The intent here is not obvious, but was widely taken as an appeal to proponents of Second Amendment rights to use violence against the Democratic presidential candidate of 2016, Hillary Clinton. It is the characteristic feature of such off-record requests that their intent is plausibly deniable. Thus, when Donald Trump was asked about (6), he claimed he had been referring, all along, to activists' power to vote Clinton out, not take her out by violent means.[13]

Off-record requests are the ambiguous command *par excellence*, because the speaker tries to have his or her cake and eat it, too: to say something without actually saying it, or, better, by apparently saying *something else.* A review of all the directives in Roman comedy turns up few incontrovertible examples.[14] This scarcity has at least two causes. First, off-record requests are the chameleons of any directive system: they are difficult to detect, because they pretend to be something other than what they are. Second, even though we know Plautus' and Terence's audiences delighted in the ambiguity of the wordplay and pun, the playwrights generally needed to communicate characters' motives unambiguously, thus obviating the use of off-record requests.

3. Conditionals.

Note that the less (3) and more (4) ambiguous requests, above, are expressed as conditionals, "if . . . then" statements. These express hypothetical states of affairs ("if it were to rain today"), and convey, in a tentative way, statements ("if you are ready [i.e., since you are ready], let's begin"), and requests ("here's the test, if you are ready to begin"). Indeed, requests conveyed with conditional sentences can convey politeness:

(7)   The Carthaginian's request that his addressee look at a token:

tesseram conferre si vis hospitalem, eccam attuli (Poen. 1047–48).

Look, I brought the (guest-friend) token, if you want to compare it with yours.

I propose now to categorize and discuss all the conditional requests in Roman comedy (there are seventy). My thesis here is that speakers choose the conditional request that best reflects their bond to the addressee. Thus, we most often find conditionals of the type "if you rub my back, I'll rub yours" in relationships where reciprocity is foregrounded. We find polite conditionals like (7), where politeness would presumably be called for: inferiors' addresses to superiors. And we find ambiguous off-record requests like (4), whenever direct expression would threaten the speaker's relationship with the addressee.

The following table lists the kinds of conditional sentence used in Plautus and Terence to convey commands, requests, and directives.[15]

Type	Examples	Frequency
1. Logical Conditional Sentence	*sed ea* [sc. *muliere*] *ut sim implicitus dicam, si operaest auribus / atque advortendum ad animum adest benignitas* (*Mer.* 14)	22
2. Future More Vivid	*<ea>m calamitatem vostra intellegentia / sedabit, si erit adiutrix nostrae industriae* (*Hec.* 31–32)	10
3. Future Less Vivid	*si aequom siet me plus sapere quam vos, dederim vobis consilium catum* (*Ep.* 257–258)	26
4. Tentative suggestions cast in *si* clauses	*si itast, tesseram / conferre si vis hospitalem, eccam attuli* (*Poen.* 1047–48)	7
5. Mixed Conditions	*id ago, si taceas modo* (*Ps.* 997)	4
6. Present Contrary to Fact	*quod tu si idem faceres, magis in rem et vostram et nostram id esset* (*Hec.* 249)	1

Table 1: Conditional Requests in Plautus and Terence: 70 total.

Types 1 and 2: Logical Conditional Sentences and Future More Vivid.

Conditionals of the type "If it rains, the ground gets wet" are standardly called "Logical Conditional Sentences."[16] In one manifestation of this type, expressing the idea "If you scratch my back, I'll scratch yours," the if clause contains a present indicative and the main clause has the future indicative: *si illud facis, hoc tibi faciam* ("if you do this, I'll do that").[17] Example (8) is typical.

(8)   Mercury addresses the audience, just prior to driving Amphitruo away from the house.

MERCURIUS   *iam ille hic deludetur probe, siquidem vos voltis auscultando operam dare. (Am. 1004–5)*

MERCURIUS   Soon he will be well and thoroughly duped, right here, if, that is, you want to put your effort to listening.

Logical Conditional Sentences in principle express a conclusion that certainly or necessarily follows, if the protasis is true.[18] With this syntactical type, Mercury definitively promises a result, the audience's entertainment (*iam ille . . . deludetur probe*), *if* the audience proves willing to listen (*siquidem vos voltis auscultando operam dare*). If, then, *si* + present indicative, future indicative promises some benefit (*bene erit tibi*) in exchange for the hearer's compliance (*si hoc facis*), its opposite, the threat, forbids (*si hoc facis*) or compels (*nisi hoc facis*) action, imposing a sanction (*male erit tibi*) on the hearer for the latter's failure to comply. Consider example (9).

(9)

EUCLIO   *nisi refers –*

LYCONIDES   *quid tibi ego referam?*

EUCLIO   *quod surrupuisti meum, iam quidem hercle te ad praetorem rapiam et tibi scribam dicam. (Aul. 759–60)*

EUCLIO	If you don't return—
LYCONIDES	What?
EUCLIO	What you took of mine, I'm really gonna seize you and take you before the praetor; slap a lawsuit on you.

Again, Euclio uses the syntax of the Logical Conditional Sentence (*nisi* + present indicative, future indicative) to stress that if his addressee does not comply (*nisi refers*), a lawsuit will definitely ensue (*tibi scribam dicam*). Of the 73 threats in Roman comedy, most (41) are like Euclio's, that is, they have a *nisi* clause containing a present indicative, precisely the structure used to convey stringent threats.[19]

By contrast, promises of the form *bene erit tibi, si* indicative, *hoc facis* express especially emphatic requests. Of the 22 directives expressed in this way (with a *si* clause containing a present indicative), almost all (20) guarantee a benefit to the addressee, as expressed in the main clause, like Mercury's *iam ille hic deludetur probe*. Let us now turn to the Future More Vivid type, exemplified in (10).

(10) The old man Callicles wants to get the truth from two maidservants.

CALLICLES	*at si verum mi eritis fassae, vinclis exsolvemini.* (*Truc.* 784)
CALLICLES	But if you tell me the truth, you'll be released from your shackles.

Most of the FMV requests are *quid pro quo* constructions, like (10): Callicles makes a promise to the maidservants, if only they will do something for him first. Yet only two of our FMV requests employ the future perfect in the *si* clause (*si feceris istuc, hoc tibi faciam*): Callicles' above, and one spoken by the prologus in Terence's *Phormio*. The same structure (*si feceris istuc, hoc tibi faciam*) is more often used to convey threats.[20] Indeed, of the threatening type *si istuc feceris, vapulabis*, I count nine in Plautus and two in Terence.[21] Interestingly, both examples from Terence come from the *Eunuch*, a play which comes closest to Plautus in many respects, including its language.[22]

To return to the two FMV requests like that at (10), these are reserved for formal situations, like the inquisition during which Callicles offers to free his maidservants, or the prologue's appeal to the audience in *Phormio* (Ter. *Ph.* 28–29). Otherwise, requests with the simple future in the *si* clause (e.g., *si auscultabis, eloquar*) are neutral in register, appearing in situations where elevated diction is expected (the dignified old man Philto advises his son, *Trin.* 300; a prologue speaks at *Hec.* 31–32), but also where it is not (the sycophant asks for the old man's attention at *Trin.* 939, Pseudolus makes a promise to his master, *Ps.* 724).[23]

Of the potentially polite conditional sentences belonging to either Type 1 ("Logical Conditional Sentences") or 2 (Future Most Vivid) that express directives, then, there are 32 total: 22 from Type 1, and 10 from Type 2 (Future More Vivid).[24] These account for about half of the conditional-sentence directives in Roman comedy. And of these 32, 27, or 84%, express a *quid pro quo*, like the messenger god's (8) or Callicles' (10).

Unsurprisingly, requests like "I'll scratch your back if you scratch mine" occur in relationships where elements of reciprocity and exchange are foremost. For example, the relationship between actors of a Roman comedy and their audiences turns on reciprocal exchange of services (the actors will entertain if the audience will pay attention). Accordingly, we find nine *quid pro quo* conditionals in actor-audience exchanges, and again, Mercury's in passage (7) is typical, as is Prologus' in passage (3), above.[25]

Where else do we find the *quid pro quo* conditional request? In the ongoing debate on Roman friendship, one side emphasizes the "fundamentally instrumental nature" of the bond, while the other claims that mutual devotion is the defining feature.[26] It is worth asking, then, if the "I'll scratch your back if you scratch mine" type features in friendship and similar bonds. Let us circumscribe our search to precisely that kind of conditional.

Now, as mentioned above, 27 of the "I'll scratch your back, if..." type belong either to syntactical type (1), the Logical Conditional Sentence, or (2), the Future More Vivid; three assume the so-called Future Less Vivid form *si hoc facias, hoc tibi faciam*, our type (3); three are cast as mixed conditions, our type (5). That makes a total of thirty-three conditionals of this kind.

Seventeen occur in relationships having a *quid pro quo* aspect that is mutually manifest to both parties: a parasite and a patron (*Cur.* 328); a captor, bargaining with captives (*Capt.* 331–32; *Truc.* 784); a slave and his master, typically in an "inversion" scene, where the slave claims superior status because he has something the *dominus* wants (*Cas.* 743, *Epid.* 728, *Ps.* 724, 1328; Ter. *Hau.* 317).[27] Fourteen occur in dialogues between strangers; for instance:

(11) A parasite posing as a freedman asks his addressee about Lycus' whereabouts.

CURCULIO *sed hunc quem quaero commostrare si potes, inibis
a me solidam et grandem gratiam.* (*Cur.* 404–405)

CURCULIO But if you show me the man I seek, You'll have earned my solid and serious goodwill.

Here the apodosis, *inibis a me solidam et grandem gratiam*, essentially promises the addressee a benefit.

None of these occur in dialogues between those who share an intimate bond, with just **two** exceptions. The first can be dealt with summarily, as an old man promises his friend the whole story, if the latter will only listen: *si taceas, loquar* (*Trin.* 148). This is a formulaic phrase, and among the *quid pro quo* directives we are considering, it occurs six other times in more or less this form (*si taceas, loquar*); all other instances occur either in dialogues between strangers or between a patron and client.[28] The second exception is even more telling. In the famous last scene of *Adelphoe*, Demea pretends to be generous and liberal, like Micio. In the prologue of this play, Micio explained his parenting philosophy: essentially, that father and son should relate in a kind of *quid pro quo* bond:

(12)

MICIO *ille quem beneficio adiungas ex animo facit, studet par referre, praesens absensque idem erit (Ad. 72–73)*

MICIO The one whom you bind to you with favors acts sincerely towards you, He's eager to return the favor, and, whether present or absent, will be the same to you.

Now, in the last scene, Demea makes a mockery of this philosophy, getting the city bachelor to give favors liberally: first to take on a poor widow as a wife to please the son (929–95), then to give a poor neighbor a plot of land (947–56), and finally to free a slave and maidservant (960–77). In return, Micio will secure these beneficiaries' good will. After all, securing others' good will through favors is Micio's distinguishing feature (passage [12], above, and *Ad.* 863–65).

Finally, Demea promises that Micio will be repaid if the bachelor gives the freed slave some money to help the latter start life as a *libertus*:

(13)

DEMEA *siquidem porro, Micio, tu tuom officium facies atque huic aliquid paullum prae manu dederis, unde utatur, reddet tibi cito. (Ad. 979–80)*

DEMEA If, Micio, you do your duty and give this man something to hand, that he could use, he'll repay you quickly.

To convince Micio to give the money, Demea promises that Micio will recover the loaned money (*reddet tibi cito*), implying that he, Demea, will ensure that repayment. It makes sense that this "If you do this, I'll do something for you" type of request should appear precisely in a scene where Demea exposes as faulty his brother's instrumental approach to familial relationships, one based on *quid pro quo*.

It is telling that such conditional requests do not, as a rule, appear in dialogues between friends. This fact, then, argues against the notion that Roman friendship had a "fundamentally instrumental nature."

Type 3: Future Less Vivid

The hypothetical *si des, gaudeam*, could be construed two ways in Early Latin, depending on the context. It may express a possibility that is, to some extent, doubtful: "If you end up giving, I'll be happy."[29] But if you have just refused to give, then *si des, gaudeam* expresses a contrafactual condition, "If you'd given it, I would be happy." I think we can find genuinely off-record requests that exploit this contrafactual meaning. De Melo translates passage (4), above, *dicam, si videam tibi esse operam aut otium* (*Mer.* 286), as a contrafactual, "I'd tell you if I saw that you have time or leisure." As explained above, the line's speaker meaning could be something like "You're busy, and I don't want to disturb you with my news." But the friend listening sees a different speaker meaning: a request for attention.

And note how Epidicus, the eponymous clever slave of Plautus' play, deploys the construction, as he suggests to two old men that he may have an idea:

(14)

EPIDICUS   *si aequom siet me plus sapere quam vos, dederim vobis consilium catum, quod laudetis, ut ego opino, uterque.* (*Ep.* 257–58)

EPIDICUS   If it were proper for me to be wiser than you, I'd give you a smart plan you'd both praise, as I think.

The audience—Epidicus' "betters"—could simply accept the overt, sentence meaning: "If it were proper to be smarter than you [but it is not], I'd offer a clever plan [but I can't or won't]." Instead, however, the target audience understands that the slave is asking them to listen to a plan. This is an off-record request partly because it passes the deniability test: Epidicus could have denied that this was a request to listen to his advice.

Chrysalus, tricky slave of *Bacchides*, similarly employs a contrafactual condition to give advice.

(15)

CHRYSALUS   *verum, ut ego opinor, si ego in istoc sim loco, dem potius aurum quam illum corrumpi sinam.* (Bac. 1039–1040)

CHRYSALUS   In my opinion, if I were in your place, I'd give the money rather than letting him be morally corrupted.

The *callidus servus* hypothesizes a world in which he, the servant, was the master, with a son in need of help. Within this now-established hypothetical world, Chrysalus imagines what exactly he, now a master, would do to help his imaginary *filiusfamilias*. Nicobulus, the actual master listening to all this, can decide how he should act on Chrysalus' words—the invented scenario posed by the slave.

Chrysalus does not come out and simply advise Nicobulus, since it would appear untoward for a servant so to advise the *paterfamilias*, who should in principle know what's best for his son. But Chrysalus can give advice without appearing to do so, for (15) would allow Chrysalus to deny any such intent if pressed.

On the whole, speakers with authority avoid using these Future Less Vivid requests with inferiors, having no need to be diffident or go off-record: a superior position enables a more direct style of speech.[30]

The three exceptions to this general rule are telling, for they use the polite form ironically to convey its opposite, an impolite request. And in each case, the speaker enjoys a position of authority over the addressee. In his eponymous play, Amphitruo suggests that his wife adopt a more restrained and prudent attitude (*saltem tute si pudoris egeas, sumas mutuom, Am.* 819). Menaechmus of the eponymous play aims a similarly biting criticism at his wife: *ni mala, ni stulta sies, ni indomita imposque animi, / quod viro esse odio videas, tute tibi odio habeas* (*Men.* 110–111). Similarly biting is the criticism-with-request in Demea's appeal to his son: *si tu sis homo, hic faciat,* "If you were a person, he [Micio] would be doing it [sc., marrying the poor next-door neighbor]" (*Ad.* 934–35).[31]

Type 4: Tentative Suggestions Expressed in *si* clauses

Of the seven examples of this type in Roman comedy, (14) is typical.

(16)   A parasite points out a symposiast's garland to a matron:
PENICULUS   *em hac abiit, si vis persequi vestigiis.* (*Men.* 566)

PENICULUS   Look, he went this way, if you want to follow his tracks.

Peniculus expresses himself in a tentative way, with a *si* clause. Perhaps because, in general, requests expressed this way are more tentative, we find all seven instances put in the mouth of an inferior addressing a superior. A passage in *Poenulus* might furnish the single exception. There, the Carthaginian guest, Hanno, cautiously asks his host to take a look at his *tessera*, "guest-friend token": *tesseram / conferre si vis hospitalem, eccam attuli,* "Look, I've brought my token, if you want to compare your own with it" (*Poen.* 1047–48; passage [7], above). Hanno, however, is an odd duck in the world of Roman comedy: he is an outsider, and shares traits with the tricky slave.[32]

71

4. Conclusion

When confronting ambiguity in our texts, we are used to dealing with two types, lexical (or semantic) and syntactic. Greek and Latin authors exploit these in striking ways. Sophocles, for instance, has Oedipus address Jocasta as *philtaton* "dearest," just before his catastrophic realization ("O dearest [*philtaton*] person of Jocasta, why have you sent me here, from the house," ὦ φίλτατον γυναικὸς Ἰοκάστης κάρα, / τί μ' ἐξεπέμψω δεῦρο τῶνδε δωμάτων, *OT* 950–51). The word simultaneously means, in this passage, both "dearest" and "very much belonging to me." Thus, *philtaton* emphasizes Jocasta in her role as *both* wife ("dearest") *and* mother to the Theban King ("very much his own"). The ambiguity behind the word is, then, a subtle foreshadowing of Oedipus' discovery, only about 200 lines in the future. Plautus can similarly exploit the ambiguous meaning of a word to create comedy, heighten the interest in a scene, and raise a thematic issue.[33]

Syntactic ambiguity is exemplified by the famous oracle given to Pyrrhus, King of the Epirotes, in Ennius: *aiio te Aeacida Romanos vincere posse*, "I say that you, son of Aeacus, can beat the Romans / I say that the Romans, son of Aeacus, can beat you" (*Ann.* 167). The ambiguity here, of course, lies in the function of the accusative embedded in an *accusativus cum infinitivo* clause.[34]

But we have been dealing with a different kind of ambiguity, that which arises when two more intents, or "speaker meanings" could be "read off" from what the speaker says, the "sentence meaning." When such ambiguous utterances *could* convey requests, in addition to one or more other "speaker meanings," we call them off record. Of the conditional sentence types we have reviewed, we find that almost all convey rather direct requests, leaving little to no room for any alternative "intents" to be inferred.

These conditional requests reflect the relationship between speaker and addressee. Of all the conditional directives that promise something in exchange for the hearer's compliance (*quid pro quo* directives), more than half occur in relationships where the element of exchange is foremost, and the rest, with two notable exceptions, occur in exchanges between strangers. The more polite conditionals (3, Future Less Vivid) and (4, Tentative suggestions cast in *si* clauses), by contrast, are usually directed by an inferior to a superior.

This brings us to our genuinely off-record requests—the ambiguous ones. We found that the Future Less Vivid, in its contrary-to-fact version, was the single type productive of these. The speaker goes off record with a request, because, expressed openly, it could challenge the existing relationship. Thus, the two slaves at (14) and (15) do not *openly* give advice to their master, because doing so would make explicit their intellectual, if not social, superiority. Safer for the slave to go off-record, then: the master can choose to understand the "speaker meaning" (offer of advice), or not. If the master were to press the slave, asking whether the lowly *servus* truly intended to presume to offer advice, the slave could always deny it. That is the value of the off-record request: the fiction of the relationship can be preserved, while both speaker and addressee tacitly, but never openly, countenance the facts that might threaten it.[35]

* * *

It is a pleasure to dedicate this essay to Fr. Reginald Foster, who brought Latin alive for me during his magical *Latinitas Aestiva* sessions on the Janiculum in the summer of 2004.

BIBLIOGRAPHY

Barrios-Lech, P. 2015. "Bilingual Pun and Epic Allusion in *Aulularia* (Plaut. *Aul.* 394–396, 736)." *QUCC* 109.1:119–136.

———. 2016. *Linguistic Interaction in Roman Comedy*. Cambridge.

Bennett, C. E. 1966 (repr.). *Syntax of Early Latin*, vol. 1: *Syntax of the Early Latin Verb*. Hildesheim.

Brown, P., and S. Levinson. 1987. *Politeness. Some Universals in Language Usage*. Cambridge.

Dickey, E. 2012. "The Rules of Politeness and Latin Request Formulae." In *Laws and Rules in Indo-European*, ed. P. Probert and A. Willi, 313–328. Oxford.

Ernout, A., and F. Thomas. 1964 (repr.). *Syntaxe Latine*. Paris.

Fontaine, M. 2007. "*Parasitus Colax* (Terence, *Eunuchus* 30)." *Mnemosyne* 60:483–489.

———. 2010. *Funny Words in Plautus*. Oxford.

Gildersleeve, B. L., and G. Lodge. 1997. *Gildersleeve's Latin Grammar*. Wauconda, IL.

Hofmann, J. B., and A. Szantyr. 1965. *Lateinische Syntax und Stilistik*. Munich.

Karakasis, E. 2005. *Terence and the Language of Roman Comedy*. Cambridge.

Kissine, M. 2012. "Sentences, Utterances, and Speech Acts." In *The Cambridge Handbook of Pragmatics*, ed. K. Jaszczolt and K. Allan, 169–190. Cambridge.

Konstan, D. 2010. "Are Fellow Citizens Friends? Aristotle versus Cicero on *Philia*, *Amicitia*, and Social Solidarity." In *Valuing Others in Classical Antiquity*, ed. R. Rosen and I. Sluiter, 233–248. Leiden.

Kühner, Raphael, and Carl Stegmann. 1912–1914. *Ausführliche Grammatik der lateinischen Sprache*. 2nd edn. 3 vols. Hanover.

Leech, G. 1983. *Principles of Pragmatics*. London.

Lindskog, C. 1895. *De Enuntiatis apud Plautum et Terentium Condicionalibus*. Lund.

Morgan, J. L. 1978. "Two Types of Convention in Indirect Speech Acts." In *Syntax and Semantics 9: Pragmatics*, ed. P. Cole, 261–280. New York.

Müller, R. 1997. *Sprechen und Sprache: Dialoglinguistische Studien zu Terenz*. Heidelberg.

Pinker, S. 2007. "The evolutionary social psychology of off-record indirect speech acts." *Intercultural Pragmatics* 4(4):437–461.

Risselada, R. 1993. *The Imperative and Other Directive Expressions in Latin: A Study in the Pragmatics of a Dead Language*. Amsterdam.

Sadock, J. M., and A. M. Zwicky. 1985. "Speech Acts Distinctions in Syntax." In *Language Typology and Syntactic Description*, ed. Timothy Shopen, 155–196. Cambridge.

Saller, R. 1982. *Personal Patronage under the Early Empire*. Cambridge.

Searle, J. R. 1975. "Indirect Speech Acts." In P. *Syntax and Semantics*, vol. 3: *Speech Acts*, ed. Peter Cole and J. Morgan, 59–82. New York.

Skutsch, O. (ed.) 1985. *The Annals of Quintus Ennius*. Oxford.

Unceta-Gómez, L. 2014. "La politesse linguistique en latin: Bilan d'une étude en cours." In *Dictionnaire Historique et Encyclopédie Linguistique du Latin*, accessible at http://www.linglat.paris-sorbonne.fr/encyclopedie linguistique:notions linguistiques:syntaxe:formules de politesse.

Toledo Martin, Rogelio. 2016. "Speech act conditionals in two works of Cicero: *In Verrem* and *Ad Atticum*." *Pallas*, 102:247–254.

ENDNOTES

[1] I have just paraphrased the traditional definition, cf. Searle (1975) 60: "cases in which one illocutionary act is performed indirectly by way of another." Kissine (2012, 170–185), however, offers qualifications. The seminal discussions are those of Grice 1975 and the aforementioned Searle 1975. The idea that indirection is any illocutionary goal (speaker intent) *not* conveyed by the sentence type (declarative, interrogative, imperative) conventionally associated with it finds rebuttal in Risselada 1993, 68–73. I find too extreme view the view of Geoffrey Leech (1983, 33), who claims that every utterance is indirect because it requires the hearer to infer the speaker's intention. In his words, "[a]ll illocutions are 'indirect' in that their force is derived by implicature."

[2] On the attention-getting function of *eho*, see Müller 1997, 105.

[3] Barrios-Lech 2016, 223, a conclusion based on analysis of master-slave interactions in Terence. But the above passages at least suggest that the same features characterize "master's talk" in Plautus, too.

[4] Ancient authors point out that more elaborated speech is polite: Eugraphius, for instance, observes that Chremes, in his long address

to Menedemus, at *Hau.* 53–74, *ut oportet apud ignotum, longa utitur oratione*: "as is suitable before someone unfamiliar, makes use of a lengthy speech" (*ad Hau.* 53). See also Demetrius (*De Elocutione* 7), who remarks in a discussion on forceful expression (δεινότης) that "orders are given concisely and briefly, every master being curt towards his slave. Supplication, on the other hand, and lamentation are lengthy": Barrios-Lech 2016, 224.

[5] I use the term "sentence meaning" to mean the literal content and "speaker meaning" to indicate the intended message: see Pinker 2007, 439.

[6] As Sadock and Zwicky (1985, 193) write in their survey of speech acts in a variety of languages, "indirection usually serves a purpose in that it avoids—or at least gives the appearance of avoiding—a frank performance of some act the speaker wishes to perform . . . most cultures find requests somewhat objectionable socially and these are conveyed by indirect means."

[7] Cic. *Amic.* 29 on the importance of *beneficia* to confirm friendship and Barrios-Lech 2016, 202–203, for further references.

[8] Brown and Levinson 1987. See Luis Unceta-Gómez, http://www. linglat.paris-sorbonne.fr/encyclopedie linguistique:notions linguistiques:syntaxe:formules de politesse, for a critical review of this and other theories of politeness. I argue for the applicability of some of Brown and Levinson's ideas to the Latin material at Barrios-Lech 2016, 32–39.

[9] Don. *ad Eu.* 864

[10] Pinker 2007, 441.

[11] Barrios-Lech 2016, 110–111.

[12] Brown and Levinson 1987, 226–227.

[13] As he said to Sean Hannity: "[t]his is a political movement. This is a strong powerful movement, the Second Amendment. Hillary wants to take your guns away. She wants to leave you unprotected in your home. And there can be no other interpretation."

[14] I reviewed all the directives in Plautus and Terence—a total of 6,520— contained in my directive database described at Barrios-Lech 2016, 25.

[15] I do not consider *si* clauses like those at *Am.* 29, *mirari non est aequom sibi si praetimet*, "it's not right for you to wonder, if he fears for himself" (cf. *Am.* 452), where the *si* clause here functions as a kind of substantive (See further K.-St. II §219, 2, and H.-Sz. II §360); nor do I look at *si* clauses that soften the directive: *si me amas, si audes* (*As.* 645–6, *Capt.*

219, *Trin.* 243). I consider only conditional sentences that convey a directive only by virtue of reading *both* the main *and* the if clause together. The database is available on my website: https://works.bepress. com/peter_barrios-lech/. The literature on conditionals is considerable; I mention only a few works in the footnotes below. Apart from the standard grammars, Toledo Martin 2016 provides a succinct overview, taking into account Speech Act and Functional Grammar approaches.

[16] E.g., in Fr. Foster's teaching grammar of choice, Gildersleeve and Lodge, §595. See also K.-St. II §212 4, H.-Sz. II §360.

[17] In the main clause, we find future and future perfects (once a future infinitive in an *AcI*); *faxo*, the sigmatic future, plus a future indicative in guarantees (*Ps.* 1328: *si is, aut dimidium aut plus etiam faxo hinc feres*); and forms of the modal verb *posse*.

[18] K.-St. II §213 (a).

[19] H.-Sz. II §360 (c.): "*nisi* (*ni*) mit Praes.—Fut. ist bei Plt. die Regel in (meist drohenden) Befehlen auf die unmittelbare Zukunft . . . in verboten aber *si* mit Fut. II – Fut." Lindskog 1895, 5–28, collects the material; the figure above, 73, is based on my own reading. My data largely confirm Lindskog's observation at 28 that "cum protasis, a nisi particula incipiens, iussum continet, praesens fere usurpatur; cum protasis a si particula incipiens interdictum continet, futurum exactum usurpatur," where *fere* should be stressed, as there are exceptions.

[20] By contrast, *si* + future perfect, future indic. (main cl.) is the preferred syntax for threats, where *si* instead of *nisi* is chosen: see e.g. Lindskog 1895, 19–20, e.g., *Mos.* 239: *nec recte si illi dixeris, iam ecastor vapulabis.*

[21] Pl. *Au.* 56, *Cur.* 726, *Men.* 856, *Mil.* 1426, *Mos.* 239, *Rud.* 759, 762, 793, *Trin.* 463; Ter. *Eu.* 800, 1063.

[22] Karakasis 2005, 145–246.

[23] The future, *si auscultabis, eloquar,* because the speaker doesn't expect the request to be carried out immediately (e.g. *Trin.* 300, Ter. *Hec.* 31–32), but elsewhere, that doesn't seem to be the case (e.g. *Trin.* 939). Lindskog 1895, 30–36, discusses *promissa* "promises," explaining why speakers might choose *si* + present indic. over *si* + future indic.: while the former are generally "involved in the present"—Mercury in passage (8) wants his audience to listen *now*—the latter, *si* + future indic., deal with a future that precedes the action in the main clause, though he concedes at 32 that "negari non potest in uno alterove exemplo cur hoc aut illud tempus ponatur, rationem perspici vix posse."

[24] I have considered threats separately, since if a speaker chooses to utter a threat, politeness is usually out of the question.

[25] So, Pl. *Mer.* 14, *Am.* 1005, *Ps.* 1333, *Trin.* 4–5, *Mil.* 80, *Trin.* 7, *Capt.* 6, *As.* 947; Ter. *Ph.* 28–29. Ter. *Hec.* 31–32 is the single exceptional instance.

[26] See, e.g., Saller 1982. 13–15. For a review of this debate, see Konstan 2010, 235–244.

[27] We have already discussed the nine that occur in prologue-actor exchanges, above.

[28] *Cur.* 328 (patron-client); *Rud.* 647, 952; *Trin.* 881, 897, 939 (strangers).

[29] K.-St. II §214 b, with some interesting observations on its use from the EL period on at p. 395, Anmerk. 1. See also Bennett I, 273–274, and Ernout 1964 §372.

[30] Fifteen addressed to superiors, 8 to equals, 3 to inferiors; see also n. 3, above, for masters' more direct style of speech with inferiors.

[31] Now, it is true that even inferiors direct these kinds of sharp criticism-with-request at superiors, but these are few in number, and follow, again, an observable pattern: *Am.* 904 (Alcumena to her husband); *Cas.* 261 (Cleostrata to her husband).

[32] See Barrios-Lech 2016, 324n56 for references.

[33] As I have argued in Barrios-Lech 2015, at *Au.* 736, Plautus puns on two possible meanings for Euclio's *liberos*, his children or his money, thus hinting at the father's perversion of his priorities, with a greater interest in his *auri aula* than in his daughter. For more on Plautus and Terence's puns, see n. 15, above.

[34] See Skutsch ad loc., who says that the oracle in *Annales* is based on the one given to Croesus in Herodotus, "telling [him] that, if he should lead an army against the Persians, great would be the empire he would destroy" (τῶν δὲ μαντηίων ἀμφοτέρων ἐς τὠυτὸ αἱ γνῶμαι συνέδραμον, προλέγουσαι Κροίσῳ, ἢν στρατεύηται ἐπὶ Πέρσας, μεγάλην ἀρχήν μιν καταλύσειν, Hdt. 1.53.5). But there the ambiguity is primarily semantic rather than syntactic, resting on the vagueness of *whose* empire Croesus will destroy, since Aristotle (*Rhet.* 3.5, 1407a) tells us that the oracle in *orat. recta* ran as follows: Κροῖσος Ἅλυν διαβὰς μεγάλην ἀρχὴν καταλύσει.

[35] For the ability of off-record requests to let speakers "get away with a relationship-threatening proposition in a way that plain speech would not," see Pinker 2007, 453–457, an essay which served as the starting point for my own.

Teleology and Tyrannicide in Cicero's *Brutus* 331

Stuart M. McManus

In early 46 BCE, Cicero was looking forward to a quiet retirement.[1] His voice was failing and his political clout was much reduced from the heady days of his consulship and his glorious return from exile a decade or so before. While he still kept abreast of the ongoing struggle between Caesar and the senatorial faction, his career in politics was over. Or was it?

Many reject this image of a former statesmen in his golden years, instead painting the orator from Arpinum as seething at the rise of Caesar and plotting the downfall of the strongman who had undermined the traditional Roman political model. This view is usually substantiated by a single passage at the end of Cicero's *Brutus*, a dialogue on the history of oratory completed sometime in the spring of 46 BCE, in which Cicero addresses Brutus directly, lamenting the political situation at Rome that had denied Brutus the oratorical career he deserved.[2] In Cicero's call for Brutus to "maintain the fame of two great houses and add to them a new luster," many have seen a purposeful ambiguity, reading the phrase as an invitation to rid Rome of Caesar by violent means. Those "two great houses" (*duo amplissuma genera*), they tell us, refer to the bloodlines of the Iunii Bruti and the Servilii. Remember L. Iunius Brutus, who expelled Tarquin; remember C. Servilius Ahala, who killed the aspiring tyrant Maelius. From this passage, J. P. V. D. Balsdon concluded darkly:

"how, except by murder, could Brutus do as well as, or even better than, these ancestors?"[3]

Yet *Brutus* 331 does not require this reading. I will argue that the former consul's final words to the dialogue's dedicatee, when read within the larger context of the work and Cicero's contemporary letters, can be interpreted as a lament within a Stoic resignation to fortune in the face of the uncertain political situation. There are even passages in the *Brutus* in which Caesar is praised in the highest terms with an eye to currying favor with the new strongman. In the dialogue, Cicero was urging Brutus not to challenge Caesar, but to continue his studies in the hope of their future usefulness, for, at the time of writing, Cicero still harbored the hope that the traditional constitutional arrangement could be revived under the victorious general. Only later did he realize that this was impossible.

Before we go on, here is the passage in full:

> *sed in te intuens, Brute, doleo, cuius in adulescentiam per medias laudes quasi quadrigis vehentem transversa incurrit misera fortuna rei publicae. hic me dolor tangit, haec me cura sollicitat et hunc mecum socium [sc. Atticum] eiusdem et amoris et iudici. tibi favemus, te tua frui virtute cupimus, tibi optamus eam rem publicam in qua duorum generum amplissumorum renovare memoriam atque augere possis. tuum enim forum, tuum erat illud curriculum, tu illuc veneras unus, qui non linguam modo acuisses exercitatione dicendi sed et ipsam eloquentiam locupletavisses graviorum artium instrumento et eisdem artibus decus omne virtutis cum summa eloquentiae laude iunxisses.*[4]

1. Identifying Ambiguities

The pro-tyrannicide reading rests on a misidentification of the real ambiguity in *Brutus* 331. Most readers have concentrated on the passage in which Cicero wishes for "a constitution of public affairs as shall make it possible for you to maintain the fame of two great houses and add to them a new luster." This they have read as a subtle suggestion to Brutus to revive Rome's earlier constitutional arrangement by doing away with Caesar. However, such a political situation was the prerequisite for Brutus to renew and outdo his family's name ("as shall make it possible..."), not the means to achieve it. Cicero was thus not calling for Brutus to restore the traditional *status rei publicae*, in which the senate was the main locus of political power and oratory was the politician's main tool, something that could arguably have been achieved by removing Caesar. Rather, he was simply stating his desire for a return to such a state of affairs, without any hint that Brutus should be the catalyst. If this were indeed a call to kill Caesar, as some have suggested, the question would then arise as to how the *respublica* was stopping Brutus from laying hands on Caesar, for tyrannicide was a legitimate act in Roman political culture.[5] If anything, all that may be deduced from this passage is that Cicero was despondent with the contemporary state of affairs (not a particularly controversial view). But he offers no hint of how it might be rectified.

If there is any ambiguity, it is rather, in my view, in Cicero's reference to Brutus' "two illustrious lineages" (*duo amplissuma genera*). Baldson and others point to the fact that Brutus identified as a member of the Iunii Bruti and the Servilii in general, and in particular as a descendant of two defenders of the *status rei publicae*, C. Servilius Ahala and L. Brutus, as is apparent from his coins of 54 BCE (Fig. 1).[6] It is also true that Cicero was well aware of this, and indeed made numerous references to this lineage, especially later in the *Phillipics*, delivered after the Ides of March.[7]

However, the logical connection between Brutus' ancestry and his involvement in the assassination is really the product of authors writing in or after 44 BCE who wished to see Brutus' actions as his destiny.[8] Furthermore, the "two illustrious lineages" in *Brutus* 331 need not refer specifically to L. Brutus and Servilius Ahala. Nineteenth-century commentators may have been correct in glossing these words as a more general allusion to the Iunii Bruti and the Servilii clans.[9] "Lineage" (*genus*) normally refers to ancestry in general, not specific ancestors (*avi*). Significantly, although L. Brutus appears briefly in the dialogue, Ahala is nowhere to be found, an odd omission if we are to believe that Cicero wished Brutus to understand the closing passage of the dialogue as a specific reference to him and his actions.

No, Brutus' "two illustrious lineages" can just as easily be read as a more general reference to the Iunii Bruti and the Servilii clans from which Brutus was descended, both amply represented in the rest of the dialogue, where they are presented as outstanding orators, apart from M. Iunius Brutus the *accusator*, who misused his talents and brought shame on his *genus*.[10] Cicero's appeal at the end of the dialogue is thus arguably part of an extended attempt to persuade Brutus to turn his attention to oratory, which Cicero presents as his young friend's birthright. If the political conditions were right and Brutus applied himself to the task, Cicero implies, he would be worthy of one of the highest compliments in epideictic rhetoric, that of having equaled or even excelled one's forebears, as Cicero would highlight in *On Duties*.[11]

Harvard Art Museums / Arthur M. Sackler Museum, The
George Davis Chase Collection of Roman Coins, Gift of George
Davis Chase, Professor of Classics and Dean of Graduate Study
at the University of Maine, 1942.176.44. Copyright: Imaging
Department © President and Fellows of Harvard College

Even if Cicero is referring explicitly to C. Iunius Brutus and
Servilius Ahala (and not to clans broadly conceived), he may not
be advocating tyrannicide. In the first place, L. Brutus had only
expelled Tarquin, and did so, not by resorting to *vis*, which might
suggest comparisons with the Ides of March, but by relying on his
skills as an orator, as Cicero in fact reminds Brutus in the dialogue.[12]
Furthermore, although L. Iunius Brutus and Servilius Ahala were
indeed involved in the downfall of tyrants, they were multifaceted
figures in the Roman imagination, evoked in differing situations
with differing meanings. In Cicero's other works, we find a variety
of depictions of these historical figures. In *On Old Age*, for example,
Cicero portrays L. Iunius Brutus as a patriot who laid down his life
for the republic, while in the oration *On His House* Cicero reminds
his audience that C. Servilius Ahala went into exile at the bidding
of the Roman people.[13] Since in 46 BCE there was no hint of Brutus'
future actions, the passage may just as plausibly be read as a call to
Brutus to go into exile himself, or to lay down his life for the state, as
Pompey had done.

It is also significant that this reference to Brutus' ancestors forms the final part of an ascending tricolon, a figure of parallelism that creates a structural analogy among its three constituent elements, reinforced by the repetition of the second person pronoun (*tibi, te, tibi*). In the first and second cola, Cicero stresses that he and Atticus support Brutus in his endeavors (*tibi favemus*) and that Brutus already had the innate virtue required of an orator (*te tua frui virtute cupimus*). These ideas are then reiterated in the final colon, where Cicero underlines his staunch support for Brutus, as well as Brutus' inherited talent for oratory. As is typical of final cola, the ideas are also developed: Cicero laments that this aim may not be immediately realizable, since a suitable *respublica* does not exist. Brutus could and did possess the requisite virtue (*virtus*), but fortune (*fortuna*) stood in his way, a state of affairs all too familiar to those versed in Stoic philosophy.[14] We see then that the final part of the tricolon is not a sudden departure in the form of a call to tyrannicide, but an extension of the two previous cola, exhorting Brutus to turn his attention to oratory by constructing an image of him as the heir to a long line of orators. Given the right political environment, not necessarily creating it himself, Brutus was destined for fame, thanks to his inherited skills and the personal support of Cicero and Atticus. Combined with the vagueness of Brutus' "two illustrious lineages," the weight of evidence therefore seems to support the reading of this ambiguous passage of the *Brutus* as a call not to tyrannicide, but to persistent study in the hope of later rewards.

2. Cicero's Attitude to Caesar in the *Brutus*

The tone of the dialogue as a whole is of course somewhat bleak, opening as it does with Cicero's reflections on the death of his great rival, Hortensius.[15] Yet, despite Cicero's obvious concern for the future of Rome, there is no hint that Brutus himself can resolve its problems, and while Cicero laments that Rome feels no need for *arma*, the weapons he refers to are the figurative rapiers of the eloquent orator-statesman.[16] More significantly, the *Brutus* does not suggest that Caesar must be sacrificed for the good of the Republic. The first direct reference to Caesar appears in a discussion of the poor memory and excessive gesturing of C. Scribonius Curio, the author of a dialogue critical of Caesar, which Cicero mocked for being laughably inconsistent. Here, Brutus is made to wonder at Curio's ineptitude: "Could his memory have been so bad that even in a written account he should not on re-reading have observed what a flagrant blunder he had made?"[17] If *Brutus* 331 is a call to tyrannicide, it is strange that Cicero went out of his way to mock one of Caesar's detractors.

A more extensive judgment of Caesar is given later in the dialogue, when Brutus asks Cicero to give an account of the abilities of contemporary orators, and especially of Caesar and M. Claudius Marcellus, "whom I know you admire." Talk of Marcellus, who had gone into self-imposed exile in Mytilene after the Battle of Pharsalus, immediately evokes in Cicero the "remembrance of our common misery," but instead of leading the discussion himself, he quickly passes the bat to Atticus. This silence on Cicero's part does not go unnoticed by Brutus, who suggests that it is the result of his general unwillingness to talk about the living, adding that there is, in any case, no real need for Cicero to express his views on Caesar, since "your judgement about his genius is well known, and his concerning you is not obscure."[18] Atticus then stresses that both he and Cicero consider Caesar "of all our orators . . . the purest user of the Latin tongue."[19] In this back and forth, there is certainly a hint that Cicero was a less-than-wholehearted supporter of Caesar, as one would expect of a man living in uncertain times, when being overtly partisan could have serious consequences. But the elision of Cicero's true feelings in a prudent *praeteritio* does not necessarily imply murderous intent.

Following this generally positive if somewhat muted endorsement of Caesar as an orator, the rest of Atticus' analysis of Caesar's style is interrupted by a series of frequent digressions on the rise of Latin eloquence, the relative merits of the orator and the military leader, and the issue of neologisms. This rather meandering discussion is perhaps another sign that Cicero, considering the uncertain political situation, was reluctant to engage in a penetrating and conclusive analysis of Caesar's career as an orator-statesman, preferring to concentrate on the minutiae of his speaking style. Again, however, the parts of the speech that do address Caesar's oratory are essentially laudatory, praising especially his purity of language, which, Atticus stresses, it is the duty of every Roman citizen to maintain.[20] If Cicero were really seeking to cast Caesar as an enemy of the *respublica Romana*, why would he single him out as an exemplary Roman citizen? Indeed, Atticus is made to praise Caesar for having added to this pure Latinity the embellishments of his early rhetorical training, so that he "seems to have placed a well-painted picture in a good light."[21]

Cicero's only detailed response in his own voice is his judgment on Caesar's famous *Commentaries* on the Gallic War. Describing them as "praiseworthy," Cicero proceeds to highlight Caesar's bare Atticist prose, an observation that must be read as a veiled criticism, given Cicero's well-known contempt for that style.[22] Cicero then quickly returns to praising Caesar, admitting that his style befits the commentary genre, which is meant to serve as notes for later historians to develop into larger works. But Cicero then goes as far as to argue that only inept scholars would take up the task of elaborating on these commentaries, since "nothing is sweeter in history than pure and lucid brevity."[23] Here, in essence, Cicero is praising Caesar's *Commentaries* as the authoritative account of the events they describe, despite his personal dislike of Caesar's aesthetic. Given that Caesar's account of the Gallic War is highly self-aggrandizing, Cicero is clearly arguing that Caesar's narrative of his own rise to prominence is not to be challenged.

Cicero even stresses the mutual respect between him and Caesar.[24] Quoting from Caesar's treatise on pure Latinity, *De analogia*, Atticus is made to declare:

> *tribueritque, mi Brute, huic nostro, qui me de illo*
> *maluit quam se dicere, laudem singularem; nam*

scripsit his verbis, cum hunc nomine esset adfatus: ac si, cogitata praeclare eloqui possent, non nulli studio et usu elaboraverunt, cuius te paene principem copiae atque inventorem bene de nomine ac dignitate populi Romani meritum esse existimare debemus; hunc facilem et cotidianum novisse sermonem nunc pro relicto est habendum? (Cic. Brut. 253)

Upon our friend here, who prefers to have me rather than himself speak about Caesar, he bestowed praise of a unique kind; for after addressing him by name in his dedication, he uses these words: "And if, to the task of giving brilliant and oratorical expression to their thought, some have devoted unremitting study and practice—wherein we must recognize that you, as almost the pioneer and inventor of eloquence, have deserved well of the name and prestige of Rome—yet are we therefore to look upon a mastery of the easy and familiar speech of daily life as a thing that now may be neglected?"[25]

Here Caesar is made a mouthpiece for the praise of Cicero himself, who had brought Latin eloquence to a peak, a fact that Brutus then reiterates, noting that such praise from the mouth of Caesar was surely worth more than the triumphs of some generals![26] Although Cicero, in a fit of false modesty, quickly calls into question Caesar's judgment, which he says may be more "friendly evidence of goodwill" than his real opinion, the motivations for the inclusion of this passage are clear: Cicero's personal vanity, of course, but also a desire to cement his affinity with the most powerful man in Rome at a time of great uncertainty. Such an appropriation of Caesar's words does not bespeak any murderous intent on the part of Cicero: quite the opposite. Rather, he is nailing his flag to Caesar's mast in the hope of rewards, or at least of staying alive.

3. Cicero's contemporary political maneuvering.

Finally, it is essential to look at the other historical evidence of Cicero's political leanings while he was composing the *Brutus*, in order to ascertain whether there is any circumstantial evidence to support the pro-tyrannicide argument. For the period after the battle of Pharsalus in August 48 BCE, which Cicero spent in self-imposed exile in Brindisium before returning to central Italy in October 47 BCE, our main sources are Plutarch's *Lives* and Cicero's own letters, which tell us much about the relationship between Cicero and Caesar. Writing several centuries later, Plutarch presents the aged statesmen as retreating from public affairs, devoting his *otium* to the philosophical pursuits of his youth, and, when Caesar returned to Rome, paying court to the newly crowned victor in the Civil War.[27] Plutarch also mentions that Cicero, just before he began to compose the *Brutus*, had a private meeting with Caesar at Tarentum, at which friendly words were exchanged.[28] In Cicero's letters—the only contemporary source available for the period of composition of the *Brutus*—Cicero appears to have decided that his days at the forefront of Roman politics were behind him, and that his best chance of securing a pleasant retirement at his beloved villa lay in pinning all his hopes on Caesar's benevolence. Writing to his friend Varro in the final days of April, just as he was putting the final touches to the *Brutus*, Cicero urged caution and patience rather than rash action.[29] His state of mind is perhaps most neatly summed up by a letter to a lawyer friend written a few weeks after he had finished the dialogue. Here he talks of politics only in terms of his successes in currying favor with Caesar, and seems to delight more than anything in his improving health, his culinary exploits, and his plan to open a school of rhetoric:

> *cum essem otiosus in Tusculano, propterea quod discipulos obviam miseram, ut eadem me quam maxime conciliarent familiari suo* [sc. *Caesari*], *accepi tuas litteras plenissimas suavitatis, ex quibus intellexi probari tibi meum consilium, quod, ut Dionysius*

*tyrannus, cum Syracusis pulsus esset, Corinthi dicitur
ludum aperuisse, sic ego sublatis iudiciis amisso regno
forensi ludum quasi habere coeperim . . . ipse melior fio,
primum valetudine, quam intermissis exercitationibus
amiseram; deinde ipsa illa, si qua fuit in me, facultas
orationis, nisi me ad has exercitationes rettulissem,
exaruisset. extremum illud est, quod tu nescio an
primum putes: plures iam pavones confeci, quam tu
pullos columbinos . . . tu istic te Hateriano iure delectas,
ego me hic Hirtiano.* (Cic. *Fam.* 9.18.1–3)

I was at my Tusculum villa enjoying a holiday, because
I had sent my pupils to meet their particular friend [i.e.
Caesar], so that they might at the same time win his
favor as far as possible for myself too, when I received
your letter so brimful of charm. I gathered from it that
you approve of my scheme—I mean my having begun,
now that the law-courts have been abolished, and I
am no longer king of the Forum, to keep a kind of
school, just as Dionysius the tyrant, after his expulsion
from Syracuse, is alleged to have opened a school at
Corinth . . . I myself am getting better, first as regards
my health, which I had lost owing to the exercise of
my lungs having been interrupted; secondly, whatever
faculty of eloquence I may have possessed, had I not
taken to this form of exercise again, would have
utterly dried up. Last comes this—though you would
probably put it first—that I have now disposed of more
peacocks than you have of pigeon-poults. While you
over there are reveling in Haterius' laws, I over here
am reveling in Hirtius' sauce.[30]

From this and other letters, Shackleton Bailey was right to
conclude that the period of Cicero's life from his return to Italy to
his delivery of his famous speech *Pro Marcello* of September 46 BCE

was characterized by relative optimism, or at least resignation, in the face of Caesar's supremacy.[31] Indeed, in the course of that year, rather than seeing Cicero's views towards Caesar hardening, we can observe Cicero, ever the calculating politician, at work devising schemes to influence Caesar and his supporters, not eradicate them. At one point, Cicero even judged himself to have been so successful in currying favor with the Caesarians that he was second only to Caesar himself in their estimations. Writing to a friend, he noted:

> *omnia promissa confirmata certa et rata sunt, quae ad reditum et ad salutem tuam pertinent: vidi, cognovi, interfui; etenim omnes Caesaris familiares satis opportune habeo implicatos consuetudine et benevolentia sic, ut, cum ab illo discesserint, me habeant proximum.* (Cic. Ad Fam. 6.12.1–2)

> All the promises bearing upon your return and restoration have been confirmed, certified, and ratified; I have seen, examined, taken part in everything. In fact, opportunely enough, I have all Caesar's intimate friends so closely bound to me by familiar acquaintance and kindly feeling that, after him, they account me next.

Although these comments are found in a letter to one of the exiled Pompeians, and therefore should be read *cum grano salis*, this letter bespeaks close contact and cooperation between Cicero and the Caesarian faction, an unlikely state of affairs if he were openly advocating assassinating their leader. This reconciliation would culminate in his oration *Pro Marcello*, delivered later in the same year, in which Cicero heaped praise on Caesar while also subtly requesting a return to the traditional Roman political system.[32]

The notion that Cicero was involved in the murder of Caesar at all stems from the allegation that Brutus cried out Cicero's name immediately after the event, a report that Cicero mentions only to deny its veracity in the *Philippics*.[33] Plutarch states firmly that Cicero played no role in the plot, as the conspirators thought him too old and lacking in mettle for such a daring move.[34] Since Cicero had turned sixty in the year the *Brutus* was published, this exclusion does not seem unreasonable. Beyond Cicero's known support for the senatorial faction (*boni*) and the alleged exclamation of his name by Brutus, there is no evidence to implicate Cicero in the plot, however convenient it may be for historians to give an important role in the events to the figure through whose writings they are forced to reconstruct them. That Cicero began to lose faith in Caesar's willingness to revive the traditional Roman model of governance a year later, in 45 BCE, is possible and indeed probable. At this point, he began to speak less of a possible revival of senatorial government and started to describe Caesar as a capricious monarch, perhaps even a tyrant. When Caesar made himself *dictator perpetuo* in early 44 BCE, Cicero cannot have reacted well.[35] But we should not read this disenchantment back into 47–46 BCE, when he was writing the *Brutus*.

4. Conclusion

In sum, the ambiguities identified by historians in *Brutus* 331 as representing a coded message from Cicero to Brutus to kill Caesar are hard to defend when the passage is read closely, placed in the context of the *Brutus* as a whole, and examined alongside other contemporary evidence. The mention of Brutus' ancestors, on which the pro-tyrannicide argument hinges, is not necessarily an explicit reference to L. Iunius Brutus and C. Servilius Ahala, who in any case were not both tyrannicides. Rather, it is a rhetorical gesture to the long line of able orators that the Iunii Bruti and Servilii had produced, with the aim of encouraging Brutus in his studies. Furthermore, Cicero's letters suggest that when he returned to central Italy and began work on the *Brutus*, he was not burning with rage against the dictator, but old, sick, and resigned to Caesar's supremacy, at least for the time being. He was a man in retirement enjoying the fruits of long political career. Indeed, this Cicero seems almost a creature of the Caesarian faction, exchanging kind words with Caesar at Brindisium, seeking to ingratiate himself with the dictator's supporters, and begging for *clementia* for his friends. Cicero's views on Caesar were to change in the next year and a half before the fateful events of 44 BCE. However, during the period of the composition, publication, and immediate reception of the *Brutus*, it would have been unthinkable for Cicero to incite Brutus to murder. In short, *Brutus* 331, although admittedly ambiguous in places, contains no secret death warrant delivered in the apparently innocuous form of a dialogue on the history of oratory.[36]

* * *

Reginaldo Foster magistro optimo, festivitate et facetiis insigni, necnon etiam Tulliani nominis vindici Stuartus McManus discipulus indignus amoris ergo hoc opusculum dono dedit.

BIBLIOGRAPHY

Balsdon, J. P. V. D. 1956. "The Ides of March." *Historia* 7:80–94.

———. 1964. "Cicero the Man." In *Cicero*, ed. T. A. Dorey, 171–214. London: Routledge & K. Paul.

Bengston, H. 1970. *Zur Geschichte des Brutus.* Munich: Verlag der Bayerischen Akademie der Wissenschaften.

Blom, H. van der. 2010. *Cicero's Role Models: The Political Strategy of a Newcomer.* Oxford: Oxford University Press.

Borszák, S. 1975. "Cicero und Caesar: ihre Beziehung im Spiegel des Romulus-Mythos." In *Ciceroniana: hommages à Kazimierz Kumaniecki*, ed. Alain Michel and Raoul Verdière, 22–35. Leiden: E. J. Brill.

Caboli, G. 1975. "Cicerone, Catone e i neoatticisti." In *Ciceroniana: hommages à Kazimierz Kumaniecki*, ed. Alain Michel and Raoul Verdière Leiden, 51–103. Leiden: E. J. Brill.

Clarke, M. L. 1981. *The Noblest Roman: Marcus Brutus and his Reputation*. Ithaca, NY: Cornell University Press.

Colish, Marcia L. 1985. *The Stoic Tradition from Antiquity to the Early Middle Ages*, 2 vols. Leiden: E. J. Brill.

Douglas, A. E., ed. 1966. *M. Tulli Ciceronis Brutus*. Oxford: Oxford University Press.

Dyer, R. 1990. "Rhetoric and Intention in Cicero's *Pro Marcello*." *Journal of Roman Studies* 80:17–30.

Gelzer, M. 1938. "Cicero's *Brutus* als politische Kundgebung." *Philologus* 93:128–31.

Gowing, A. 2000. "Memory and Silence in Cicero's *Brutus*." *Eranos* 98:39–64.

Groebe, P. 1920. "Die Abfassungszeit des *Brutus* und der *Paradoxa* Ciceros." *Hermes* 55:105–107.

Gutgesell, M. 1997. "Die Münzpropaganda des Brutus im Jahre 54 v. Chr." *Numanistiches Nachrichenblatt* 46:223–228.

Habicht, C. 1990. *Cicero the Politician*. Baltimore: Johns Hopkins University Press.

Hendrickson, G. L. 1906. "The *De Analogia* of Julius Caesar; Its Occasion, Nature, and Date, with Additional Fragments." *Classical Philology* 1:97–120.

Kytzler, B., ed. 1986. *Cicero: Brutus*, 3rd ed. Munich: Artemis.

Lintott, A. 1999. *Violence in Republican Rome*. Oxford: Oxford University Press

———. 2008. *Cicero as Evidence: A Historian's Companion*. Oxford: Oxford University Press.

Meier, C. 1980. *Die Ohnmacht des allmächtigen Dictators Caesar*. Frankfurt am Main: Suhrkamp.

Mitchell, T. N. 1991. *Cicero: The Senior Statesman*. New Haven, CT: Yale University Press.

Ortmann, U. 1988. *Cicero, Brutus und Octavian, Republikaner und Caesarianer: ihr gegenseitiges Verhältnis im Krisenjahr 44/43 v. Chr.* Bonn: Habelt.

Osgood, J. 2009. "The Pen and the Sword: Writing and Conquest in Caesar's Gaul." *Classical Antiquity* 28:328–58.

Piderit, K. W., ed. 1862. *Brutus de claris oratoribus: für den Schulgebrauch erklärt.* Leipzig: Teubner.

Rawson, E. 1975. *Cicero: A Portrait.* London: Allen Lane.

Robinson, E. A. 1951. "The Date of Cicero's Brutus." *Harvard Studies in Classical Philology.* 60:137–146.

Rossi, R. F. 1953. "Bruto, Cicerone e la congiura contra Cesare." *Parola del Passato* 8:26–47.

Stockton, D. L. 1971. *Cicero: A Political Biography.* London: Oxford University Press.

Shackleton Bailey, D. R. 1971. *Cicero.* London: Duckworth.

Sumner, G. V. 1973. *The Orators in Cicero's* Brutus: *Prosopography and Chronology.* Toronto: University of Toronto Press.

Winterbottom, M. 2002. "Believing the *Pro Marcello.*" In *Vertis in usum: Studies in Honour of Edward Courtney,* ed. J. F. Miller, C. Damon, and K. Sara Myers, 24–38. Munich: Saur.

ENDNOTES

1   For this view, see Rawson 1975, 257; Rossi 1953; Stockton 1971, 269–77; Mitchell 1991, 272–73. All translations are taken from the relevant Loeb editions.

2   There has been some debate as to whether the work was completed before or after April 46 BCE, when the news of Caesar's victory at Thapsus reached Rome, although the weight of evidence seems to support an earlier dating, see: Robinson 1951; Groebe 1920; Caboli 1975, 67n33; Gowing 2000, 62–64.

3   Balsdon 1958, 91; Balsdon 1964, 198. The author of what is still the authoritative commentary on the *Brutus* also had murder on his mind, seeing a more sinister message lurking beneath this "compliment and exhortation to Brutus as philosopher and orator": Douglas 1966, 233. See also: Lintott 1999, 55; Lintott 2008, 309; Kytzler 1986, 277; Meier 1980, 211. A few have challenged this rather teleological view, but for most scholars this passage at the end of the *Brutus* seems sufficient to prove Cicero's desire to plunge a knife into the dictator, either in person

or vicariously through Brutus: Bengston 1970, 14–15; Ortmann 1988, 69n1; Clarke 1981, 24–25.

4   Cic. *Brutus*, 331.

5   Lintott 1999, 53–58.

6   Brutus' later coinage from around 42 BCE (after the Ides of March) also bore images of him and L. Iunius Brutus: Gutgesell 1997. The most cited instance of Brutus' self-identification with the figures is in Cicero's letters, where we learn of a family tree devised by Atticus for Brutus in August 45 BCE. Cic. *Ad Att.* 13.40.1: *ubi igitur φιλοτέχνημα illud tuum quod vidi in Partheone, Ahalam et Brutum?* On the *stemma* see also Nepos, *Atticus* 18.3.

7   Cic. *Phil.* 1.13, 2.26, 2.114, 3.8–11, 4.7–8, 6.8–9, 7.11, 10.14, 10.25. It is notable that the most significant instance of Cicero stressing Brutus' lineage is designed to counter Antony's claims that he himself had been behind the assassination (Cic. *Phil.* 2.26): *Etenim, si auctores ad liberandam patriam desiderarentur illis actoribus, Brutos ego impellerem, quorum uterque L. Bruti imaginem cotidie videret, alter etiam Ahalae? Hi igitur his maioribus ab alienis potius consilium peterent quam a suis et foris potius quam domo?*

8   Plut. *Brutus* 2.1; Cassius Dio 44.12; Appian *Bell. Civ.* 2.112. Blom 2010, 97–98.

9   Piderit 1862, 198.

10   Cic. *Brutus*, 53, 107, 130, 175, 222 (Iunii Bruti); 78, 97, 135, 161, 162, 164, 169, 206, 223, 269 (Servilii), 130 (M. Iunius Brutus).

11   Cf. *Rhet. ad Her.* 3.13. Cic. *De off.* 1.115–120.

12   Cic. *Brutus* 53: *Quis enim putet aut celeritatem ingeni L. Bruto illi nobilitatis vestrae principi defuisse? qui de matre savianda ex oraculo Apollinis tam acute arguteque coniecerit; qui summam prudentiam simulatione stultitiae texerit; qui potentissimum regem clarissimi regis filium expulerit civitatemque perpetuo dominatu liberatam magistratibus annuis legibus iudiciisque devinxerit; qui collegae suo imperium abrogaverit, ut e civitate regalis nominis memoriam tolleret: quod certe effici non potuisset, nisi esset oratione persuasum.* Kytzler 1986, 277, argues that Cicero's characterization of L. Brutus as freeing Rome from the *perpetuo dominatu* of the kings was a reference to the Caesar's title *dictator perpetuo*, and so reads this as another incitement to tyrannicide. But the *Brutus* predates Caesar's taking on this title by some two years (Cic. *Phil.* 2.87).

13 Cic. *De sen.* 75: *cum recorder non L. Brutum, qui in liberanda patria est interfectus.* Cic. *De domo sua* 86: *et C. Servilius Ahala, cum essent optime de re publica meriti, tamen populi incitati vim iracundiamque subierunt, damnatique comitiis centuriatis cum in exsilium profugissent.*

14 On Cicero and the Stoic tradition, see Colish 1985, I, 61–158.

15 The political context is stressed by *praeteritio*: Cic. *Brutus*, 10–11. See Gelzer 1938, 128–31.

16 Cic. *Brutus* 7: *Equidem angor animo non consili, non ingeni, non auctoritatis armis egere rem publicam, quae didiceram tractare quibusque me assuefeceram quaeque erant propria cum praestantis in re publica viri tum bene moratae et bene constitutae civitatis.*

17 Ibid. 219: *Tantamne fuisse oblivionem, inquit, in scripto praesertim, ut ne legens quidem umquam senserit quantum flagiti commisisset?* On Curio's attacks on Caesar see Suet. *Div. Iul.* 9.2, 49.1, 52.3.

18 Cic. *Brutus*, 248–51. On Marcellus see Sumner 1973, 138.

19 Cic. *Brutus* 252.

20 Ibid. 252–62.

21 Ibid. 261: *Caesar autem rationem adhibens consuetudinem vitiosam et corruptam pura et incorrupta consuetudine emendat. Itaque cum ad hanc elegantiam verborum Latinorum—quae, etiam si orator non sis et sis ingenuus civis Romanus, tamen necessaria est—adiungit illa oratoria ornamenta dicendi, tum videtur tamquam tabulas bene pictas conlocare in bono lumine. Hanc cum habeat praecipuam laudem, in communibus non video cui debeat cedere. Splendidam quandam minimeque veteratoriam rationem dicendi tenet, voce motu forma etiam magnificam et generosam quodam modo.* The analogy between rhetoric and painting is of course common in Cicero (cf. Cic. *De inv.* 2.2–4). In the *Brutus*, Hortensius' decline is described in terms of the fading colours of a picture (320): *Primus et secundus annus et tertius tantum quasi de picturae veteris colore detraxerat . . .*

22 Cicero openly mocks the Atticists in the dialogue for their double standards, as they embraced Lysias but not Cato the Elder, see: Cic. *Brutus*, 63–9.

23 Ibid. 262: *Tum Brutus: Orationes quidem eius mihi vehementer probantur. Compluris autem legi atque etiam commentarios, quos idem scripsit rerum suarum. Valde quidem, inquam, probandos; nudi enim sunt, recti et venusti, omni ornatu orationis tamquam veste detracta. Sed dum voluit alios habere parata, unde sumerent qui vellent scribere*

historiam, ineptis gratum fortasse fecit, qui illa volent calamistris inurere: sanos quidem homines a scribendo deterruit; nihil est enim in historia pura et inlustri brevitate dulcius. On Caesar's aims in the *Commentaries*, see Osgood 2009.

24 Cic. *Brutus*, 161–2, 189–90.

25 See Hendrickson 1906, 110–19.

26 Cic. *Brutus* 254–5: *Tum Brutus: Amice hercule, inquit, et magnifice te laudatum puto, quem non solum principem atque inventorem copiae dixerit, quae erat magna laus, sed etiam bene meritum de populi Romani nomine et dignitate. Quo enim uno vincebamur a victa Graecia, id aut ereptum illis est aut certe nobis cum illis communicatum. Hanc autem, inquit, gloriam testimoniumque Caesaris tuae quidem supplicationi non, sed triumphis multorum antepono.*

27 Plut. *Life of Cicero*, 40.

28 Ibid. 39.

29 Cicero *Ad fam.* 9.2.4: *tibi igitur hoc censeo, latendum tantisper ibidem, dum effervescit haec gratulatio et simul dum audiamus quem ad modum negotium confectum sit; confectum enim esse existimo. Magni autem intererit qui fuerit victoris animus, qui exitus rerum; quamquam quo me coniectura ducat habeo, sed exspecto tamen.*

30 Cicero also famously made this pun in *Verr.* 2.1.121; see also the Introduction.

31 Shackleton Bailey 1971, 198–99.

32 Cic. *Pro Marc.* 25, 33, etc. On the sincerity of the *Pro Marcello* see Rawson 1975, 219; Dyer 1990, 17–30; Winterbottom 2002, 33–34. In another contemporary letter, despite clearly not being happy with the developing Caesarian monarchy, Cicero was careful not to single out Caesar personally for criticism: *Ad fam.* 7.28.3: *Nec vero nunc quidem culpa in eo est, in cuius potestate omnia sunt—nisi forte id ipsum esse non debuit—sed alia casu, alia etiam nostra culpa sic acciderunt, ut de praeteritis non sit querendum.*

33 Cic. *Phil.* 2.30. This tradition is also found in Cassius Dio, 44.20.

34 Plut. *Life of Cicero* 42.

35 Habicht suggests convincingly that Cicero had begun to lose hope that Caesar would revive the traditional political model after May 45 BCE, when Cicero returns to using regal vocabulary to describe Caesar for the first time since the Civil War. But Habicht is not justified in concluding from this and *Ad Att.* 13.40.1 that: "It seems beyond doubt

that Caesar's assassination was on Cicero's mind by the summer of 45 and that he focused on Brutus": Habicht 1990, 73–74. Borszák (1975, 34) sees the ambiguous words of *Ad Atticum* 12.45.3 (May 45 BCE) as a sign of Cicero's wishing Caesar dead. Scholars frequently quote Cicero's later letters to Trebonius and Cassius as evidence of his support and involvement in the plot (*Ad Fam.* 10.28.1, 12.4.1). However, the use of the unreal conditional seems to suggest that this is a *post eventum* statement of support rather than a reflection of any role or knowledge of the plot (12.4.1): *Vellem Idibus Martiis me ad coenam invitasses: reliquiarum nihil fuisset.*

[36]   Habicht 1990, 76.

Praeteritio and Cooperative Ambiguity

Rachel Philbrick

nuper cum morte superioris uxoris novis nuptiis locum vacuefecisses, nonne etiam alio incredibili scelere hoc scelus cumulavisti? quod ego praetermitto et facile patior sileri, ne in hac civitate tanti facinoris immanitas aut exstitisse aut non vindicata esse videatur. praetermitto ruinas fortunarum tuarum quas omnis proximis Idibus tibi impendere senties: ad illa venio quae non ad privatam ignominiam vitiorum tuorum, non ad domesticam tuam difficultatem ac turpitudinem, sed ad summam rem publicam atque ad omnium nostrum vitam salutemque pertinent. (Cic. *Cat.* 1.14)

Recently, when you had made your previous wife's position vacant for a new bride, didn't you pile yet another unbelievable crime on top of this crime? This I pass over, and I am content to keep silent about it so that such a horrendous act might not seem to have existed in this city, or at least not seem to have gone unpunished. I pass over the ruin of your fortune, the full weight of which you will feel looming over you on the next Ides. I come instead to those matters that

99

pertain not to the private ignominy of your vices, not to your personal financial problems and moral depravity, but to the highest interests of the state and to the life and safety of us all.

In this passage from the opening section of his exposure of the Catilinarian conspiracy to the Roman senators, Cicero accomplishes something remarkable. He manages to introduce into his attack on Catiline several nasty allegations under the pretext of *not* discussing those very issues. He begins by insinuating that Catiline not only murdered his wife (bad enough!) but afterward committed a second, equally terrible (but unspecified) crime. He merely mentions this double crime before declaring that he wishes to "pass over" it, to move on to more important matters. Before arriving at those more important matters—the republic and the senators' lives and safety—he also "passes over" four other unseemly aspects of Catiline's character: his lost wealth, his private vices, his domestic distress, and his moral depravity. In the process of limiting the scope of his prosecution—declaring what he *won't* talk about—Cicero paints a rather sordid picture of Catiline that falls outside the bounds of what will be a denunciation based narrowly on *periculum*. He has adroitly slandered his target while maintaining the pretense that he has done no such thing.

The rhetorical strategy that Cicero deploys so effectively here is known as *praeteritio*. As we can see in the Ciceronian example, the orator who uses it manages to hide something in plain sight. That which he claims he will not utter lies undeniably before his audience. How, exactly, does he manage to pull off this trick, without appearing self-contradictory or mendacious? This paper examines the precise interpretive mechanisms that enable *praeteritio* to succeed. In the end, the orator's successful use of *praeteritio* depends on an audience that is cooperative and willing to read ambiguity into a statement that is unambiguous.

1. The deceit of *praeteritio*.

The rhetorical term *praeteritio* comes from *praeterire* ("to pass over"), a common verb for introducing the device. The trope, which is also known by the Greek name *paraleipsis* (παράλειψις) and was defined in Greek rhetorical handbooks by the 4th century BCE, came to be called by the Latin term *praeteritio* by at least the 3rd century CE (in the rhetorical handbook of Aquila Romanus).[1] Latin writers of the classical period generally use the term *occultatio*, a name that relies on the metaphor of hiding something in plain sight.

The earliest attested definition of *occultatio* comes from the *Rhetorica ad Herennium*, the oldest extant Latin handbook of rhetoric (written perhaps ca. 86–82 BCE).[2] The unknown author defines *occultatio* in the following way:

> *occultatio est cum dicimus nos praeterire aut non scire*
> *aut nolle dicere id quod nunc maxime dicimus.* (4.37)

> *Occultatio* is when we say that we are passing over, or
> that we don't know or don't want to say, that which we
> are now precisely saying.

This definition highlights the contradictory nature of *praeteritio*, which requires the speaker to say what he will not say. The author's repetition of *dicimus* here underscores the contradiction: articulating what will go unspoken requires a speech act.[3]

The handbook's author then hints at the etymology of *occultatio*, describing the reasons why an orator might use the device:

> *haec utilis est exornatio si aut ad rem quam non*
> *pertineat aliis ostendere, quod occulte admonuisse*
> *prodest, aut longum est aut ignobile, aut planum non*
> *potest fieri, aut facile potest reprehendi; ut utilius sit*
> *occulte fecisse suspicionem quam eiusmodi intendisse*
> *orationem quae redarguatur.*

> This ornament is useful for a subject which it is not pertinent to reveal openly to others, because there is benefit in suggesting it obscurely, or because open expression would be long or sordid, or cannot be made clear, or can be refuted easily; as a result, it is more useful to have created suspicion obscurely than to have devised a speech of the kind that may be disproven.

The repetition of *occulte* suggests the deceitfulness of *praeteritio*. The orator or writer who uses it must hide his point to sneak it by his audience. Like the Trojan horse, it conceals within it the opposite of what it professes to be on the surface.

If we were feeling ungenerous, we could call a speaker who uses *praeteritio* a liar. Cicero, for example, promises not to address the issue of Catiline's financial distress, but still mentions it twice (*ruinas fortunarum tuarum, domesticam tuam difficultatem*). He similarly alludes to Catiline's questionable morality (*privatam ignominiam vitiorum tuorum, turpitudinem*). *Praeteritio* looks a lot like *reticentia* or *recusatio*—rejection of a topic—except that, in the act of professing to reject the topic, the speaker in fact lingers on what will be "omitted." *Praeteritio* also differs from the related strategy of passing over topics to return to them at a later time, or not to burden the audience with unnecessary detail, a practice Quintilian recommends for reducing the length of a speech. As an example of real omission, he cites the following line of Cicero's: "Fulcinius dies; there are indeed many things (*multa*) which are in this matter, but I will pass them over (*praetermittam*) because they are separate from the case."[4] The refusal to elaborate on the vague *multa* distinguishes this use of *praetermittere* from *praeteritio*.

If we were inclined more favorably toward a speaker like Cicero, we might call his words *ironic*: they claim to signify a meaning that is the opposite of the meaning they actually express (*praeteritio* was often classified as a subcategory of irony by ancient theorists).[5] Quintilian defends irony generally against the charge of deceit by asserting that "although it asserts and feels one thing, it nevertheless does not pretend something else, for everything around it is usually straightforward."[6] But whether we read *praeteritio* as deceitful or ironic, the device is contradictory at its core. That which the speaker denies saying is nevertheless said.

2. Obscuring with ambiguity.

The adroit speaker by necessity finds ways to obscure *praeteritio*'s contradictory nature. Cicero sometimes introduces the "unmentionable" information *before* stating that he will pass over the topic. In the passage from the *First Catilinarian* quoted above, he begins by phrasing the damning charge as a question directed at Cataline (*nuper cum morte superioris uxoris novis nuptiis locum vacuefecisses, nonne etiam alio incredibili scelere hoc scelus cumulavisti?*), which he follows with the declaration, "This I pass over" (*quod ego praetermitto*). The relative pronoun *quod* refers to the entirety of the preceding question, the details of which have been introduced to the audience without any claims about their veracity.

Another strategy for obscuring the inherent contradiction of *praeteritio* is to introduce structural ambiguity into the sentence. In English, for example, one could say: "I won't say how John lost all of his money at the casino."[7] The success of this statement as an instance of *praeteritio*, as Henkemans (2009) points out, depends on the potential ambiguity of the English word *how*. In this case, the original sentence can either mean "I won't say *in what way* John lost his money" or "I won't say *the fact that* John lost his money." The first possible meaning is straightforward, merely omitting the details of John's loss. (Was it at roulette or blackjack?) The second is self-contradictory in a way that, in this bald expression, would aggravate the sensibilities of most readers or listeners. The ambiguity of *how*, though, obscures the contradictory option and allows both meanings to be accepted by the audience.

Do we find similar structural ambiguities in Latin instances of *praeteritio*? In classical Latin, this particular ambiguity is far less common than in English. The first meaning ("I won't tell you *in what way* John lost his money") would be expressed by an indirect question, while the second ("I won't tell you *the fact that* John lost his money") would be expressed through indirect statement, usually with the accusative-plus-infinitive construction. Although *praeteritio* can be accomplished through both indirect question and indirect statement, the two constructions are rarely confused. Cicero's speeches demonstrate the range of constructions that verbs of "passing over" can introduce:[8]

(1) with accusative object:
   praetermitto ruinas fortunarum tuarum (*Cat.* 1.14)
   I pass over the ruin of your fortune.

(2) with accusative and infinitive (*oratio obliqua*):
   omitto nihil istum versum pertinuisse ad illum (*Pis.* 75)
   I disregard that this verse had nothing to do with him.

(3) with *de*:
   non quaero unde cccc. amphoras mellis habueris . . .
   omitto de melle (*Verr.* 2.2.183)
   I do not ask you where you got the 400 amphorae of honey . . . I disregard the honey.

(4) with object clause:
   mitto quod aliena, mitto quod possessa per vim, mitto quod convicta ab Apollonidensibus, mitto quod a Pergamenis repudiata, mitto etiam quod a nostris magistratibus in integrum restituta, mitto quod nullo iure neque re neque possessione tua. (*Flacc.* 79)
   I omit the fact that [these estates] belonged to someone else, I omit that they were acquired through force, I omit that your ownership of them was refuted by the citizens of Apollonis, I omit that they were repudiated by the citizens of Pergamum, I omit also that they were restored in their entirety by our magistrates, I omit

that they were yours by no law either of ownership or of possession.

(5) with indirect question:
omitto quam haec falsa, quam levia, praesertim cum omnino nulla causa iusta cuiquam esse possit contra patriam arma capiendi. sed nihil de Caesare. (Phil. 2.53)
I omit how false, how trivial, these [pretexts] were, especially since no one has any reason that is just for taking up arms against his country. But nothing about Caesar.

The success of the *praeteritio* in the first four examples relies on treating as fact the information that is not to be discussed. Thus, in (1), Catiline's financial ruin is taken for granted, an indisputable fact that Cicero—and, it is implied, his audience—need not spend time and words elaborating. The example in (4), which uses object clauses introduced by *quod*, demonstrates a more elaborate construction, which nevertheless follows the same strategy. The object clause offers the speaker the space for more elaborate constructions of details he intends to pass over.

The fifth construction represents a different tactic. Example (5) from the second *Philippic* shows how a successful *praeteritio* can be achieved through reference to degree or detail. Cicero promises not to go into detail about the degree to which Caesar's pretexts were false and trivial, thereby implying that they were *to some degree* false and trivial. To state that they are in any degree (*quam*) false and trivial is to effectively label them as such. The *cum*-clause that follows, in which Cicero denies that any reason for civil war can be legitimate, confirms this implicit statement.

These Ciceronian methods of introducing *praeteritio*, then, do not depend on the same structural ambiguity as does the English example. As Latin evolved, though, an ambiguity of that sort did in fact emerge. The conjunction *ut*—which could always introduce direct and indirect questions—came to be used as a common means of introducing indirect speech. This linguistic development can be seen already in authors of the early imperial period. Hyginus, one of Augustus' freedmen and a man of great learning (serving as prefect of the Palatine library), used this construction in his *On Astronomy* when describing the constellation Arctophylax (Boötes): *de hoc fertur* <u>*ut*</u> *sit Arcas nomine, Callistus et Iovis filius* ("it is said about him <u>that</u> he is named Arcas, the son of Callisto and Jupiter").

Aware of the developing flexibility of *ut*, we can see potential ambiguity in several instances of Ovidian *praeteritio*. In Book 3 of the *Tristia*, in a poem that details the harshness of the Scythian winter (the snow never melts, the winds level buildings), Ovid concludes his catalogue of climatological oddities with the following *praeteritio*:

> *quid loquar,* <u>*ut*</u> *vincti concrescant frigore rivi,*
> *deque lacu fragiles effodiantur aquae? (Tr.* 3.10.25–6)

Why should I say <u>how/that</u> the streams congeal, bound by cold, and the brittle water is dug out of the pool?

Most readers are likely inclined to read the *ut* that follows *loquar* in the first line as "how," introducing an indirect question. In light of Hyginus' *ut*, however, we can appreciate the possible ambiguity of Ovid's *ut*. Although someone might object that Ovid has contradicted himself however we interpret that *ut*, since we could easily understand the cause of the rivers congealing to be the result of the binding cold (*frigore*), Ovid certainly has not said as much on the subject as he could. He will, in fact, return to the topic of frozen waters in a late exilic composition in the *Epistulae ex Ponto*, providing a lengthy explanation of the physics behind the freezing of the Black Sea— complete with reference to the relative densities of water bodies (*Pont.* 4.10.37–64).

The same potentially ambiguous structure is found in book 4 of the *Metamorphoses*. Here Ovid gives one of his internal narrators, Alcithoë (one of the three Myneid sisters who tell stories instead of worshipping Bacchus, for which they are punished with transformation into bats), a rather lengthy passage of *praeteritio*, in which she lists the stories she has decided *not* to tell as a prologue to her tale of Salmacis. One of the stories she passes over is that of the otherwise-unknown Sithon:

> *nec loquor ut quondam naturae iure novato*
> *ambiguus fuerit modo vir, modo femina Sithon.* (*Met.* 4.279–80)

> Nor will I say how/that, when formerly the law of nature had been changed, the ambiguous Sithon was now a man, now a woman.

In this case, the ambiguity of *ut* fits nicely, not only with the deceitfulness of *praeteritio* in general, but even more with the ambiguity of Sithon's gender in this instance. Sithon's double identity has a parallel in the possible double reading of the *ut* clause.

This sort of structural ambiguity is not, however, a requirement for authors to use *praeteritio* successfully, as is clear from the wide range of structures introduced by verbs of passing over and the many examples already examined. In the next section, I will consider a much deeper sort of ambiguity that resides in the audience of *praeteritio*.

3. Cooperative ambiguity.

Since structural ambiguity is not the only (or even the primary) tool Latin authors use to resolve *praeteritio*'s inherently contradictory nature, the resolving (or obscuring) of that contradiction must happen elsewhere. It is ultimately effected not by the speaker but by the audience. To understand how this happens, we must first delve into some principles of how linguistic communication works.

In a series of lectures delivered in 1967, Paul Grice set out his theory of the Cooperative Principle that generally governs effective communication.[9] This principle runs: "Make your contribution such as is required, at the stage at which it occurs, by the accepted purpose or direction of the talk exchange in which you are engaged" (Grice 1989, 26). Grice outlined four maxims that a "cooperative" contribution should follow, and which participants in a conversation by default expect will be observed:[10]

    A. The cooperative principle
        Be cooperative.
    B. The maxims of conversation
        (1) Quality: Be truthful
            (i) Don't say what is false.
            (ii) Don't say what lacks evidence.
        (2) Quantity
            (i) Don't say less than is required.
            (ii) Don't say more than is required.
        (3) Relation: Be relevant.
        (4) Manner: Be perspicuous.
            (i) Avoid obscurity.
            (ii) Avoid ambiguity.
            (iii)Be brief.
            (iv) Be orderly.

Grice further developed the concept of "implicature," a term he used to designate meaning inferable from contextual information when any of the maxims is violated. (This concept shares characteristics with Quintilian's defense of irony: "it does not pretend something else, for everything around it is usually straightforward." Both Quintilian and Grice argue that a statement's non-surface meaning—what Grice calls its non-natural meaning—can be gleaned readily from the form of that statement.)

    Even this briefest of introductions to the Gricean maxims should reveal that *praeteritio* flouts several of them. Most glaring is its violation of the maxim of Quality: when a speaker claims that he will pass over a topic, which then he still mentions, he has "said what he believes to be false" (B.1.i). If he uses this trope in order to introduce charges that could be easily refuted (as the author of the *Rhetorica ad Herennium* suggests, see above), he has "said that for which he lacks sufficient evidence" (B.1.ii). And if he uses *praeteritio* to show something that does not pertain to the subject (again, *Rhetorica ad Herennium* 4.37), then he violates the maxim of Relevance.

How then does a cooperative audience make sense of an utterance that so clearly violates the cooperative principle of communication? As Grice formulates the question: "How can [the speaker's] saying what he did say be reconciled with the supposition that he is observing the overall Cooperative Principle?" (Grice 1989, 30). One way (Grice's proposal) is to understand that the speaker is signaling the presence of an implicature. In the case of *praeteritio*'s violation of Relevance, this may often be the case. When Cicero exclaims, "But nothing about Caesar" (*sed nihil de Caesare, Phil.* 2.53, quoted above), he is claiming that a discussion of Caesar is not relevant to his discussion of Antony. A cooperative listener, however, may surmise that Cicero is *implicating* the opposite: that Caesar's actions, and Antony's knowledge of or involvement in them, are very relevant to Cicero's denunciation of Antony.

When, however, *praeteritio* violates the maxim of Quality, as it usually does, implicature does not provide a satisfying answer to our question. In his discussion of the first maxim (B.1.i), Grice offers four examples of violations: irony, metaphor, meiosis (litotes), and hyperbole (Grice 1989, 34). These tropes use non-literal language to implicate meaning. Here we see again the connection between irony and *praeteritio*, now framed in a slightly different way: both irony and *praeteritio* violate the cooperative maxim "Don't say what is false." But there exists an important difference. While an ironic statement *implicates* the opposite (e.g., saying "He's a fine friend" when speaking about a business rival), *praeteritio directly states* the opposite (is self-contradictory). Grice's theory of implicature therefore falls short of a complete explanation of this device.

I would suggest that a cooperative audience has another way to reconcile *praeteritio*'s violation of the first maxim of Quality: by transferring the violation from one maxim to another. It is far easier to make sense of an utterance that violates one of the other maxims, for instance, the maxim B.4.ii, "avoid ambiguity." A cooperative listener will credit the speaker with use of ambiguity before she will conclude that the maxim of Quality has been violated. Accordingly, the word that introduces the *praeteritio*—the very word that contains the contradiction—is often interpreted by the cooperative listener as ambiguous, as containing a meaning that dissolves the contradiction.

The results of this cooperative process are visible in the extended meanings that verbs of *not saying* acquired in Latin. Many verbs that introduce *praeteritio*—including *praetermittere* and *praeterire*, but also *silere, tacere,* and *(non) dicere*—have a primary meaning of "making no utterance" but acquired extended meanings of "making no extended reference to." We have clear examples of the results of this process in one of Cicero's speeches against Verres:

> *omne illud tempus quod fuit antequam iste ad magistratus remque publicam accessit, habeat per me solutum ac liberum. sileatur de nocturnis eius bacchationibus ac vigiliis; lenonum, aleatorum, perductorum nulla mentio fiat; damna, dedecora, quae res patris eius, aetas ipsius pertulit, praetereantur; lucretur indicia veteris infamiae; patiatur eius vita reliqua me hanc tantam iacturam criminum facere. (Verr. 2.1.33)*

That entire span of time before he entered into the magistracy and the republic, let him have it from me exempt and free. Let there be silence about his nocturnal revels and all-nighters; of pimps, gamblers, panders let no mention be made; let the losses, the disgraces—which his father's estate and his age accomplished—be passed over; let him earn the reward of his old bad reputation; the evidence of the remainder of his life allows me to forgo all those accusations.

On hearing a statement like Cicero's "of pimps, gamblers, panders let no mention be made," listeners must in fact *introduce* ambiguity in order to engage with the speaker cooperatively. A hyper-literal (uncooperative) reader or listener of this sentence would point out that Cicero's appeal for *nulla mentio* has been violated by Cicero himself, since the three genitives (*lenonum, aleatorum, perductorum*) fairly constitute a *mentio*. But a cooperative reader or listener will read ambiguity into the idea of *nulla mentio* in order to accept Cicero's statement. A cooperative reader may think to herself, "How many words, really, amount to a *mentio*? Surely he could have said more about those pimps and gamblers, but he did after all stop himself."

The same process occurs in the case of *silere* ("to keep silent, make no noise"), which is the verb in this passage that most glaringly suggests contradictory *praeteritio*. Cicero does make some noise when he refers specifically to the "nocturnal revels and all-nighters" that Verres enjoyed. After Cicero, *silere* is used commonly to mean more than maintaining a literal silence. It could be used as a synonym for *nullam mentionem facere*, either with *de* (as here) or transitively, and in this capacity it became a common marker of *praeteritio*. When Horace, in an ode praising Augustus, makes a list of all the divinities he will *not* pass over in his encomium of the *princeps*, *silere* is the first verb he uses: *neque te silebo/ Liber* ("nor will I say nothing of you, Liber," *Odes* 1.12.21-2). The verb *tacere*, broadly synonymous with *silere*, came to have this same praeteritic function. Ovid's Alcithoë (already quoted above) uses it to dismiss her first story idea:

> *"vulgatos taceo" dixit "pastoris amores*
> *Daphnidis Idaei, quem nymphe paelicis ira*
> *contulit in saxum: tantus dolor urit amantes." (Met.*
> 4.276–8)

"I pass over in silence," she said, "the well-known loves of Daphnis, the shepherd from Mount Ida, whom a nymph turned into a rock because of her anger over a mistress. Such a great anguish burns lovers."

Alcithoë, in true Ciceronian fashion, accomplishes more than "silence" with her *praeteritio*. She manages to summarize the story of Daphnis and also to include the story's "moral" (*tantus dolor urit amantes*). The juxtaposition of *taceo* and *dixit* in line 276 highlights the contradictory nature of Alcithoë's statement. She is "silent," yet she "spoke." The poet-narrator, who has orchestrated this juxtaposition, seems to be subtly pointing out the inherent contradiction that *praeteritio* contains.

Even the verb *dicere* ("to say") can introduce *praeteritio*. We saw above how the author of the *Rhetorica ad Herennium* uses *dicere* three times in his definition of *praeteritio*, in a way that emphasizes the contradiction inherent in the device. To say what you are not going to say strikes us as listeners or readers as too contradictory to be acceptable, as with the earlier example sentence "I won't say the fact that John lost all of his money." But Cicero uses even *dicere* to introduce *praeteritio*. In his defense of Cluentius, Cicero declares, "I do not say (*non dico*) at this time, judges, a fact that I'm not sure should be said (*dici*)—that he [Staienus] was condemned for treason."[11] In another speech, he varies this strategy only slightly, affirming that "I shall not say (*non dicam*) at this point that our ancestors always complied with tradition in peace, with utility in war."[12] Of course, he has just said that very thing. A cooperative audience, however, will read ambiguity into the idea of "speaking," just as it does with the idea of "making mention" and "keeping silence." As a result, *dicere* came to encompass an array of meanings that our English verb "to say" does not, including "to tell, describe" and "to affirm, say 'yes'" (antonym of *negare*)." So, while Cicero may literally be *saying* things about Staienus and Roman ancestors, he can be seen as technically not *dicens* in the sense that he is not relating these points in detail.

The locus of *praeteritio's* ambiguity is the human audience, for it lies with the audience to judge whether Cicero or Alcithoë or any other speaker truly has "passed over" the subjects they claim they will not mention. This means that each recipient of the *praeteritio* must grapple with any apparent contradiction, and different audience members may have different standards for what constitutes "silence" or "a mention."

4. Passing over Vergil's Fifth *Georgic.*

One of Latin literature's best-known instances of *praeteritio* provides a clear example of this subjective response. The last book of Vergil's didactic poem on farming, the *Georgics*, treats bees and beekeeping, but about a quarter of the way in, Vergil digresses to describe what he will *not* be addressing in his work:

> *atque equidem, extremo ni iam sub fine laborum*
> *vela traham et terris festinem advertere proram,*
> *forsitan et pinguis hortos quae cura colendi*
> *ornaret canerem biferique rosaria Paesti (Georg.*
> 4.116–119)

> And I, if I were not now furling my sails near the farthest limit of my labors and hurrying to turn my ship to land, perhaps I would sing of the care of cultivation that embellishes fertile gardens and the rose beds of twice-bearing Paestum.

If he only had more time, Vergil declares, he would turn his attention to gardens and their upkeep. If Vergil had written only the four lines above before moving on to his discussion of bees, this passage would possibly be classed as *recusatio*, a refusal to address a certain topic. After all, it is the *cura colendi*, the act of cultivation, rather than the fact of gardens that he declines to address. To put it in the terms of our original example English sentence, Vergil here asserts that he "won't tell us *in what way* gardens are kept" (not "the fact that gardens are kept").[13] But in the lines that follow, Vergil digresses and describes many details of gardens and their upkeep, using the figure of the Old Man of Tarentum as an exemplar of that *cura colendi*. Taken as a whole, this passage (lines 116–48) constitutes an extended example of *praeteritio.*

Vergil caps this extended *praeteritio* with a reiteration of his opening statement, that the topic of gardens is what he will be passing over:

> *verum haec ipse equidem spatiis exclusus iniquis*
> *praetereo atque aliis post me memoranda relinquo.*
> (*Georgics* 4.147–8)

> But I am passing over these matters, excluding them because of inadequate space, and I leave them to others after me to mention.

Using conventional verbs of *praeteritio* (*praetereo, relinquo*) and citing a textbook reason for avoiding the topic (lack of space; cf. the second passage from the *Rhetorica ad Herennium* above), Vergil asserts his claim not to have "sung of" (cf. *canerem*, 119) these matters.

If we probe the specific language of Vergil's gardening digression, we find that he deftly treats the very topic he has said he has no time to address. In so doing, he presents us with an especially complex example of the verbal sidestepping characteristic of *praeteritio*.[14] In the opening lines of the passage, Vergil enumerates those topics he does not have time to discuss: *horti* and *rosaria* (quoted above), but also specific plants, both edible (endive, wild celery, cucumbers; 4.120–22) and decorative (narcissus, acanthus, ivy, myrtle; 122–24). The waterways that nourish these plants are also mentioned prominently (*rivis*, 4.120; *virides . . . ripae,* 121). When he turns to describing the Old Man's garden (125–46), which exemplifies the benefits and bounty of a private garden, Vergil subtly echoes these same topics (despite *tacuissem*, 123) without repeating any specific detail. Like the *horti* he will pass over, the Old Man's garden is watered by a river (the Galaesus, 126). He also grows vegetables (not particularized, as earlier, but referred to collectively as *olus*, 130) as well as fruit-trees (a feature of gardens not mentioned in the *praeteritio*). He also grows roses (*rosam*, 134) and other decorative flowering plants—not the narcissus and myrtle mentioned earlier, but lilies, vervain, and poppies (131), and hyacinths (137).

The opening *praeteritio* and the description of the Old Man's garden are stitched together most explicitly by a marked verbal parallel in the poet's references to the narcissus and hyacinths. The narcissus that the poet will not sing of is called "late blooming" (*sera comantem*, 122), while the Old Man "trimmed the bloom" (*comam tondebat*, 137) of the hyacinths in his garden. Both phrases depend on a metaphorical meaning of *coma* (literally "hair") to describe the foliage or bloom of a plant. This strikingly anthropomorphic language—which will become standard among Latin poets, but is first attested in this passage—draws attention to itself in both places. The metaphor of "hair" may also remind us that both Narcissus and Hyacinth were once young men with actual hair, transformed into flowers under disturbing circumstances.[15] This allusion to this twin pair of mythological figures parallels the doubleness of this passage's two gardens, the one that Vergil will not sing and the Old Man's.

What do we make of the fact that Vergil addresses the very topics—and occasionally with noticeable similarity of language—that he told us he would not treat? Should we charge him with hypocrisy? He has escaped obvious contradiction by carefully avoiding direct repetition of his language from the *praeteritio*, but he has still spent thirty lines describing gardens (and one man's garden in particular).

The success of Vergil's *praeteritio* hinges on the ambiguity of the verb *canere*. Its primary sense, "to sing," is equally applicable to humans, birds, and musical instruments. Its direct object (either implied or stated) is usually some word for "song" or an equivalent. So Ennius can speak of "the verses that the fauns and the soothsayers used to sing" (*versibus quos olim Faunei vatesque canebant* [16]). Just as often, though, *canere* takes as its object a non-song word, as famously found in the opening line of the *Aeneid*: *arma virumque cano*. In such cases, *canere* more precisely means "to sing of," i.e., "to make something or some person the subject of one's singing."[17] In the example from the *Aeneid*, *arma* ("arms") and *virum* ("the man") are the subjects of the poet's song, the topics that the subsequent twelve books will treat.

These two meanings of *canere* explain how Vergil, in the *Georgics*, can claim not to have "sung of" gardens, even though he devotes thirty lines to the topic. *Horti* have not been the subject of his song; they are not his *carmen*'s true topic, beekeeping. Instead, *horti* have been a brief digression, although one that plays an important role in the poem's program.[18] So, even if it can be said that Vergil *versus de hortis cecinit*, he can make a legitimate claim that *non hortos cecinit*. The formal subjects of his song remain fields, trees, animals, and bees, as he tells Maecenas in the poem's opening lines:

> *quid faciat laetas segetes, quo sidere terram*
> *uertere, Maecenas, ulmisque adiungere uitis*
> *conueniat, quae cura boum, qui cultus habendo*
> *sit pecori, apibus quanta experientia parcis,*
> *hinc canere incipiam.* (*Georgics* 1.1–5)

> What makes the fields fertile, Maecenas, under what
> star it is appropriate to turn the soil and to join vines
> to elms, what is the care of cattle, how to keep flocks,
> how much experiential knowledge there is for frugal
> bees—from here I begin to sing.

One way to read Vergil's *praeteritio* corresponds to how we interpreted Cicero's use of the device: as a mechanism for introducing additional material, on a subject outside of the bounds he has set for himself at the poem's outset, into the structure of the *Georgics*. We can read in Vergil's careful parallelism between the opening lines of *praeteritio* and the description of the Old Man's garden that now-familiar technique of saying what you say you won't say. Vergil's use of close synonyms and avoidance of actual repetition reveal a self-consciousness about the potential contradiction between his asserted *recusatio* and the Tarentine digression. Within this reading of the *praeteritio*, it appears that Vergil never intended to "sing" anything more about gardens.

There is an alternative way to read this passage that makes it less designing, less "ironic." In this view, the *praeteritio* is a literal representation of Vergil's plan for the poetry book. One commentary on the *Georgics* assesses the horticultural *praeteritio* as "a graceful interpolation, sketching the plan of what might have been a fifth Georgic."[19] This reading of Vergil's *canerem* has a long history that began within a generation after Vergil's death. Columella (4 –c. 70 CE) actually wrote a "fifth book" on gardens to fill the gap left by Vergil. Columella's 12-book treatise, *De Re Rustica*, follows in the venerable Roman tradition of instructional writing on agriculture. Like Cato's *De Agri Cultura* and Varro's *Res Rustica* (important source texts for Vergil as he wrote the *Georgics*), Columella's treatise is written in prose—except for the tenth book, on gardens, which Columella wrote in dactylic hexameter, citing Vergil as his inspiration:

> *quare cultus hortorum, quorum iam fructus magis in usu est, diligentius nobis, quam tradidere maiores, praecipiendus est, isque, sicut institueram, prorsa oratione prioribus subnecteretur exordiis, nisi propositum meum expugnasset frequens postulatio tua, quae praecepit, ut poeticis numeris explerem Georgici carminis omissas partis, quas tamen et ipse Vergilius significaverat posteris se memorandas relinquere.* (RR. 10.3)

Therefore, I must teach the cultivation of gardens (whose products are now in greater demand) more carefully than my predecessors have handed down, and I would add this to my earlier books in prose, as I had intended to do, if your repeated appeals had not overcome my resolve and bid me to complete in meter those parts of the *Georgics* which Vergil omitted and which, as he himself had intimated, he left to later writers to mention.

Columella's deliberate echoing of Vergil's own words (*aliis post me memoranda relinquo, Georgics* 4.148) at the end of this declaration of purpose shows him picking up where Vergil left off, composing the book that Vergil didn't have time to write. Columella reveals himself as a cooperative reader who could take *praeteritio* at face value. And he allows us to see how words like *canere*, which are used to introduce *praeteritio*, accrue a range of meanings that are at times contradictory, through the ongoing exchanges between authors and more and less cooperative audiences.

* * *

I would like to thank Reggie for the lasting influence he has had on my approach to and appreciation of the Latin language. It has been ten years since I attended his Schola Aestiva Latinitatis, but it remains one of the touchstones of my career. He has also influenced my approach to addressing letters to friends, for whom no fewer than five colors of ink are acceptable.

BIBLIOGRAPHY

Conington, J. and H. Nettleship, eds. and comm. 1979. *The Works of Virgil*. Hildesheim; New York: G. Olms.

Corbeill, Anthony. 2002. "Rhetorical Education in Cicero's Youth." In *Brill's Companion to Cicero: Oratory and Rhetoric*, ed. James May, 23–48. Leiden; Boston: Brill.

Goldstein, David. 2013. "Wackernagel's Law and the Fall of the Lydian Empire." *Transactions of the American Philological Association* 43 (2):325–347.

Grice, Paul. 1989. *Studies in the Way of Words*. Cambridge, MA: Harvard University Press.

Habinek, Thomas. 2005. *The World of Roman Song: From Ritualized Speech to Social Order*. Baltimore; London: The Johns Hopkins University Press.

Henkemans, A. Francisca Snoeck. 2009. "The contribution of *praeteritio* to arguers' confrontational strategic maneuvers." In *Examining Argumentation in Context: Fifteen Studies on Strategic Maneuvering*, ed. Frans H. van Eemeren, 241–255. John Benjamins Publishing Company.

Huang, Yan. 2015. "Neo-Gricean Pragmatic Theory of Conversational Implicature." In *The Oxford Handbook of Linguistic Analysis*, Second Edition, ed. Bernd Heine and Heiko Narrog, 615–639. Oxford University Press.

Johnson, W. R. 1969. "Tact in the Drusus Ode: Horace, *Odes* 4.4." *California Studies in Classical Antiquity* 2:171–181.

Lausberg, Heinrich. 1998. *Handbook of Literary Rhetoric: A Foundation for Literary Study*, ed. David E. Orton and R. Dean Anderson. Leiden; Boston: Brill.

Thomas, Richard F. 1982. *Lands and Peoples in Roman Poetry: The Ethnographical Tradition*. Cambridge Philological Society.

Usher, S. 1965. "*Occultatio* in Cicero's Speeches." *The American Journal of Philology*, 86 (2):175–192.

ENDNOTES

[1] Aquila (*De Figuris Sententiarum et Elocutionis* 8) describes *praeteritio* as follows: "The use of this figure is frequent when, as though passing over something, we nonetheless say it" (*frequens est huius figurae usus, ubi quasi praetermittentes quaedam nihilo minus dicimus*). See Lausberg 1998, §882–886.

[2] On the dating of the *Rhetorica ad Herennium*, see, e.g., Corbeill 2002, 33.

[3] The verb *dicere* conveys not merely "saying" ("speaking") but "expressing with authority" or "insisting on the validity of" (see Habinek 2005, 63), meanings that enhance the contradiction of the definition: *occultatio*

119

asserts the validity of the act of passing over *as well as* the act of disclosing.

4   Quintilian, *I.O.* 4.2.48–49, quoting Cicero, *Pro Caecina* 11 (*moritur Fulcinius; multa enim quae sunt in re, quia remota sunt a causa, praetermittam*). Although Cicero here uses one of the signal words of *praeteritio* (*praetermittam*), his refusal to detail the *multa* distinguishes this technique from true *praeteritio*. Cf. Usher 1965, 176–7, on the distinction between *praeteritio* and *reticentia*.

5   Cf. Lausberg 1998, §902. In the *Rhetorica ad Alexandrum*, one of the earliest surviving rhetorical handbooks, the two concepts seem to be conflated under the heading εἰρωνεία (εἰρωνεία δ' ἐστὶ λέγειν τι προσποιούμενον μὴ λέγειν, 21). Irony is important to the interpretation of *praeteritio* in Johnson 1969, 172–3.

6   Quintilian, *I.O.* 9.2.45: *quamquam aliud dicit ac sentit, non aliud tamen simulat, nam et omnia circa fere recta sunt*. His definition of irony ("one must understand the opposite of what is said," *contrarium ei quod dicitur intellegendum est, I.O.* 9.2.44) closely resembles the definition of *praeteritio* found, *inter alia*, in the *Rhetorica ad Herennium*.

7   Example from Henkemans 2009, 245, modified.

8   The most common words for introducing *praeteritio* in the speeches of Cicero are *mittere* (29 times) and *omittere* (37 times), while *praeterire* and *praetermittere* are used 8 and 10 times respectively (Usher 1965, 179).

9   Grice's ideas have been debated and modified, but neo-Gricean principles still stand as central tenets of pragmatics today; see Huang 2015, 615–18. They remain largely unexplored within the field of classics, but for a recent use of Gricean maxims to interpret a classical text, see Goldstein 2013.

10   The following scheme is modeled on the simplified version outlined by Huang 2015, 616. Cf. Grice 1989, 26–29.

11   *Non dico hoc tempore, iudices, id quod nescio an dici oporteat, illum maiestatis esse condemnatum* (*Pro Cluentio* 99).

12   *Non dicam hoc loco maiores nostros semper in pace consuetudini, in bello utilitati paruisse* (*De Imperio Gnaei Pompei* 60).

13   The Latin, however, is (fittingly) ambiguous: *rosaria* in line 119 can be taken either as the object of *ornaret* (along with *hortos*) or as the object of *canerem*. I have translated it as the object of *ornaret*, but if we read it as the object of *canerem*, Vergil has made two statements ("I would

sing of *how to care for* gardens" and "I would sing of rose gardens"), the second of which is more contradictory than the first.

[14] Cf. the first type of praeteritic strategy described by Henkemans 2009, 244: "in which the speaker puts forward an alternative assertion, which at first sight seems to be a different statement, but on closer inspection turns out to be the same thing in the context at hand."

[15] Cf. Ovid, *Metamorphoses* 3.339–510 (Narcissus) and 10.155–219 (Hyacinthus).

[16] Ann. fr. 207 Skutsch. In the Latin, Skutsch prints vorsibus (instead of versibus).

[17] So Liddell and Scott.

[18] Cf. Thomas 1982, 56–59.

[19] Conington and Nettleship n. ad 116–148. They speculate (n. ad 148) that Vergil "thought a rural poem could not be extended beyond four books without weariness to himself and his readers, or that he recoiled from the difficulty of minute botanical description."

Dido's (?) Tears: A Brief History of a Sorrowful Ambiguity

Jessica Seidman

> Mainly, of course, they are his tears;
> but there are moments in the poem
> when it is well not to be too sure;
> and there are readers, also, who had
> better not be too sure at any time; and
> anyhow they are not his tears only, but
> hers too, if we need to think so, and,
> again, if we need to think so, the very
> fountain of tears of all the world.[1]

The character of Dido may be most closely associated with the theme of "hopeless love," but "grievous weeping" would not be far behind. Dido famously weeps her way through much of *Aeneid* 4. Just thirty lines into the book, we already find her "overflowing" with teary confusion (*sinum lacrimis implevit obortis*, "she filled her breast with the tears which had sprung up," 4.30), and once the flood gates are open, there's seemingly no closing them: Dido swears by her tears (4.314), uses them in angry rhetorical questions (4.369), weeps in frustration (4.413–14), weeps by proxy (4.437–8), reminisces about weeping (4.548), and even pauses to weep before killing herself (4.649). The wells have dried up by the time we encounter her in the Vergilian afterlife of book 6, but the same cannot

123

be said of her literary afterlife: her tears continue to drench Aeneas' sword as she stands on the pyre in Ovid's *Heroides* (7.185).

Dido's lachrymosity has complicated the interpretation of line 4.449: *mens immota manet, lacrimae volvuntur inanes*, "his mind remains unmoved, the tears roll down, useless." The Latin is simple enough for a first-year student, but it would seem to be missing a critical bit of information: *whose* tears? A characteristically tearful Dido (413) has just sent her sister, "bearing her tears" (*talisque miserrima fletus/fertque refertque soror*, 437–8), to reason with Aeneas, who "feels the cares deep in his great heart" (*magno persentit pectore curas*, 448), even as he rejects Anna's petitions. Servius Auctus sums up the possibilities: *quidam tamen "lacrimas inanes" vel Aeneae, vel Didonis, vel Annae, vel omnium accipiunt*, "Nevertheless, some read the 'useless tears' as those of Aeneas, or of Dido, or of Anna, or of all." As I hope to show here, this confusion has been remarkably productive, as generations of readers have reflected their own unique perspectives through their interpretations of the line. Indeed, in their commentaries, both Austin and O'Hara have suggested that ambiguity was precisely Vergil's goal. "Virgil is purposely ambiguous, and why may he not remain so?" observes Austin.[2]

"Because the line isn't ambiguous at all!" retorts a chorus of classical scholars whose work on the line goes back at least 150 years. Indeed, although roughly equal numbers assign the tears to Aeneas and to Dido, they all agree that the "answer" is obvious and that the other side is clearly wrong. In his 1876 commentary, Conington observes, "*Lacrimae* can only be the tears of Dido, as represented and shared by Anna;"[3] over a hundred years later, Moles adds only "Obviously."[4] In his more polemical article, Hudson-Williams insists that it is "mere perversity" to regard the tears as shed by anyone other than Dido, and "to the attentive reader the poet's careful language presents no ambiguity."[5] Critics who argue that the tears belong to Aeneas are no less animated, often employing exactly the same language. Convinced that it is Aeneas who weeps, Horsfall critiques the other side's "intensely perverse view"[6] and characterizes Hudson-Williams's argument as "one of the least convincing articles on Virgil known to me."[7] Pöschl likewise insists on Aeneas' tears, noting that "no other interpretation is acceptable."[8] Echoing Hudson-Williams's language—if not his ultimate conclusion—Lyne argues that "context here in fact disallows ambiguity."[9]

Although most scholars have been content to find fault with each other's interpretations, a few have placed the blame squarely on the poet himself. "While the reasons for [assigning the tears to Dido] seem conclusive to me," writes Keith, "it must be admitted that Vergil by a certain carelessness of words opened up the possibility of another view."[10] In an article on incomplete lines in Vergil, under the heading "Poor Additions," Steele is even less kind: "If [the tears are] Dido's, they are misplaced, as they come at the end of a description of Aeneas. If they are his, they are not in harmony with 'mens immota manet,' and in either case the words, like the tears, are inane."[11] It is ambiguous whether the line is purposely or unintentionally ambiguous—or, indeed, whether it is ambiguous at all.

Rather than adding yet another voice to this centuries-old "whose tears" debate, this paper examines what has been at stake in the answer and how the identity of the weeper has had exegetical consequences far beyond line 449, involving particularly Augustine's approach to this ambiguous ambiguity. We will begin by taking a close look at the Latin of line 449 itself and the lines immediately preceding it, and by reviewing the modern arguments that have been advanced identifying Aeneas or Dido respectively as the source of the *lacrimae*. Austin has famously observed that "the line is ruined by a chill analysis;"[12] we'll try not to let the analysis get too chilly before turning to the warm hearth of Augustine's reception.

1. Tears of frustration: The modern debate.

Critics from the fourth century to the twenty-first have seen little ambiguity in the Latin of *Aeneid* 4.449, despite intense disagreement about the proper interpretation. Nearly all modern English translations, however, have preserved precisely the ambiguity of the

Latin line, studiously avoiding the possessive pronouns "his" or "her" before "tears," which would easily render the supposed clarity that critics see in the Latin. In Mandelbaum's we find "his mind cannot be moved; the tears fall, useless;" in Lombardo's, "but his mind does not move, / And the tears that fall to the ground change nothing;" in Fagles's, "His will stands unmoved. The falling tears are futile;" in Ruden's, "But tears did nothing; his resolve endured." Either these translators, unlike the critics, find Vergil's Latin quite ambiguous, or they believe that their English renderings are themselves perfectly unambiguous without resorting to possessives.

As mentioned above, the story is quite different among the literary critics, though the essential arguments for assigning the tears to Aeneas and to Dido have been roughly the same for the last 150 years. The first point of contention has to do with the syntax of line 449 itself: *mens immota manet, lacrimae volvuntur inanes*. In the context, everyone agrees that the *mens* must belong to Aeneas ("*his* mind remains unmoved"); those in the "Aeneas' tears" camp point out that Latin precludes the possibility of a new, different subject for the second half of the line without an expressed word to indicate the change. As Horsfall puts it, for the tears to belong to Dido, "[an] exceptionally awkward change of subject is required that Virgil does not habitually leave to the reader's fantasy."[13] Opponents respond that this is a chill analysis indeed, that Latin is far more flexible than these critics suppose, and even that "the addition of any word specifically designating the author of the tears could only be the work of a novice,"[14] which Vergil most certainly was not.

The strongest support for the "Aeneas' tears" side is the simile that immediately precedes the line (4.437–449):

> *talibus orabat, talisque miserrima fletus*
> *fertque refertque soror. sed nullis ille movetur*
> *fletibus aut voces ullas tractabilis audit;*
> *fata obstant placidasque viri deus obstruit auris.*
> *ac velut annoso validam cum robore quercum*
> *Alpini Boreae nunc hinc nunc flatibus illinc*

eruere inter se certant; it stridor, et altae
consternunt terram concusso stipite frondes;
ipsa haeret scopulis et quantum vertice ad auras
aetherias, tantum radice in Tartara tendit:
haud secus adsiduis hinc atque hinc vocibus heros
tunditur, et magno persentit pectore curas;
mens immota manet, lacrimae volvuntur inanes.

[Dido] begged her with such words, and so her most unhappy sister
relates such weeping again and again. But he is moved
by no weeping, nor does he bend to hear any words;
the fates stand in the way and the god blocks the man's
ears, quietly at peace.
And just as when the Alpine north winds,
with gusts now on this side now on that, struggle amongst themselves
to uproot a strong oak, with its ancient trunk; there is
a creaking sound,
and lofty branches strew the ground as the trunk is shaken;
the tree itself clings to its rocks and roots itself as deeply in the world below
as it stretches with its canopy to the heavenly sky:
not at all differently is the hero tossed here and there by the onslaught of
words, and he feels the cares deep in his great heart;
his mind remains unmoved, the tears roll down, useless.

On *frondes* (444), Servius notes *sicut lacrimae Aeneae,* "just like the tears of Aeneas," paving the way for what West would later term a "multiple correspondence simile:" the *fletus* Anna relates in 439 become the *flatus* striking the tree in 442; the tree itself (*ipsa*, 445) corresponds to Aeneas' mind (*mens*, 449), while the shaken trunk (*concusso stipite*, 444) is his heart (*pectore*, 448); finally, as Servius noted, the fallen branches (*frondes*, 444) are Aeneas' tears (*lacrimae*, 449).[15] Since every other part of the tree has a clear parallel in the description of Aeneas, the branches should represent his tears. As Quinn observes, "Unless we are prepared to believe Virgil spoilt the coherence of his simile in its last three words, we must give the tears to Aeneas."[16] Keith counters that the tears do not fit with the rest of the elements in the simile, which represents an "inward or spiritual quality of Aeneas"—his *mens* and *pectus* as aspects of his spirit, not physical body parts—and to equate the leaves with actual tears would introduce "a purely physical element quite incongruous with the spiritual idea developed just above, and certainly not in Vergil's usual style."[17] Hudson-Williams adds that critics who have advanced this argument are "seemingly unfamiliar with the aspect of rolling tears" and that "it is hard to believe that a thought so alien to Virgil's sense of propriety could ever have occurred to him."[18]

The most compelling argument for "Dido's tears" is the pairing of words and tears throughout this episode. The combination first appears at line 413 (*in lacrimas . . . precando*), right before Dido sends Anna to Aeneas. They are connected again in line 437 (*talibus [dictis] . . . fletus*) and again at 439 (*fletibus . . . voces*). In all of these cases, both the words and the tears belong to Dido (perhaps as related by Anna). So when we see *vocibus* on line 447, again referring to Dido, Vergil has primed us to expect "tears" nearby—and we find them in *lacrimae* on 449. Contextually, Vergil has prepared us for these to be Dido's tears, unifying the whole episode with a chiastic arrangement of the pair in 439 with the pair in 447/449.[19]

These, then, are the essential arguments that scholars have been making regarding line 449 since the mid-nineteenth century. Many of these points have a veneer of logical objectivity, supported as they are by parallel passages, appeals to the norms of Latin syntax, and close attention to poetic devices. The reader may be surprised, however, to observe how many of these arguments include a more overtly personal, impassioned appeal, amounting to something like "Vergil just wouldn't *do* that!" These scholars have internalized a strong sense not only of Vergil's poetics, but also of the character and message of his work, a sense they support with their various readings of line 449. Hudson-Williams characterizes these more subjective "feelings" about the line quite negatively as "the personal whims and prejudices" of critics,[20] but this judgment dismisses the very brilliance of line 449: through this ambiguity, Vergil has created as many subjective positions as he has readers, who, for two millennia, have found themselves and their concerns reflected in a mere six words. As we will see in the case of Augustine, the line is a sort of empty vessel, ready to be filled with the ever-shifting identities of a single reader.

2. Empty tears: Augustine's ambiguous identity.

Augustine offers a very direct interpretation of *Aeneid* 4.449 in book 9 of *De Civitate Dei*. Here Augustine is explaining that Platonists and Stoics have essentially the same beliefs about emotions; they simply use different vocabulary (9.4.1–3). Everyone—even the wise man—is subject to *phantasiae*, the causes of fear and sadness, but wise men are able to control their responses to these feelings with rational precepts (9.4.7–10). For Augustine, the paragon of this Stoic wisdom is Aeneas in line 449:

> *ita mens ubi fixa est ista sententia nullas perturbationes, etiamsi accidunt inferioribus animi partibus, in se contra rationem praevalere permittit; quin immo eis ipsa dominatur eisque non consentiendo et potius resistendo regnum virtutis exercet. talem describit etiam Vergilius Aenean, ubi ait*

> *mens immota manet; lacrimae volvuntur inanes.*
> (9.4.11)

Thus, when that understanding is firmly entrenched, the mind allows no disturbances to prevail against it contrary to reason, even if they happen in the lower parts of the soul; but the mind is not for a second overpowered by them and it affirms the authority of virtue by not assenting to these impulses but rather by resisting. Vergil also describes Aeneas this way, when he says

> His mind remains unmoved; his tears roll down empty.

Like most modern commentators, Augustine appears to see no ambiguity in the *lacrimae* whatsoever. For Augustine, they belong to Aeneas, end of story. Even for those inclined to agree with Augustine, his unequivocal assignment of the tears to Aeneas may come as a surprise. Dido is not mentioned in *De Civitate* at all, whereas in the first book of the earlier *Confessions*, Augustine connects his own tears with Dido explicitly. Indeed, the odd resonance between this offhand reference to *Aeneid* 4.449 and that vivid moment from Augustine's childhood goes well beyond Augustine's familiarity with (and love of) the *Aeneid* and the general theme of weeping, as "emptiness"— explicitly, the word *inanis*—plays a critical role in the *Confessions* passage as well:

> *unde tamen et hoc nisi de peccato et <u>vanitate vitae</u>, qua caro eram et spiritus ambulans et non revertens? nam utique meliores, quia certiores, erant primae illae litterae, . . . quam illae, quibus tenere cogebar Aeneae nescio cuius errores, oblitus errorum meorum, et plorare Didonem mortuam, quia se occidit ab amore, cum interea me ipsum in his a te morientem, deus, vita mea, siccis oculis ferrem miserrimus. quid enim miserius misero non miserante se ipsum et flente Didonis mortem, quae fiebat amando Aenean, non*

flente autem mortem suam, quae fiebat non amando te, deus? (Conf.1.13.20–21)

But where did I get this [preference for literature over basic skills] except from sin and the vanity/ emptiness of life, by which I was flesh and "wind, going and not returning?" For those early studies [i.e., basic skills] were assuredly better because they were more unerring, . . . more unerring than those studies which forced me to remember the wanderings of some Aeneas, forgetful of my own wanderings, and to wail for dead Dido because she killed herself for love, when meanwhile, in pursuing these things, I was allowing myself to die apart from you, my God, my life; my eyes were dry, myself most pitiful. [21] For what is more pitiful than a pitiful man who does not pity his very self and weeps for the death of Dido, which happened because of her love for Aeneas, but who does not weep for his own death, which happened because of his lack of love for you, God?

Augustine concludes,

peccabam ergo puer, cum illa inania istis utilioribus amore praeponebam vel potius ista oderam, illa amabam. iam vero unum et unum duo, duo et duo quattuor odiosa cantio mihi erat, et dulcissimum spectaculum vanitatis equus ligneus plenus armatis, et Troiae incendium, atque ipsius umbra Creusae. (1.13.22)

And so I sinned as a boy, when I preferred those empty things in my affection to those more useful things, or rather I hated the latter, I loved the former. But then the chant "one and one are two, two and two are four" was hateful to me and <u>the sweetest show of vanity/emptiness</u> was the wooden horse <u>filled</u> with armed men and the burning of Troy and "the shade of Creusa herself."

Here Augustine is playing on themes of "emptiness" and "fullness": his childhood enthusiasm for the stories of the *Aeneid*, which he characterizes as *illa inania*, "those empty things," and *dulcissimum spectaculum vanitatis*, "the sweetest show of emptiness," itself arises *vanitate vitae*, "from the emptiness of life." At least two of the *Aeneid* episodes with which Augustine concludes continue the theme of emptiness: the Trojan horse has been hollowed out so that it might be "filled" with men, while Creusa is merely an insubstantial "shade" that Aeneas is unable to grasp. Since this moment of tearfulness for Augustine is also characterized as *inanis*, it is worth considering what that word might connote in this context.

Augustine contrasts *inania* with *utilioria*, suggesting that *inanis* might mean something like "lacking practical value," but the fierceness of Augustine's self-critique in this moment calls for something more dire. The image of the empty Trojan horse "filled with armed men" reminds the reader of the ways in which things that are empty and hollow in themselves can become vehicles for harm and, perhaps, sin. That is, the *Aeneid* itself is no more harmful than an empty wooden horse, but it can become a weapon if "filled" with interpretations that promote sin. Because Augustine felt a very close connection to the *Aeneid* from childhood, his personal identification with the characters offered a dangerous opportunity for this type of harmful interpretation. In the same way that line 449 allows the possibility for the tears to belong to Aeneas or Dido, the characters Aeneas and Dido themselves are empty vessels for Augustine to fill with his own identity and those of other people in his life, transforming the story of the *Aeneid* into his own story.

The potency of Augustine's *inanis* helps us to make an important distinction. As we have seen, most scholars today believe that there is a right and a wrong interpretation of line 449, though they cannot agree on which is which. Similarly, Augustine also recognizes that there are right and wrong ways to "fill in" these characters, but he distinguishes the two in a strikingly different way. In his view, what really matters is whether one identifies with a weeping Dido or a weeping Aeneas, particularly as one runs the risk of becoming empty oneself, a mere *umbra*, like Creusa.[21]

Who, then, is Augustine in our ambiguous, weepy narrative? On a first reading of the passages above, it is clear that the young Augustine felt a strong identification with Dido in her distress. Dido's grief over the loss of Aeneas offers Augustine himself a model for weeping over the loss of Dido. This empathic response has struck some modern readers as odd: "While it seems strange for a boy to identify with the suicidal leanings of the great queen of Carthage, it is precisely by internalizing set roles that Augustine comes to understand and interpret his own emotions."[22] Indeed, even in denouncing his childhood foolishness, Augustine reprimands himself, not for identifying with Dido, but for not identifying with her fully enough. As the adult Augustine reflects on his youth, he recognizes that he was similar to Dido not only in his weepiness, but also in his (spiritual) deadness as a result of his own actions, a type of suicide; Augustine should not have wept *for* Dido because he himself *was* Dido.

This makes it all the more surprising that, in this very section of the *Confessions*, Augustine also presents himself as a weepy Aeneas. After recalling his relentless and sinful pursuit of praise, he writes, "And I was not weeping for these things, and I was weeping for Dido, 'dead and having pursued the final ends by the sword,' I myself pursuing your most distant creation, even as you were abandoned, and 'dust going unto dust,'" *et haec non flebam, et flebam Didonem extinctam ferroque extrema secutam, sequens ipse extrema condita tua relicto te, et terra iens in terram (Conf.* 1.13.21). Here Augustine is quoting *Aeneid* 6.457, in which Aeneas addresses Dido: "Unhappy Dido, and so a true message had come to me, / that you had died and had pursued the final ends by the sword?" *Infelix Dido, verus mihi nuntius ergo / venerat extinctam ferroque extrema secutam?* Here in

Aeneid 6, there is no ambiguity whatsoever: Aeneas "poured down tears and addressed her with sweet love" (*demisit lacrimas, dulcique adfatus amore est*, 6.455). In appropriating Aeneas' words for himself, Augustine shifts his identification from a weeping Dido to a weeping Aeneas. As Camille Bennett has observed, this shift corresponds to a recognition by the more mature Augustine that "in weeping, like Aeneas, for Dido, he unwittingly acknowledged himself to be not the abandoned but the abandoner, whose *errores* took him from his love."[23] Augustine is able to occupy the roles of both the injured and the one who has committed the injury; the ambiguity of the tears in the *Aeneid* perfectly matches the ambiguity of Augustine's own identification, as he achieves the resonance of both the *lacrimae* of Dido and the *lacrimae* of Aeneas.

This approach to the ambiguity is different from the interpretations of the modern critics surveyed earlier in two significant ways. First, where most modern critics insist upon an "either/or" interpretation of the line, Augustine's hermeneutic of subjectivity fully embraces a "both/and" approach. The second difference is the hermeneutic itself: Augustine's interpretation in the *Confessions* is guided in no small part by the ways that he can see himself in the text, first in the character of Dido and later in the character of Aeneas. Perhaps this is not far from the "personal whims and prejudices" that Hudson-Williams decries, but for Augustine, the subjectivity is not something to hide; rather, it is the whole point. The characters are empty spaces for each of us to inhabit; if we do this properly, they will illuminate the plot lines of our own lives and our proper relationship with God.

As Augustine reaches the climax of the *Confessions* with the death of Monica in book 9, he suggests that, just as he has inhabited the tearful space of Dido and Aeneas at different moments, so the reader can profitably identify with the tearful protagonist of his own narrative. As he watches his mother lie dying in a room in Ostia, Augustine struggles to hold back tears, and we find a near-perfect instantiation of his later interpretation of *Aeneid* 4.449:

premebam oculos eius, et confluebat in praecordia
mea maestitudo ingens et transfluebat in lacrimas,
ibidemque oculi mei violento animi imperio resorbebant
fontem suum usque ad siccitatem, et in tali luctamine
valde male mihi erat. (Conf. 9.12.29)

I closed her eyes, and a huge wave of grief flowed into
my heart and was flowing into tears, and at the same
time, by the forcible power of my mind, my eyes kept
holding back their flow until they were completely
dry, and I felt truly awful in such a struggle.

But at last, Augustine allows himself to weep:

et libuit flere in conspectu tuo de illa et pro illa, de
me et pro me. Et dimisi lacrimas quas continebam, ut
effluerent quantum vellent, substernens eas cordi meo.
et requievit in eis, quoniam ibi erant aures tuae, non
cuiusquam hominis superbe interpretantis ploratum
meum.

And it was a relief to weep in your sight about her and
for her, about myself and for myself. And I released
the tears that I used to hold back, so that they flowed
as much as they wished, scattering them beneath my
heart. And my heart rested in them, since your ears
were present there, not those of some person who
would interpret my grief in arrogance. (*Conf.* 9.12.33)

On the one hand, Augustine seems to embody the Stoic Aeneas of
De Civitate, the one who rationally does not lose sight of ultimate
goal, even as he responds emotionally to the *phantasia* of personal
loss.[24] At the same time, the ambiguity of identification persists, as
Augustine weeps both *about* (*de*) his mother and *for* (*pro*) his mother,
about himself and *for* himself. *De* suggests an objective view from the

135

outside, as though Augustine has watched his mother's death and his own agony on stage: these are external events that he can weep *about*. *Pro*, on the other hand, suggests identification, a "standing in the place of:"[25] Augustine weeps *as* his mother and *as* himself. The tears are his own *and* hers, as he slips in and out of the characters of his *Aeneid* model and his own story. Indeed, Augustine instructs his own readers with nearly the same words in book 10: *flete mecum et pro me flete qui aliquid boni vobiscum intus agitis, unde facta procedunt*, "Weep with me and weep for me, you who pursue anything good within yourselves from which [good] deeds issue" (*Conf.*10.30.50). Just as Augustine himself steps in and out of the empty characters of Aeneas and Dido, his younger self and his mother, so now he urges his own readers to fill the spaces he has created in the characters of his own work, weeping both alongside him and as him, identifying with a grief all share, even as they pursue the good. There are, it seems, enough tears for everyone.

3. Conclusion: Translating tears.

I mentioned earlier that nearly all modern English translations avoid explicitly assigning the tears to Aeneas or to Dido. C. Day Lewis's 1952 Oxford translation is the lone exception:

> Even thus was the hero belaboured for long with every
> kind of pleading, and his great heart thrilled through
> and through with the pain of it; resolute, though, was
> his mind; unavailingly rolled her tears.

Lewis's introduction focuses primarily on the poetic challenge of translation and presents little in the way of critical interpretation of the text. But just as modern critics have claimed access to Vergil's mind, and as Augustine saw into Aeneas' heart, so Lewis longs for a kind of contact with the poet:

That leads us straight into the mystique of translating. To catch the tone of the original, there must be some sort of affinity between you and him: neither skill in versification nor perceptive scholarship is enough . . . Translation . . . is a matter of love, skill, and luck. Without the luck, you cannot reach through the words and thoughts of your original and make contact with the man who wrote it.[26]

"Reaching through the words" of 4.449, Lewis found Dido.

When Oxford republished Lewis's translation in 1986, Jasper Griffin added an introduction and notes, including this note on Lewis's translation of 4.449: "*her tears*: the Latin more naturally means 'his tears': a point not without importance." Of course, Lewis's translation was not altered, thus leaving the reader in a state of *aporia*, unable to choose between the allegedly "less natural" translation actually present on the page and the "perceptive scholarship" relegated to the endnotes. The book itself reifies the history of the problem: the meaning is perfectly clear in the translation and perfectly clear in the notes; but what to do when a single text points in opposite directions?

Lewis dedicated his translation to W. F. Jackson Knight, "who went through my translation with me, line by line, correcting, suggesting, encouraging,"[27] and who also wrote the epigraph at the start of this paper:

Mainly, of course, they are his tears; but there are moments in the poem when it is well not to be too sure; and there are readers, also, who had better not be too sure at any time; and anyhow they are not his tears only, but hers too, if we need to think so, and, again, if we need to think so, the very fountain of tears of all the world.

We would do well, I think, to follow his advice: to be sure and not sure; to see the tears as his, as hers, and as all the world's; and to know that the truth is not any less true just because it is what we need it to be.

* * *

This paper is, of course, dedicated to Fr. Reginald Foster, who always scoffs at "Dido's tears," but on one very hot July afternoon in Ostia, standing on the spot where Monica died, brought me and many of my fellow students to tears with the sweetness of his love for Augustine's Latin. My deepest gratitude to him for filling the empty spaces with his playfulness and passion. None of it was in vain.

BIBLIOGRAPHY

Austin, R. G. 1955. *P. Vergili Maronis Aeneidos Liber Quartus*. Oxford: Clarendon Press.

Bennett, Camille. 1988. "The Conversion of Vergil: The Aeneid in Augustine's Confessions." *Revue des Études Augustiniennes* 34:47–69.

Conington, John. 1876. *P. Vergili Maronis Opera*. Vol. II. London: Whittaker & Co.

Desmond, Marilynn. 1994. *Reading Dido: Gender, Textuality, and the Medieval Aeneid*. Minneapolis: University of Minnesota Press.

Dryden, John. 1909. *Virgil's Aeneid*. New York: P.F. Collier and Son. http://oll.libertyfund.org/titles/1175.

Edwards, Mark. 2009. *Sound, Sense, and Rhythm: Listening to Greek and Latin Poetry*. Princeton: Princeton University Press.

Fagles, Robert. 2008. *The Aeneid: Virgil*. Reprint edition. New York: Penguin.

Fontaine, Michael. 2016. "Freudian Bullseyes in the Classical Perspective: The Psycholinguistics of Guilt in Virgil's *Aeneid*." In *Wordplay and Powerplay in Latin Poetry*, ed. Phillip Mitsis and Ioannis Ziogas, 131–149. Berlin: de Gruyter.

Henry, James. 1878. *Aeneidea: Critical, Exegetical, and Aesthetic Remarks on the Aeneis*, Vol. II. London: Williams and Norgate.

Horsfall, Nicholas. 1988. Review of *Homo Viator: Classical Essays for John Bramble*, ed. Michael Whitby et al. *The Classical Review* 38.2:383–385.

———. 1995. "Aeneid." In *A Companion to the Study of Virgil*, ed. Nicholas Horsfall, 101–216. Leiden: Brill.

Hudson-Williams, A. 1990. "*Lacrimae Illae Inanes.*" In *Virgil*, ed. Ian McAuslan and Peter Walcot, 149–156. Oxford: Oxford University Press.

Keith, Arthur L. 1928. "Vergil, Aeneid 4.449." *The Classical Weekly* 21, no. 15:113–114.

Knight, W. F. Jackson. 1968. *Roman Vergil*. New York: Barnes & Noble, Inc. First published 1944 by Faber.

Lewis, C. Day. 1952. *The Aeneid of Virgil*. Oxford: Oxford University Press.

Lombardo, Stanley. 2005. *Virgil: Aeneid*. Indianapolis: Hackett.

Lyne, R. O. A. M. 1987. *Further Voices in Vergil's Aeneid*. Oxford: Clarendon Press.

Mandelbaum, Allen. 1961. *The Aeneid of Virgil*. New York: Bantam.

Martindale, Charles. 1993. "Descent into Hell: Reading Ambiguity, or Vergil and the Critics." *Proceedings of the Virgil Society* 21:111–150.

MacCormack, Sabine. 1998. "'The Tears Run Down in Vain': Emotions, Soul, and Body." In *The Shadows of Poetry: Vergil in the Mind of Augustine*, 89–131. Berkeley: University of California Press.

Mackie, C. J. 1988. *The Characterisation of Aeneas*. Edinburgh: Scottish Academic Press.

McCarthy, Michael C. 2009. "Augustine's Mixed Feelings: Vergil's 'Aeneid' and the Psalms of David in the 'Confessions.'" *The Harvard Theological Review* 102, no. 4:453–479.

Moles, John. 1987. "The Tragedy and Guilt of Dido." In *Homo Viator: Classical Essays for John Bramble*, ed. Michael Whitby et al., 153–161. Bristol: Bristol Classical Press.

O'Hara, James J. 2011. *Vergil: Aeneid Book 4*. Newburyport, MA: Focus Publishing.

Page, T. E. 1902. *The Aeneid of Vergil, Books I–VI*. London: MacMillan & Co.

Pease, Arthur Stanley. 1935. *Publi Vergili Maronis Aeneid Liber Quartus*. Cambridge, MA: Harvard University Press.

Pöschl, Viktor. 1962. *The Art of Vergil: Image and Symbol in the Aeneid*. Ann Arbor: University of Michigan Press.

Quinn, Kenneth. 1963. *Latin Explorations: Critical Studies in Roman Literature*. London: Routledge and Paul.

Ramage, Carol L. 1970. "'The Confessions of St. Augustine: The Aeneid' Revisited." *Pacific Coast Philology* 5:54–60.

Ruden, Sarah. 2008. *The Aeneid: Vergil*. New Haven: Yale University Press.

Schelkle, Karl Hermann. 1939. *Virgil in der Deutung Augustins*. Stuttgart and Berlin: W. Kohlhammer.

Servius. 2004. *Servius' Commentary on Book Four of Virgil's* Aeneid. Trans. and annotated by Christopher M. McDonough, Richard E. Prior, and Mark Stansbury. Wauconda, IL: Bolchazy-Carducci.

Steele, R. B. 1910. "Incomplete Lines in the Aeneid." *The Classical Journal* 5, no. 5:226–231.

Vergil. 1969. *Opera*. Ed. by R. A. B. Mynors. Oxford: Oxford University Press.

Werpehowski, William. 1991. "Weeping at the Death of Dido: Sorrow, Virtue, and Augustine's 'Confessions.'" *The Journal of Religious Ethics* 19, no. 1:175–191.

West, David. 1969. "Multiple Correspondence Similes in the Aeneid." *The Journal of Roman Studies* 59:40–49.

Woods, Marjorie. 2003. "Weeping for Dido: epilogue on a premodern rhetorical exercise in the postmodern classroom." In *Latin Grammar and Rhetoric: From Classical Theory to Medieval Practice*, ed. Carol Dana Lanham, 285–294. London: Continuum.

Ziolkowski, Eric J. 1995 "St. Augustine: Aeneas' Antitype, Monica's Boy." *Literature and Theology* 9, no. 1:1–23.

ENDNOTES

1 Jackson Knight 1968, 251.
2 Austin 1955, 135. See also O'Hara 2011, 69: "Whose tears these are is unclear, probably deliberately."
3 Conington 1876, 304.
4 Moles 1987, 158n12.
5 Hudson-Williams 1990, 152.
6 Horsfall 1988, 384.
7 Horsfall 1995, 125.
8 Pöschl 1962, 46.
9 Lyne 1987, 164n35.
10 Keith 1928, 114.
11 Steele 1910, 230.
12 Austin 1955, 135.
13 Horsfall 1995, 125.
14 Hudson-Williams 1990, 152.
15 West 1969, 44–45. These are the correspondences West finds "particularly noteworthy," but he points out others as well.
16 Quinn 1963, 41n1.
17 Keith 1928, 113.
18 Hudson-Williams 1990, 153.
19 Keith 1928, 113; Hudson-Williams 1990, 151–52.
20 Even as he offers some of the best examples himself; Hudson-Williams 1990, 149.
21 "To imitate something not oneself . . . is to become '*adumbratus*,' to be a shadow, a resemblance of some other thing," Bennett 1988, 50.
22 McCarthy 2009, 461. As Woods (2003, 285–94) has noted, rhetorical exercises that encouraged boys to sympathize with angry and hurt women were common through the premodern period, and Woods herself has experimented with such exercises in her own classroom.
23 Bennett 1988, 56.
24 See Ziolkowski 1995, 13n70, arguing that Augustine assigns the tears to Aeneas in *De Civitate* as a justification for his own tears at the death of Monica.
25 This meaning of *pro* is most explicit in Lewis & Short II.B.2 ("in the place of"), but, I would argue, it is also implicit in the definitions "on behalf of" (II.B.1) and "the same as" (II.B.3). All three suggest varying

degrees and types of identification, of viewing oneself as representative of another or, as I have framed it in this discussion, sharing a space with another. When an orator pleads "on behalf of" his client, he is substituting his own words and *dignitas* for the accused. Certainly "pray on behalf of us" and "[you] pray instead of us" are distinctly different translations (both *ora pro nobis*), but both ask the addressee to *represent* the speaker.

26   Day Lewis 1952, 9.
27   Day Lewis 1952, 10.

Vivas Hinc Ducere Voces: Hearing Horace's *Satires* in his *Ars Poetica*

Jennifer Ferriss-Hill

H orace's *Ars Poetica* ("Art of Poetry") was revered throughout the Middle Ages, Renaissance, and Early Modern period. This 476-line verse epistle, ostensibly written at the request of the Piso family for a handbook on how to write drama, served as *the* manual for practicing poets, provided a blueprint for efforts at "updated" rules for literary composition, and has inspired numerous translators and imitators.[1] The earnestly didactic function of the poem, itself part of a tradition that included Aristotle's *Poetics* and Neoptolemus of Parium's *Art of Poetry*,[2] was never in serious doubt[3]— not, that is, until recently, when scholars began to look with suspicion upon all manner of claims that Horace casually attempts to pass off at face value throughout his writings, including even details of his own parentage and childhood.[4] The *Ars Poetica*'s tenacious grip on its hallowed status may strike the modern reader as surprising, since on the one hand Horace's signature wryness is everywhere on display, and on the other there is much in the poem that rankles as too naïve to be believably serious. I show here that the *Ars Poetica* is both profoundly satirical (even of the literary critical tradition in which it purports to participate) and yet in its own way serious—though not necessarily about literature. A key and illuminative ambiguity lies in the fact that alongside poetic composition, Horace also and alternately speaks of painting and sculpting, even living. As a result, the more he insists upon literature as the poem's exclusive purview, the more this façade begins to degrade. As I read it, far from being a narrowly circumscribed *Art of Poetry*, the *Ars Poetica* in fact encompasses all human endeavor,[5] and as such becomes ultimately rather more of an *Ars Vivendi* ("Art of Living") than has been recognized. Ethics and conduct thus come to the fore, and it is in this that we may see Horace's earliest work, his first book of *Satires* (or, as he referred to them, *sermones*, "conversations"), reflected in what presents itself as his last.[6] Just as the *Satires* give advice for living that contains encoded prescriptions for writing, so the *Ars Poetica* may, in turn, be read as a cipher for how to live masquerading as a guidebook on how to write.

The *Ars Poetica* begins with a striking vignette of a creature with a human head, a horse's neck, and colorfully feathered limbs; a beautiful woman (as the head turns out to be) with a black fish-tail:

> *humano capiti cervicem pictor equinam*
> *iungere si velit et varias inducere plumas*
> *undique collatis membris, ut turpiter atrum*
> *desinat in piscem mulier formosa superne,*
> *spectatum admissi risum teneatis, amici?*
> *credite, Pisones, isti tabulae fore librum*
> *persimilem cuius, velut aegri somnia, vanae*
> *fingentur species, ut nec pes nec caput uni*
> *reddatur formae. "pictoribus atque poetis*
> *quidlibet audendi semper fuit aequa potestas."* (Hor.
> *AP* 1-10)

> If a painter should wish to join a horse's neck to a human head and make colorful feathers grow from limbs gathered from every-which-where, so that what is a beautiful woman up on top ends horribly in a black fish, would you hold back your laughter, friends, when you have been let in for a viewing? Believe me, Pisos, just like that painting would be a book whose images are fashioned to be empty, like a sick man's

dreams, such that neither head nor foot can be related
to a single form. "Painters and poets have always had
the same opportunity to dare whatever they wish."

Although readers who know the poem as the *Ars Poetica* come to it
with the natural expectation that its focus will be poetry,[7] the opening
privileges painting (moreover, of a failed sort) over writing: *pictor*
("painter") appears prominently in the opening line, *librum* ("book")
follows *tabellae* ("painting") in line 6, and Horace's imaginary
interlocutor objects that "painters and poets" (in that order) "have
always had the same opportunity to dare whatever they wish" (9–10).
One of the poem's most famous and frequently excerpted phrases, *ut
pictura poesis*, "poetry is like painting" (361), likewise positions poetry
second. If the poem's opening leaves us feeling unsatisfied, even
perplexed, surely this is by design, for Horace, deft poet that he is, does
not merely want to lecture his readers about the importance of unity
and harmony. Rather, in performing an opening that is disjointed
and baffling, and to which we, addressed in the second person plural
(*teneatis*), have been admitted as viewers (*spectatum admissi*), he
compels us to *feel* the effects of art that lacks these guiding principles,
and gives us permission to laugh (*risum*)—laughter being the most
heartfelt and unfalsifiable form of critique and, paradoxically, one
that can be delivered only by true friends (*amici*). When propriety is
violated by artists, the result is both absurd and unsettling. When it
is violated by writers, we are left to imagine what that result would
entail, for Horace gives us no visualization of it, only the generalizing
advice, *denique sit quidvis, simplex dumtaxat et unum*, "in short, let
it be anything you wish, as long as it is straightforward and a single
thing" (23).

Horace then moves on to a second central tenet of the *Ars Poetica*,
the idea that in attempting to avoid one vice a person is liable to
commit its opposite. Again, painting is king:

> *brevis esse laboro,*
> *obscurus fio; sectantem levia nervi*

145

deficiunt animique; professus grandia turget;
serpit humi tutus nimium timidusque procellae.
qui variare cupit rem prodigialiter unam,
delphinum silvis appingit, fluctibus aprum:
in vitium ducit culpae fuga, si caret arte. (25–31)

I strive to be brief, I become obscure; sinews and spirit fail the one who chases smooth things; having professed great things, he becomes swollen; he who is too safe and fearful of the storm creeps on the ground; he who desires to vary a single theme unnaturally paints a dolphin in the woods, a boar on the waves. The avoidance of fault leads to error, if done artlessly.

The closing words, *si caret arte*, are more barbed than they might appear, for Horace continues, "take up material, you who write, that is well-matched to your strengths, and consider at length what your shoulders would refuse to carry, what they would be strong enough to bear" (*sumite materiam vestris, qui scribitis, aequam / viribus et versate diu quid ferre recusent, / quid valeant umeri*, 38–39). Resurfacing periodically (e.g., 263–69, 291–94, 366–90), Horace's reminders that successful creative endeavor requires a robust awareness of one's limitations as an artist are rather insistent: so much so, in fact, that one wonders whether the young scions of the illustrious Piso family—the poem's addressees and so, in a sense, its first readers—were starting to squirm in discomfort.[8] Horace's gambit is bold, not least because offending one's addressees is generally inadvisable. A possibly more important dynamic, however, involves Horace's implicit claim that he stands as an *amicus* to the Piso family, and that as their friend, any criticisms he directs at them are not only genuine and true, but cannot be left unvoiced.[9]

The reader who perseveres through Horace's ecphrases on the visual and plastic arts is rewarded, at long last, by some advice that pertains to literature. Characters must, Horace stresses, speak in a manner that befits their age and sex, station in life and origin:

si dicentis erunt fortunis absona dicta,
Romani tollent equites peditesque cachinnum.
intererit multum divusne loquatur an heros,
maturusne senex an adhuc florente iuventa
fervidus, et matrona potens an sedula nutrix,
mercatorne vagus cultorne virentis agelli,
Colchus an Assyrius, Thebis nutritus an Argis.
aut famam sequere aut sibi convenientia finge. (112-19)

If the words of the one speaking are not in harmony
with his fortunes, the Roman knights and foot soldiers
will raise a cackle. It will matter a great deal whether
a divinity is speaking or a hero, whether a mature
old man or one still hot with blooming youth, and a
powerful married woman or a busy nurse, whether an
itinerant merchant or the cultivator of a little plot of
land that grows green, a Colchian or an Assyrian, one
reared at Thebes or at Argos. Either follow tradition
or create things that are consistent with themselves.

ne forte seniles
mandentur iuveni partes pueroque viriles,
semper in adiunctis aevoque morabimur aptis. (176-78)

So that old men's parts are not by chance entrusted to
a young one, nor men's parts to a boy, we will always
take our time over traits associated with and fitted to
an age.

Moreover, comedy and tragedy each have their own register (89–91),
and surprises are met by the spectators with ridicule (104–5, 113; cf.
5). Throughout these sections Horace plants explicit declarations,
proverb-like, of the ideas illustrated in the vignettes: "create things
that are consistent with themselves" (*sibi convenientia finge*, 119) and
"let it be self-consistent" (*sibi constet*, 127).

147

Horace's use of characters, the living creations of a writer, to bring life to his prescriptions is not idle, and certainly not in a poem that begins with the word *humano*. The *Ars Poetica*'s opening word is especially striking in that the conjunction *si*, which we would expect to see in this first position, is forced to wait until the second line to take its place in the sentence. But in the case of Horace, who is and would have been familiar to readers of the *Ars Poetica* as a satirist (as well as, of course, a lyric poet), it can come as no surprise that he has humans and their behaviors firmly in his sights. So it is that his twin concerns with "that which is fitting" and with the need to avoid extremes are not limited to the *Ars Poetica* and its ostensible sphere of writing; they manifest themselves also in the *Satires*, where they are applied in the first place to living. In Horace's earliest poems we may therefore see the ambiguities of the *Ars Poetica* acting in reverse—a parallelism that invites us to read such ambiguities and ironies not as simple, saying one thing and meaning another, but as more nuanced and fluid, containing many possible readings that forever jostle against one another for supremacy.

In *Satires* 1.1, conventionally dubbed "The Race for Wealth and Position,"[10] Horace criticizes the human bent for avarice: "Neither the seething summer heat nor the winter deters you from profit," he says, "not fire, sea, nor sword, nothing stands in your way, until no other man should be richer than you" (*te neque fervidus aestus / demoveat lucro neque hiems, ignis, mare, ferrum, / nil obstet tibi, dum ne sit te ditior alter, Sat.* 1.1.38–40). He interrogates his interlocutor, "What joy can it give you to bury fearfully a huge mass of silver and gold furtively in the ground?" (*quid iuvat immensum te argenti pondus et auri / furtim defossa timidum deponere terra?* 41–42). The interlocutor, characteristically dim-witted, eventually cuts in with, "What would you have me do, then? Live like Maenius or Nomentanus?" (*quid mi igitur suades? ut vivam Maenius aut sic / ut Nomentanus?* 101–2), conjuring up two figures who are presumed to be proverbial wastrels. Horace retorts:

> *pergis pugnantia secum*

frontibus adversis componere. non ego, avarum
cum veto te fieri, vappam iubeo ac nebulonem;
est inter Tanain quiddam socerumque Viselli,
est modus in rebus, sunt certi denique fines
quos ultra citraque nequit consistere rectum. (102–7)

You persist in comparing things that battle against each other with opposing brows. When I forbid you to be greedy, I'm not ordering you to become a good-for-nothing and an idler; there is something between Tanais and the father-in-law of Visellus, there is moderation in things, there are certain limits, in short, beyond or before which Right does not wish to stand.

Several figures in the next poem, *Satires* 1.2, "The Folly of Running to Extremes," exemplify the same failings:

dum vitant stulti vitia, in contraria currunt.
Malthinus tunicis demissis ambulat; est qui
inguen ad obscaenum subductis usque facetus.
pastillos Rufillus olet, Gargonius hircum.
nil medium est. sunt qui nolint tetigisse nisi illas
quarum subsuta talos tegat instita veste;
contra alius nullam nisi olenti in fornice stantem.
(24-30)

When foolish men avoid vices, they run towards their opposites. Malthinus walks about with his tunic hanging low; another has his elegantly hiked up all the way to his obscene groin. Rufillus reeks of breath-fresheners, Gargonius of a goat. There is no mean. There are those who will not touch any women except those whose ankles are covered by a dress with its

149

fringed garment; on the other hand, another touches
only one standing in a reeking brothel (lit., "archway").

A third poem, 1.3, "On Mutual Forbearance," describes at length
a single individual who is internally inconsistent:

> *nil aequale homini fuit illi; saepe velut qui*
> *currebat fugiens hostem, persaepe velut si*
> *Iunonis sacra ferret; habebat saepe ducentos,*
> *saepe decem servos; modo reges atque tetrarchas,*
> *omnia magna loquens, modo "sit mihi mensa tripes et*
> *concha salis puri et toga, quae defendere frigus*
> *quamvis crassa, queat"* . . .
> *nil fuit umquam*
> *sic impar sibi.* (9–15, 18–19)

There was nothing balanced in that man; often he
would run about as if fleeing an enemy, at other times
[carefully] as if he were carrying Juno's sacred objects;
sometimes he had two hundred slaves, sometimes
ten; now he would speak of kings and tetrarchs, all
manner of great things, now he would say, "Just let me
have a three-legged table and a shell of pure salt and
a toga, which, though coarse, can protect against the
cold." . . . Nothing was ever so inconsistent with itself.

Thematic parallels between these passages from *Satires* 1.1–3
and the *Ars Poetica* are obvious in the overall impression of people
rushing madly about, thoughtlessly making their way through life.
But compelling textual parallels also emerge. Horace precedes and/or
concludes the excerpts above with maxims that frame the vignettes
and demarcate them as significant, and these maxims are found,
reconfigured, throughout the *Ars Poetica*. The selection from *Satires*
1.3 begins, *nil aequale homini fuit illi* (9), and ends with *nil fuit
umquam sic impar sibi* (18–19), phrases that we will later find in the

more compressed and generalizing forms, *sibi convenientia* (*AP* 119) and *sibi constet* (*AP* 127), similarly mirroring each another. What was in the *Satires* a criticism of human behavior, however, turns out also to have foreshadowed advice pertaining to artistic activity in the *Ars Poetica*. Likewise, *dum vitant stulti vitia, in contraria currunt* (*Sat.* 1.2.24) becomes *in vitium ducit culpae fuga, si caret arte* (*AP* 31), with *vitium* repeated, the position of the preposition *in* shifted, and *stulti* (denoting a quality attributed to people) reworked as *si caret arte* (where *ars*, the traditional counterpart to *ingenium*, "inborn talent," defines any creative undertaking, whether through its presence or its absence). Finally, *est modus in rebus* (*Sat.* 1.1.106), further explicated through a personification of "Right" with its feet firmly planted within certain bounds (106–7), and *nil medium est* (*Sat.* 1.2.28) anticipate the *Ars Poetica*'s continually stated need for moderation, and Right's reprise of its personified form (*AP* 25, 367). While the *Satires*' overt focus is human behavior and the *Ars Poetica*'s is literature, the dichotomy is far from straightforward, for in the ancient Greco-Roman tradition, the conceit that the poet's creations necessarily reflected his true self was a widespread one, memorably encapsulated in Seneca's phrase, *talis oratio qualis vita* (*Epist.* 114; to paraphrase, "style is the man"), and familiar also from Catullus' rejection of the notion (16.3–4, "You thought me insufficiently chaste from my verses, because they are rather soft," *me ex versiculis meis putastis, / quod sunt molliculi, parum pudicum*).

Horace plays with this duality throughout his *Satires*, and although Freudenburg was able as recently as 1993 to write that the "metaphorical possibilities" of the collection "remain virtually unexplored" (186), the last two decades have seen a surge of interest in reading Augustan poetry in metaliterary ways. Such implied meanings can be seen, for example, when Horace professes his oh-so-traditionally-Roman rustic humility, saying, "I go home to a dish of leek and chickpea and oilcake. My dining needs are tended to by three slave-boys, and a white stone slab supports two cups and a ladle; a cheap salt shell is there too, and an oil flask with a shallow bowl, plain Campanian ceramic ware" (*domum me / ad porri et ciceris refero laganique catinum.* / *cena ministratur pueris tribus et lapis albus* / *pocula cum cyatho duo sustinet; astat echinus* / *vilis, cum patera guttus, Campana supellex, Sat.* 1.6.114–18). This avowal of domestic homeliness also alludes and lays claim to Roman Satire, an earthy genre then in its infancy and consequently much given to (at least half-ironic) hand-wringing about its unworthiness as poetry.[11] When he notes the silliness of preferring to fill a cup or jug of water from a huge river rather than from a little spring (*Sat.* 1.1.54–60)—on the surface a warning against greed, since a person is likelier to drown in the river—it is hard not to see resonances of the rich tradition of flowing water as a metaphor for poetry, ranging from Pindar (cf. Hor. *Carm.* 4.2.5–8) to Callimachus' muddy Assyrian river (*Ap.* 108–9) and Horace's own marked preference for clear and slender trickles.[12] In his two books of *Satires*, Horace's eye is fixed upon humanity: what Juvenal would later describe as, "whatever men do—vows, fear, anger, pleasure, joys, to-ing and fro-ing" (*quidquid agunt homines, votum, timor, ira, voluptas,* / *gaudia, discursus,* 1.85–86). As we have come to appreciate, however, Horace's "ethical principles are fully consistent with his aesthetic principles," and "every lesson he teaches on the proper style of life contains a second literary application on the proper style of poetry."[13] This reciprocity enriches the *Satires*, which might otherwise read as a tiresome litany of moral failings. What we are now realizing is that it also enriches the *Ars Poetica*, though acting in reverse, and thus forming a mirror to the *Satires*, as Horace seems playfully to perform his own mandate for self-consistency.

Horace nods at the coherence of poetry and lifestyle, ethics and art, throughout the *Ars Poetica*. Writers, if they are to be successful, should provide both pleasure and instruction, and what they write must be more than simply believable, it must be as close as possible to reality:

> *aut prodesse volunt aut delectare poetae*
> *aut simul et iucunda et idonea dicere vitae.* . . .
> *ficta voluptatis causa sint proxima veris.* (333–34, 338)

> Poets wish either to be useful or to delight, or to say
> things that are at once both pleasing and suitable to
> life. . . . Let things crafted for the sake of pleasure be
> very close to true ones.

Horace imagines himself a whetstone (*ergo fungar vice cotis*, 304),
shaping and sharpening others, and he curiously extends the
metaphor to its logical end: just as a whetstone makes steel keen but is
itself incapable of cutting (*acutum / reddere quae ferrum valet exsors
ipsa secandi*, 304–5), so Horace claims, "I myself, writing nothing,
will teach the gift and duty" (*munus et officium nil scribens ipse
docebo*, 306). Much puzzled over, these words are traditionally taken
to mean that Horace did not write tragedy, the genre in which the *Ars
Poetica* purports to give instruction, but they again serve to minimize
the importance of writing, demoting it to a mere portion, though
an important one, of other pursuits. The words that follow, which
clarify *munus et officium*, support this view, for Horace's interest is
"from where resources are obtained, what nourishes and molds the
poet, what is becoming, what not, where virtue carries one, where
error" (*unde parentur opes, quid alat formetque poetam, / quid deceat,
quid non, quo virtus, quo ferat error*, 307–8). As Horace draws his
final poem to a close, he is more explicit about how one can make a
character's words consistent with his or her age, sex, nationality, and
occupation—a hallmark of the best writing, as introduced already at
112–19 and 176–78:

> *respicere exemplar vitae morumque iubebo*
> *doctum imitatorem et vivas hinc ducere voces.*

> I will command the learned copier to look to the
> example of life and of customs, and to draw from
> here living voices. (317–18)

Thus it is only through careful study of life (and, we may well
imagine, Horace's own *Satires* with their studies of life) that a writer

can avoid dissonance and incongruity in his creations. At the heart of all this lies wisdom, *sapere*, which is, crucially, said to be "the starting point and source of writing properly" (*scribendi recte sapere est et principium et fons, AP* 309)—"writing properly" (*scribendi recte, Sat.* 1.4.13) being the very thing that Horace says his generic ancestor Lucilius, "chatty and lazy" (*garrulus atque piger,* 12), is not up to the task of doing on account of these shortcomings in his temperament. Thus is made apparent the multivalence of Horace's prescriptions in the *Ars Poetica*, as life (*vita,* 317) and writing (309) are both revealed to have reason and wisdom (*sapere*) at their core, if done properly (*recte*).

Teaching, ever-present in the *Ars Poetica*, is a key theme also of the *Satires*, with Horace oddly regressing from the role of instructor to that of student, and moreover a student subject to lessons from increasingly "inept teachers."[14] Horace's father is an early pedagogue in this series. We encounter Horace *senior* in *Satires* 1.4, where the poet attempts to pass him off as a mere ex-slave turned auctioneer,[15] who nevertheless nobly molds his son's habits and character through their shared observation of the society around them:

> *insuevit pater optimus hoc me,*
> *ut fugerem exemplis vitiorum quaeque notando.*
> *cum me hortaretur parce, frugaliter atque*
> *viverem uti contentus eo quod mi ipse parasset,*
> *"nonne vides Albi ut male vivat filius utque*
> *Baius inops? magnum documentum ne patriam rem*
> *perdere quis velit." a turpi meretricis amore*
> *cum deterreret, "Scetani dissimilis sis."*
> *ne sequerer moechas, concessa cum Venere uti*
> *possem, "deprensi non bella est fama Treboni."* (105–14)

My excellent father trained me in this way, that I should flee from vices by noting examples of each. When he was encouraging me to live sparingly, frugally, and content with that which he himself had supplied me with [he would say], "Surely you see how poorly the son of Albius lives, how Baius lacks resources? It is a powerful lesson that one should not wish to lose one's inheritance." When he was deterring me from the foul love of a whore [he would say]: "Don't be like Scetanus." [He warned] that I should not pursue adulterous affairs, when I could enjoy lawful love [saying]: "The reputation of Trebonius, caught red-handed, is not pretty."

Horace fondly concludes, "thus he fashioned me, a boy, with his dictums" (*sic me / formabat puerum dictis*, 120–21). As Leach (1971) has shown, Horace's father, whom the poet himself dubs *pater optimus*, "excellent father," is hardly more substantial and nuanced than one of the father types familiar from Terentian comedy. Her insight precipitated an avalanche of doubts regarding other "facts" Horace reports about his upbringing. Even more suspicious is that Horace himself reprises this paternal role throughout his hexameters, culminating in the *Ars Poetica*. As Horace and his father watch and learn from Albius' son and Baius, Scatenus, and Trebonius in the *Satires*,[16] so do we. And we observe Rufillus, Gargonius, Malthinus, the further unnamed offenders of *Satires* 1.2 and 1.3, and a succession of dim-witted interlocutors, anonymous and otherwise, without perhaps realizing consciously that we have been cast in the role of young Horace, whom a father-figure (now Horace himself) is teaching by offering to our view moral counterexamples.

In the *Ars Poetica*, Horace embraces and proclaims his professorial role (306), which goes hand in hand with his paternal one, and he is explicit about the fact that life is the best, the only, source for compelling characters, those with "living voices" (*vivas . . . voces*, 318). So Horace has become not exactly his own father, but rather the stock father figure he gave us in *Satires* 1.4; and Horace educates not his own son, but young writers, filial stand-ins. These surrogate sons are not merely hypothetical: having invoked the *Pisones* (6), Horace makes much of them as father and sons, first addressing them as a group (*pater et iuvenes patre digni*, "father and sons worthy of the[ir] father," 24), and then separating out the elder son for extra, individualized tutoring:

> o maior iuvenum, quamvis et voce paterna
> fingeris ad rectum et per te sapis, hoc tibi dictum
> tolle memor, certis medium et tolerabile rebus
> recte concedi. (366-69)

O elder of the youths, although you are still being shaped towards the right and you are wise in yourself, take up mindfully this pronouncement for yourself, that mediocrity and bearableness are rightly allowed to certain things.

The advice that follows is once again pointedly critical: Horace reminds his now-singular addressee that while a mediocre lawyer may do just fine, neither gods nor men will countenance a mediocre poet (369–73); that those not gifted in athletic pursuits wisely abstain from them, though poetry is not granted the same respect (379–82); and that free birth, equestrian standing, and a life free of vice (qualities, we may imagine, of the Piso boys) are not in and of themselves sufficient to guarantee that Minerva will cooperate and provide artistic inspiration (383–86). The passage is packed with gems: *si paulum summo decessit, vergit ad imum* ("if it comes down a little from its peak, it heads to the depths," 378), used to sum up how thick perfume and contrived delicacies spoil an otherwise enjoyable banquet (374–76), resumes the idea of line 31, *in vitium ducit culpae fuga, si caret arte*. Horace finishes with his famous advice that any literary effort with ambitions of longevity should be put aside for nine years (386–90), since "a voice sent out does not know how to come back" (*nescit vox missa reverti*, 390). We have been made to feel that the paternal voice by which Horace describes the elder Piso son as still being shaped (*quamvis et voce paterna fingeris*) is not merely that of the youth's biological father, but also Horace's own (much as he was himself shaped by *his* father's words, *me formabat . . . dictis*). And just as the advice-dispensing voice is multivalent, so, too, are its prescriptions, which appear literary, but apply at the same time to living. The verb *fingere*, likewise, we have seen applied on the one hand to fashioning young men (367), and on the other to fashioning images (8) and narratives (119). While pretending to be a literary guide, then, Horace is also unavoidably a moral one in this final poem of his life, since the font of inspiration in both spheres of activity is one and the same: behavior on view in the surrounding world.

Despite the reverence with which it has been regarded, there is plainly much in the *Ars Poetica* to cast doubt upon the poem's stated *raison d'être*, and we may well wonder why Horace asks us to swallow the premise that this verse epistle is an instruction manual for drama written under commission for the Piso family. The poet tips his hand in his superfluous reminders that actions must either take place on stage or be reported after the fact (any third option in drama is difficult to envision); that certain events, such as murders and metamorphoses, may not be shown before the audience (an article of faith since the earliest days of Greek tragedy); and even, remarkably, that the five-act structure is best (all Greco-Roman drama, as far as we can tell, had five acts; *AP* 179, 185–87, 189–90). If injunctions such as these ring tinny, it is not because Horace is being stridently prescriptive (Brink 1971, 245) or because he bothered to arrange some "more or less random reflections" (Fairclough 1926, 442) into lines of dactylic hexameter. Rather, such grave yet vacuous pronouncements seem designed to arrest the reader, compelling him to ponder what Horace might really have been up to in his *Ars Poetica*—this poem that is both so satirical and so like the *Satires*.

One answer may be to view the *Ars Poetica* as one of two bookends to Horace's career. Although material and ideas applied to literature in the *Ars Poetica* appear in the *Satires*, as well as in the *Epistles* and *Odes*,[17] it is nevertheless with the earliest *Satires* that the *Ars Poetica* most deeply intersects, as shown above: that is, with the first three poems of book 1 (the "diatribe satires," as they are often termed) and further 1.4, Horace's first programmatic satire.[18] This correspondence has not been noticed before, but it is unlikely to be accidental. It would appear, then, that while Horace began his hexameter writings with his finger firmly pointed at human foibles, and critiqued them in terms that have metaliterary resonances, as has been increasingly recognized, so he concluded his poetic oeuvre by turning his eye to poetry itself, having by this stage attained the requisite standing[19] to make (what appears to be) a contribution to the august tradition of literary treatises harking back to Aristotles' *Poetics*. All the while, however, Horace never loses sight of the human element that informs literature. The *Ars Poetica* may therefore be read as his earliest satires writ large(r) and transferred into the poetic arena. Since what he presents as poetic advice is consequently rather dubious, the material of the *Ars Poetica* clearly exists within the context of a larger Horatian schema, in which living and writing are to be governed by the same, interchangeable dictates—a not-unexpected move from a writer of satire, who begins the final poem of his life with the word *Humano* and invites us, his friends (we flatter ourselves in thinking), in for a laugh at the incongruity caused by a failure in visual artistry (*spectatum admissi, risum teneatis, amici?*). Just as literary meanings are generated for the ostensibly moral *Satires*, such ambiguities elicit extraliterary meanings from the *Ars Poetica*, where we further see Horace grappling with fluid family roles and relationships, his own dependent place in the Roman social hierarchy, and the paradox that frank criticism is best delivered by a true friend.

*   *   *

Reggie changed the way I think about Latin. Privileged to attend the *Aestiva Romae Latinitas* during the summer after my freshman year of college, I was too awed to attend the *seniores* sessions, opting instead for the *iuniores* class and, of course, the meetings *sub arboribus*. More than from our field trips or from my own walks about the city of Rome, my most vivid memories of that summer are from the classroom: Reggie's dramatic growls, his constant reminders that "just one letter, friends" can separate a mood or case from another, or his exhortation (a form of which found its way into this paper: *scribendi recte sapere est et principium et fons*), *sapere aude*, "dare to be wise/bold!" Without being able to pinpoint the proximal cause, I remember that summer as the time I finally understood what it meant not merely to translate, but actually to *read* (not to mention speak) Latin. I remember, of course, that Reggie does not think much of Virgil (or Aeneas, to be exact); though I have tried, I cannot recall his feelings on Horace (of course, we did read *O fons Bandusiae* "*in situ*"), but I hope he finds something worthwhile in these pages.

BIBLIOGRAPHY

Barchiesi, Alessandro, and Andrea Cucchiarelli. 2005. "Satire and the Poet: The Body as Self-Referential Symbol." In *The Cambridge Companion to Roman Satire*, ed. Kirk Freudenburg, 207–23. Cambridge: Cambridge University Press.

Bramble, J. C. 1974. *Persius and the Programmatic Satire: A Study in Form and Imagery.* Cambridge: Cambridge University Press.

Brink, C. O. 1971. *Horace on Poetry: The 'Ars Poetica.'* Cambridge: Cambridge University Press.

———. 1963. *Horace on Poetry: Prolegomena to the Literary Epistles.* Cambridge: Cambridge University Press.

Brunt, P. A. 1965. "*Amicitia* in the Late Roman Republic." *PCPS* 11:1–20.

Cody, John V. 1976. *Horace and Callimachean Aesthetics.* Brussels: Latomus, Revue d'études latines.

Fairclough, H. R. 1926. *Horace: Satires, Epistles and Ars Poetica.* London: Heinemann.

Ferriss-Hill, Jennifer L. 2015. *Roman Satire and the Old Comic Tradition.* Cambridge: Cambridge University Press.

Fraenkel, Eduard. 1957. *Horace.* Oxford: The Clarendon Press.

Freudenburg, Kirk. 1993. *The Walking Muse: Horace on the Theory of Satire.* Princeton: Princeton University Press.

Friis-Jensen, Karsten. 2007. "The Reception of Horace in the Middle Ages." In *The Cambridge Companion to Horace*, ed. Stephen Harrison, 291–304. Cambridge: Cambridge University Press.

Frischer, Bernard. 1991. *Shifting Paradigms: New Approaches to Horace's Ars Poetica*. Atlanta: Scholars Press.

Gowers, Emily. 2012. *Horace, Satires: Book I*. Cambridge: Cambridge University Press.

———. 1993. *The Loaded Table: Representations of Food in Roman Literature*. Oxford: Oxford University Press.

Günther, Hans-Christian. 2013. "Horace's Life and Work." In *Brill's Companion to Horace*, ed. Hans-Christian Günther, 1–62. Leiden: Brill.

Hardie, Philip. 2014. "The *Ars poetica* and the Poetics of Didactic." *MD* 72 (*New Approaches to Horace's Ars poetica*, ed. Attila Ferenczi and Philip Hardie):43–54.

Hauthal, Ferdinandus. (1866) 1966. *Acronis et Porphyrionis Commentarii in Q. Horatium Flaccum*. Berlin: J. Springer. Reprint, Amsterdam: P. Schippers.

Keane, Catherine. 2006. *Figuring Genre in Roman Satire*. New York: Oxford University Press.

Kiessling, Adolf, and Richard Heinze. (1914) 1984. *Q. Horatius Flaccus: Briefe*. Berlin: Weidmann. Reprint, Zürich: Weidmann.

Laird, Andrew. 2007. "The *Ars Poetica*." In *The Cambridge Companion to Horace*, ed. Stephen Harrison, 132–43. Cambridge: Cambridge University Press.

Leach, Eleanor Winsor. 1971. "Horace's *Pater Optimus* and Terence's Demea: Autobiographical Fiction and Comedy in *Sermo* 1.4." *AJPhil.* 92:616–32.

McGann, Michael. 2007. "The Reception of Horace in the Renaissance." In *The Cambridge Companion to Horace*, ed. Stephen Harrison, 305–17. Cambridge: Cambridge University Press.

Mette, Hans Joachim. 1961. "'Genus tenue' und 'mensa tenuis' bei Horaz." *MH* 18:136–39.

Mitsis, Phillip. 1993. "Committing Philosophy on the Reader: Didactic Coercion and Reader Autonomy in *De Rerum Natura.*" *MD* 31 (*Mega nepios: il destinatario nell'epos didascalico*): 111–28.

Money, David. 2007. "The Reception of Horace in the Seventeenth and Eighteenth Centuries." In *The Cambridge Companion to Horace*, ed. Stephen Harrison, 318–33. Cambridge: Cambridge University Press.

Möller, Melanie. 2004. *Talis Oratio – Qualis Vita: Zu Theorie und Praxis mimetischer Verfahren in der griechisch-römischen Literaturkritik.* Heidelberg: Universitätsverlag Winter.

Nisbet, Robin. 2007. "Horace: Life and Chronology." In *The Cambridge Companion to Horace*, ed. Stephen Harrison, 7–21. Cambridge: Cambridge University Press.

Rudd, Niall. 1989. *Horace: Epistles Book II and Epistle to the Pisones ('Ars Poetica').* Cambridge: Cambridge University Press.

Rutherford, Richard. 2007. "Poetics and Literary Criticism." In *The Cambridge Companion to Horace*, ed. Stephen Harrison, 248–61. Cambridge: Cambridge University Press.

Shackleton Bailey, D. R. (ed.). 2001. *Q. Horatius Flaccus opera.* Münich: K. G. Saur.

Tarán, Leonardo, and Dimitri Gutas. 2012. *Aristotle, Poetics: Editio Maior of the Greek text with Historical Introductions and Philological Commentaries.* Leiden: Brill.

Tarrant, Richard. 2007. "Ancient Receptions of Horace." In *The Cambridge Companion to Horace*, ed. Stephen Harrison, 277–90. Cambridge: Cambridge University Press.

Tate, J. 1928. "Horace and the Moral Function of Poetry." *CQ* 22:65–72.

White, Peter. 1978. "*Amicitia* and the Profession of Poetry in Early Imperial Rome." *JRS* 68:74–92.

Zetzel, J. E. G. 1980. "Horace's *Liber Sermonum*: The Structure of Ambiguity." *Arethusa* 13.1:59–77.

ENDNOTES

1   See Laird 2007, 132–33 ("an object of imitation, as well as a code of practice, for Renaissance poets and playwrights"; "a kind of literary 'Magna Carta' for norms and principles . . . well into the eighteenth century"), Friis-Jensen 2007, 300–2, McGann 2007, 305, Money 2007, 321. Horace was a standard school author in late antiquity (see Tarrant 2007), but nothing can be said for certain about the extent of the readership for the *Ars Poetica* in that period.

2   See Tate 1928 and Laird 2007, 133–34, on Horace's debt to Neoptolemus; on the state of Aristotle's *Poetics* in the Roman period, see Tarán and Gutas 2012.

3   Friis-Jensen 2007, 292, 300, notes that it was even exempted from the usual classification of *"ethica"* ("works on morality") given to many Classical texts to justify their usefulness and (thus) preservation in the Christian milieu. The turn against the traditional "straight" reading begins in earnest with Brink 1963, and Frischer 1991 is seminal; see also Hardie 2014 for a recent view on the *Ars Poetica* in relation to Lucretius and to Virgil's *Georgics*, as well as the many thought-provoking and insightful essays in the 2014 volume of *MD*, which Hardie co-edited with Attila Ferenczi.

4   See n. 15.

5   These ambiguities are themselves contained within the Greek verb ποιεῖν, "make, produce, bring about, do." In Latin *poetica* and English "poet" and "poem," however, ποιεῖν is reduced to a single arena of "creating."

6   *Satires* 1, Horace's poetic debut, was published in 35/34 BCE, and followed some five years later by *Satires* 2 and the *Epodes*. The *Ars Poetica*, on the other hand, belongs to the opposing pole of Horace's life, poetic and otherwise: though its exact date is disputed (recent scholars, including Nisbet 2007, argue for publication in 15 BCE), it is generally agreed to have been Horace's last work before his death in 8 BCE, and was perhaps never published in his lifetime.

7   We admittedly do not know what Horace himself called the poem (works often took their titles from their opening words or line[s]), but Quintilian, a grammarian working at the end of the first century CE, already referred to it as *ars poetica* (*Inst. praef.*) and *liber de arte poetica* (8.3.60). Frischer 1991, 5–16, is useful on the alternative titles (*Epistula*

ad Pisones, Epist. II.3) and their histories; as he points out, each one preconditions a different set of expectations in the reader.

8   The possibility of reading Horace in the *AP* as critical of the Pisones has generally been overlooked or dismissed (so Brink 1971, e.g., 307, 372–84), but Kiessling-Heinze 1914 (e.g., ad 385) perceive these same strains, though they do not elaborate upon their importance for reading the poem as a whole. Memmius, to whom *De rerum natura* is dedicated, provides a useful comparandum: portrayed by Lucretius as "superstitious, intellectually limited, and prone to infantile fears" (Mitsis 1993, 125), he may be read well as an ironic addressee.

9   *Amicitia* ("friendship") was for the Romans a formal category of relationship, typically predicated on a similar social status and on common aspirations, though not always (particularly in the case of patron-poet friendships); see further Brunt 1965, White 1978.

10   These titles attached to the *Satires* are recent inventions, but helpful in summing up each poem's main topic.

11   Gowers 1993 has done much to mainstream the metaliterary aspects of cooking and eating in Roman literature.

12   See Freudenburg 1993, 187–90, Ferriss-Hill 2015, 173–74, 179.

13   Freudenburg 1993, 186. See further Mette 1961, Bramble 1974, Cody 1976, Gowers 1993, Möller 2004, Rutherford 2007, 253.

14   Barchiesi and Cucchiarelli 2005, 215; see also Zetzel 1980, who examines Horace's bumbling persona in the *Satires*, and Keane 2006, 115, who sees Horace's "teacher-satirist" persona being developed in *Satires* 1 and marginalized in *Satires* 2.

15   Though long taken at face value as autobiographical fact, Horace's self-identifier *libertino patre natus* ("born from a freedman father") is rendered suspicious not only in being pointedly repeated three times in *Satires* 1.6 (6, 45, 46; also at *Epist.* 1.20.20, and cf. *Sat.* 1.6.58, *non . . . claro natum patre*), but also in being a virtual translation of a line from a Greek generic forefather, the writer of Cynic diatribe, Bion of Borysthenes (fr. 1, ἐμοῦ ὁ πατὴρ μὲν ἦν ἀπελεύθερος); see Freudenburg 1993, 5, 14, and 205.

16   As Gowers 2012, 177, points out, these names, in that they suggest "'Man A,' 'Man B'" (and Man S, Man T), reek of the poet's invention.

17   At *Sat.* 2.2.54–64, for example, Horace contrasts gluttons and gourmands with one Aufidienus/Avidienus, parsimonious to a fault, beginning with the warning, "In vain you will avoid that vice if you

turn yourself foully towards another" (*frustra vitium vitaveris illud, / si te alio pravum detorseris*, 54–55), and concluding with, *hac urget lupus, hac canis, aiunt* ("On this side a wolf presses, on that one a dog, as they say"—the Latin equivalent to our "stuck between a rock and a hard place"). In *Epist.* 2.2, Horace speaks of the need to exercise moderation in spending money (190–94), and sums up ten lines later that the ideal is to be "in second place to the leaders, [but] always ahead of the last" (*extremi primorum, extremis usque priores*, 204) in strength, natural talents, physical appearance, moral virtue, station in life, and wealth.

[18] In fact, I suspect many scholars would be hard pressed to assign an excerpted passage to the *Satires*, *Epistles*, or *Ars Poetica*, so similar are these works in meter, tone, concerns, and general *Weltanschaung*. The late antique commentator Porphyrio (ad Hor. *Sat.* 1.1 and *Epist.* 1.1.1) already saw the similarities between Horace's satirical and epistolary hexameters, describing the former as a conversation (*sermo*) with someone who is present and the latter as a conversation with someone who is absent, and suggesting that they differ in title alone (see further Ferriss-Hill 2015, 43–44).

[19] After all, Horace had written the *Carmen Saeculare*, the hymn that was performed at the *ludi saeculares* of 17 BCE, staged by Augustus to inaugurate his new age.

Coniecturalem Artem Esse Medicinam: Ambiguity and Uncertainty in Disease Diagnosis and Treatment in Celsus' *De Medicina*

Katharine van Schaik

I n 1889, celebrated physician Dr. William Osler delivered a valedictory address, entitled "Aequanimitas," to the graduates of the University of Pennsylvania's Medical College. Drawing this concept from a story in the *Historia Augusta* about Antoninus Pius' last words (12.6), Osler translated *aequanimitas* as "imperturbability" and emphasized the importance of this virtue for those young physicians who would soon face the uncertainties of their occupation:

> A distressing feature in the life which you are about to enter, a feature which will press hardly upon the finer spirits among you and ruffle their equanimity, is the uncertainty which pertains not alone to our science and arts but to the very hopes and fears which make us men. In seeking absolute truth we aim at the unattainable, and must be content with finding broken portions.[1]

Osler's concerns have found a modern expression in studies of what has been called "ambiguity tolerance." This term, as the name suggests, describes the ability of medical professionals (including students) to confront and to contend with the ambiguity they encounter in daily practice. This ability is quantifiable, according to many current studies.[2] Medical professionals should be concerned with their ability to tolerate ambiguity because robust "ambiguity tolerance" facilitates better relationships between healthcare providers and patients, and, therefore, better outcomes for patients. The underlying assumptions of these articles—eloquently described by Osler more than a century earlier—are that medical practice is inherently ambiguous, and that medical practitioners must be prepared to deal with this potentially distressing feature of their vocation.

Physicians who lived millennia before Osler had already noted the troubling ambiguities of medical diagnosis and treatment. They too wrote about patients they had seen and treated, in an effort to reduce those ambiguities in encounters with future patients. For example, many texts of the Hippocratic Corpus, in particular *On the Nature of Man, Epidemics, Aphorisms,* the surgical treatises, and *On the Nature of Women,* acknowledge the uncertainties physicians face in treating patients: what diagnosis is correct, and what treatment is suitable?[3] Writing in Latin about the Greek medical tradition, the Roman encyclopedist Aulus Cornelius Celsus (first century BCE–first century CE) also explores ambiguities in medicine. He undertook the challenge of rendering into Latin concepts that had acquired particular meanings in Greek over the preceding four to five centuries. Fögen and Langslow, among others, have explained Celsus' methods of translation, explanation, and development of a Latin technical medical vocabulary. My aim here is to show how he also presents medicine as the art of contending with ambiguity. I argue that Celsus employs a well-developed and consistent lexicon to characterize the ambiguity that is inherent in the art of medicine, and to reflect upon how medical practitioners might learn to manage, or at least cope with, this ambiguity.

1. The conjectural art that deceives: *fallere* and the physician.

Discussing various signs that are important for diagnosing a disease and prognosing its course, Celsus offers a story about Asclepiades, a physician who lived in Rome at the end of the second century BCE. Asclepiades, encountering a funeral procession on its way out of the city, realized that the putatively deceased man was "misdiagnosed" as dead by his physicians and was in fact still alive. In Celsus' view, the story demonstrates that physicians are sometimes to blame for these sorts of diagnostic errors, though not always: *illa tamen moderatius subiciam, coniecturalem artem esse medicinam, rationemque coniecturae talem esse, ut, cum saepius aliquando responderit, interdum tamen fallat.* ("However, I more reservedly would add that medicine is a conjectural art, and the logic of conjecture is such that, although it corresponds with reality most of the time, nevertheless, it does sometimes deceive us," 2.6.16.)[4] In sympathizing with the apparently mistaken physician of the "deceased" man, Celsus employs a verb he often uses to characterize the danger of the *ars medicina*: *fallere*, "to deceive."

As an encyclopedist, Celsus aims to explain the *ars medicina* comprehensively: the schools of its practitioners and their histories and theories; disease types and classification schemes; the manifestations and courses of systemic and local diseases; and treatments dietetic, pharmacologic, and surgical. Despite these neat and clear descriptions and classification schemes, however, scruple also compels him to acknowledge that even experienced physicians can be at a loss in the face of uncertain observations or unexpected outcomes. One of the words that appears frequently in *De Medicina* to emphasize this ambiguity is *fallere*, which we might choose to render as "to deceive," "to disappoint," or even "to cheat." In this section, we will consider how Celsus' employment of the word sheds light on his beliefs about the ambiguities and uncertainties that characterize the field of medicine.

First we should say a word about the concepts of ambiguity, uncertainty, and deception, all of which connote a disjunction between expectation and observed reality. In this short essay, I understand "ambiguity" to refer to a situation in which multiple interpretations of a given scenario are possible and known, but a "most suitable" interpretation cannot be (at least at first) precisely identified. Ambiguity implies uncertainty as to which interpretation of the facts is most appropriate. Indeed, precision in an ambiguous situation is still possible, in that precise interpretations can be known and provisionally ascribed, but the suitability or correctness of these interpretations cannot be identified in the absence of additional information. Applied to medicine, this idea is summarized by an adage frequently invoked by modern senior physicians cautioning residents and medical students about drawing conclusions too hastily: "If you hear hoof beats, it's probably horses, but it could be zebras."

In a medical context (and in the context of this paper), the term "ambiguity," as defined above, applies to the situation in which a patient presents with a medical history and a certain set of symptoms, and a physician must identify the specific disease(s) from which the patient may be suffering. In many cases—especially in antiquity, when physicians had fewer and less effective diagnostic tools than we have today—the presentation is ambiguous: for example, at least two specific diseases may be possible culprits. To refer to this scenario in terms of the analogy provided above, the ambiguous presentation is the sound of hoof beats, and the two possible culprits are horses and zebras. The uncertainty is resolved with time, additional observations, treatment by educated guess based on experience (e.g., horses are commoner than zebras), and trial and error. Here, I take ambiguity to be the recognized existence of at least two possible interpretations of the symptom; uncertainty is not knowing which possible interpretation, if any, is more "correct."

Deception (*fallere*) fits into this framework insofar as a physician may decide on an initial interpretation of ambiguous symptoms— that is, he may make a provisional disease diagnosis—that turns out to be incorrect. In this case, we could say that he was "deceived" by the ambiguous circumstances, since he failed to choose the correct diagnosis. He was uncertain about which course of action was correct, and he made the wrong choice because of ambiguous and (as they now prove to be) deceptive symptoms and signs. Celsus wants to remind his readers that such "deception" occurs sometimes because a physician is insufficiently trained, but sometimes as an unavoidable consequence of the ambiguity that is characteristic of medicine, as subsequent analysis of forms of *fallere* and its associated adjective (fallax) will show.

The evaluation of symptoms and signs and the classification of conditions can be treacherous. Modern physicians distinguish between signs (hundreds of different "objective" indications, such as a heart murmur heard in a particular location of the chest, a dilated pupil, or pain in response to pressure on a particular spot of the abdomen) and symptoms (the patient's "subjective" description of existing problems, such as a cough, pain, or ringing in the ears). Physicians writing before and during the time of Celsus observed varying degrees of distinction between what we today call "signs" and "symptoms," and I will not explore these distinctions here, to avoid becoming mired in the epistemological debates of the fifth to the first century CE that informed Celsus' work.[5] Instead, I will simply emphasize that many ancient physicians (though not all) considered the pulse much as modern physicians consider a traditional "sign":[6] the pulse was a part of the patient's body and bodily functions that the physician could observe and classify "objectively" himself, without interference from the patient's "subjective" experience of disease. It is therefore noteworthy that in book 3, Celsus cautions that signs like the pulse are so fraught with ambiguities and uncertainties that the best course of treatment is not clear:

> *Venis enim maxime credimus, **fallacissimae** rei, quia saepe istae leniores celerioresve sunt et aetate et sexu et corporum natura. Et plerumque satis sano corpore, si stomachus infirmus est, nonnumquam etiam incipiente febre, subeunt et quiescunt, ut inbecillus is videri possit,*

cui facile laturo gravis instat accessio. Contra saepe eas concitare solet balneum et exercitatio et metus et ira et quilibet alius animi adfectus, adeo ut, cum primum medicus venit, sollicitudo aegri dubitantis, quomodo illi se habere videatur, eas moveat. Ob quam causam periti medici est non protinus ut venit adprehendere manu brachium, sed primum desidere hilari vultu percontarique, quemadmodum se habeat, et si quis eius metus est, eum probabili sermone lenire, tum deinde eius corpori manum admovere. Quas venas autem conspectus medici movet, quam facile mille res turbant. Altera res est, cui credimus, calor, aeque **fallax***: nam hic quoque excitatur aestu, labore, somno, metu, sollicitudine.* (3.6.5–7)

For we trust greatly in pulses, **a most deceptive** thing, because they are often slower or faster by the influence of age or sex or the nature of the body. And commonly, when the body is sufficiently healthy, if the stomach is weak, and even sometimes with a fever beginning, the pulse sinks and grows quiet, with the result that the patient, who easily bears the severe onset pressing upon him, could appear feeble. In contrast, the bath and exercise and fear and anger and any other affectations of the spirit are accustomed to excite pulses, to such an extent that, when the physician first arrives, the worry of the sick man, unsure about whatever it seems to him that he has, disturbs his pulses.[7] Because of this, the experienced physician does not seize the patient's forearm with his hand immediately upon arrival, but first sits down with cheerful countenance and inquires specifically after how the patient is feeling, and if he has any fear. He soothes him with pleasant conversation, and only then does he move his hand toward the patient's body.

170

And indeed, if the sight of the physician disturbs the
pulses, how easily a thousand things agitate them.
Another, equally **deceptive** thing, we have come to
believe, is heat [i.e., when the patient's body feels, to
the physician, unusually warm or hot]: for this is also
excited by external heat, by physical exertion, by sleep,
by fear, and by worry.

Metrics such as the pulse and the sensation of heat are useful
for classifying diseases and determining treatment; yet, as Celsus
acknowledges, they can be unreliable, because their interpretation
depends on the physician, the patient, and other circumstances that
are not necessarily connected to the illness. A physician may note a
weak pulse and ascribe it to an illness, when the more proximate cause
is hunger. Likewise, an incautious physician may note a fast pulse and
believe the patient is ill, when in fact anxiety is responsible for the
temporary increase in pulse rate: the pulse is *fallacissimus*, and *calor*
is *fallax*, too. More than one interpretation of these ambiguous signs
and symptoms is possible. Certainly, these are important signs for a
physician trying to decide how he should treat his patient, and they are
not useless—but Celsus cautions readers about the context in which a
physician can or should interpret these signs. Their meaning can be
ambiguous, especially without awareness of the patient's situation.
The possibility of identifying contexts in which misinterpretations
are more likely does not necessarily prevent such misinterpretations
from occurring: *Neque tamen ignorare oportet in acutis morbis
fallaces magis notas esse et salutis et mortis* ("Nevertheless, we ought
not ignore the fact that in acute diseases, more [than in chronic ones]
the signs of both health and death are deceptive," 2.6.18). Despite
the stark dissimilarity between the two possible ultimate outcomes
(health or death), the signs that suggest which outcome is more likely
are cruelly unclear. All we know, writes Celsus, is that the signs of an
acute disease are more ambiguous than those of a chronic one.

Determining appropriate treatment is just as hazardous as
identifying the nature of the problem. A patient may seem to be

the kind for whom a particular remedy is suitable, only to expire unexpectedly after receiving it. While Celsus praises the virtues of bloodletting, for example, he simultaneously notes that the procedure is not *always* useful: sometimes, patients die from it. Experience itself emphasizes the ambiguous nature of bloodletting, and an inexperienced physician runs the risk of failing to know that the rule is that there is no rule: *Postea vero usus ostendit nihil in his esse perpetuum . . . maxime tamen in his medicus inperitus falli potest, . . .* ("But *usus* later showed that nothing holds universally in these cases . . . Yet especially in these cases may the inexperienced physician be deceived," 2.10.2-3). We will return to the issue of *usus* and experience in the conclusion: for now, it is important to recognize that (1) both experienced and inexperienced physicians face ambiguities and can interpret these ambiguities incorrectly, and (2) that *fallere* indicates the presence of such ambiguities.

Indications for surgical procedures are also characterized by the likelihood that they will deceive (*fallere*) the practitioner—but in these cases, the verb shows another aspect of ambiguity in medicine. In *De Medicina*, Celsus describes how some surgical procedures are undertaken with less haziness than others regarding their indications, and with a fairly clear view of the anatomical landscape in which they are performed. In other words, some surgical procedures are easier than others. He writes that cataract surgery, for example, has a reasonable hope of success: even a *mediocriter peritus* physician can be fairly sure of how he moves the needle (7.7.14). For the patient who has a stone in the bladder, however, Celsus offers numerous qualifications about the specific kind of patient who should undergo the procedure to remove it. Even if he has the right kind of patient, the physician should only operate if the pain is so severe that the patient risks dying from it (7.26.2). About this risky procedure, Celsus warns, *non quo non interdum etiam temeraria medicina proficiat, sed quo saepius utique in hoc fallat, in quo plura et genera et tempora periculi sunt* ("Of course, even an overly bold treatment is sometimes successful, but more often it completely disappoints where there are many kinds of danger, and dangerous times of the year," 6.26.2).

Here, by its opposition to *proficiat*, *fallat* implies the idea of "failure" or "disappointment": the physician hopes the treatment will work, but this hope proves elusive more often than not. A physician may try to help a patient in agony from a bladder stone, but both patient and physician should be aware that their decision to operate rests on limited information. The physician does not necessarily know where in the genitourinary tract the stone is, for example (6.26.2ff.): pain is obviously present, but so are other, unknown factors. Celsus tries to limit the deleterious effects of these unknowns by describing the kinds of patients for whom the risky procedure of "cutting for stone" should be considered, in contrast to the broader patient population he deems eligible for relatively safer cataract surgery. Such qualification may be understood as an effort to reduce the ambiguity and uncertainty surrounding a physician's decision to operate and the outcome of the procedure.

In sum, Celsus uses *fallere* throughout his text to emphasize the point he made about Asclepiades in the beginning of book 2: patients present physicians with situations that can be interpreted in different ways. As we have seen, *fallere* emphasizes the deceptive nature of signs, which can present interpretive ambiguities. In the context of therapeutic decision making and intervention, *fallere* underscores the unpredictability of treatment outcomes: even patients who seem good candidates for a particular procedure can be deceptive, in that a poor outcome can unexpectedly result.

2. Additional words linked to ambiguity: *Dubito, dubius, dubitatio, incertus,* and *perpetuus*

Fallere is not the only word Celsus uses to illustrate the ambiguity of medicine. He also employs a cluster of words meaning "doubt": *dubito*, *dubius*, and *dubitatio*. In the preface, these "doubt" words emphasize that different schools of medical thought regard ambiguities of human health and disease through different lenses.[8] For those who believe hidden causes must be investigated to treat patients successfully, the role of etiology is "not to be doubted" (*neque esse dubium*, 1.pr.14). The Empiricists, on the other hand, argue that signs and symptoms are so ambiguous that theorizing will not help to identify their meaning. Celsus writes that the Empiricists believe *si scientiam hanc non subiciat evidens causa, multo minus eam posse subicere, quae in dubio est* ("if an evident cause does not provide knowledge, much less can a cause which is in doubt provide it," 1.pr.31). *Dubius* appears together with *incertus* in 1.pr.52, again to emphasize the Empiricists' wariness of excessive speculation about ambiguous symptoms. Less frequently, *incertus* itself is also used to indicate the difficulty of interpreting symptoms and determining treatment (cf. 1.pr.31, 1.pr.52, 2.1.8, 3.2.3, 3.12.1, and 8.1.21). In the context of exploring the approaches of different medical sects to the acquisition and interpretation of medical knowledge in his preface, Celsus uses doubt words to emphasize that physicians' conceptualization and handling of ambiguity are key differences among schools of medical thought. Ambiguity is a fundamental part of medicine, and doctrinal differences emerge from debates over how to manage it.

In the books that follow the preface, Celsus employs doubt words to qualify the circumstances under which treatments should be applied. Although words indicating doubt sometimes occur alongside negatives in a way that might suggest certainty (2.pr.1, 2.10.8, 2.14.2, 3.2.7, 7.7.8, 7.19.11, 7.23.1), this combination is often found in a context that discusses the variability of ostensibly similar diagnoses and treatments. For example, *nihil habet dubii* (7.7.8) comes after a description of how one treatment can yield different outcomes. *Nihil dubî est* introduces a particular surgical procedure that should be followed, but the subsequent sentences qualify the circumstances under which the procedure can or should be done (7.23.1; compare the situation described in 7.19.11, with *neque dubium est*). Grammatically, these qualifications are presented as groups of if/then statements. The specific treatment that should be provided is not in doubt, but a physician must follow Celsus' series of if/then statements to determine if his patient is a candidate for this treatment. Such categorization of patients and efforts to provide an algorithmic approach to treatment can be understood both as acknowledgement of the ambiguity and uncertainty in disease diagnosis and treatment, and as attempts to combat them. Despite these efforts to circumscribe room for error, however, Celsus occasionally admits that physicians just cannot know exactly what has happened, is happening, or will happen in every situation: the pairing *potest . . . dubitari* emphasizes ambiguity in determining the reasons for recovery (was it treatment or luck? 7.pr.1), and this phrase is also used to explain that a lack of signs makes it difficult to know the extent of an injury (8.4.2).

In one case, a doubt word is linked to another word that Celsus uses to characterize the tricky task of doctoring, with *dubitatio* and *fallere* appearing together in a discussion of critical days. The concept of critical days emerged in the Hippocratic texts and persisted through the medieval period, recurring in various forms in the writings of many medical authors, including Galen.[9] In general, the term referred to days on which a physician could expect certain kinds of changes in a disease state. While the Hippocratic texts emphasize the importance of noting the days on which these changes occur, they do not offer extensive commentary on how to identify these critical days. Galen (writing after Celsus) provides this kind of instruction, linking the chronological patterns of change in the state of a disease to the physicians' processes of diagnosis and treatment. Even during Celsus' time, however, physicians employed and debated the idea of critical days, noting the chronological changes in a disease state in relation to the onset of the illness.

Application of ideas about critical days to the treatment of illness also involved the mapping of a disease course onto systems of days deemed important for prognosing and observing the patient's condition. Celsus, however, points out the challenges in interpreting the method of applying critical days to a given patient's condition: *Est autem alia etiam de diebus ipsis dubitatio, quoniam antiqui potissimum impares sequebantur, eosque, tamquam tum de aegris iudicaretur, κρίσιμους nominabant* ("Moreover, there is another *dubitatio* about the days themselves, because the ancients especially paid attention to the odd days, and these days they were accustomed to call critical,[10] as though on these days the course of the disease would be determined for sick people," 3.4.11). Celsus proceeds from here to show the inconsistencies in Hippocrates' method of identifying critical days, concluding that *nihil rationis* is to be found in the system of critical days. Again calling attention to aspects of the field of medicine that can be perceived differently by different observers, he says: *antiquos tum celebros admodum Pythagorici numeri fefellerunt* ("at that time Pythagorean numbers greatly deceived many ancients," 3.4.15). Instead, Celsus argues, physicians should observe their patients and then decide how to treat, without concerning themselves with the extent to which the symptoms and signs align with the so-called "critical days," a system that is characterized by *dubitatio* and therefore capable of deception. Celsus concludes by suggesting that a physician should wait to intervene until the fever has passed completely, or, in the case of a long fever, for at least half of the time the fever is expected to last. He notes that this procedure *in omnibus ita servandum est* ("should be observed in all matters," 3.4.18), and characterizes this precept as *per omnia febrium genera perpetua* ("universal for all kinds of fevers," 3.5.1). This instance is notable, since Celsus more frequently uses *perpetuus* to emphasize that diagnoses and treatments often are not so uniformly determined and applied.

Since treatments are not all universal, the physician's challenge is knowing when the disease he confronts requires the "standard protocol," and when a different approach is warranted. Celsus recognizes that patients differ, and a close look at how he uses the word *perpetuus* in application to diseases, treatments, and rules for treatment shows his awareness of the tension inherent in applying general rules to specific patients. Commenting on the role of experience in medicine, Celsus warns readers at the outset that ... *vix ulla perpetua praecepta medicinalis ars recipit* ("the art of medicine ... admits of scarcely any universally-applicable teachings," 1.pr.63). Discussing fevers and various other diseases, symptoms, signs, and treatments, he reiterates his point over and over: *paene perpetua sunt* (1.3.1), *perpetuum in omnibus non est* (1.3.7), *non est perpetuum* (1.3.18), *usus ostendit nihil in his esse perpetuum* (2.10.2), *tamen ne id quidem perpetuum est* (2.10.9), *nihil autem horum utique perpetuum est* (3.4.7), *adeo tamen nihil perpetuum est* (5.26.25). One must take into account the natural variations in patients and diseases—observation and experience (*usus*) are crucial. And even as Celsus cautions physicians to watch patients and to adjust treatments accordingly, he concedes at the end of a description of a tongue surgery: *Adeo in medicina, etiam ubi perpetuum est, quod fieri debet, non tamen perpetuum est id, quod sequi conuenit.* ("So in medicine, even where there is a universal regarding what ought to be done, nevertheless what happens to result is not universal," 7.12.4). Even when there is no ambiguity in diagnosis and treatment, the outcome is still uncertain.

3. Managing ambiguity: *Usus* and experience.

Celsus' acknowledgement of the ambiguity inherent in patient-to-patient variability is not new. The Hippocratic writers recognized that although medicine is a τέχνη, it is limited by the doctor's challenge of grasping the patients' variable and subjective symptoms and the natures of the diverse patients he treats.[11] The key to overcoming this ambiguity is experience (ἐμπειρία).[12] In Latin, Celsus uses three terms to convey the sense of the Greek ἐμπειρία: *experimentum, experientia,* and *usus.*[13] As we will see, *usus* for Celsus is an especially integral component of the physician's battle against ambiguity.

Experientia appears in the preface, where Celsus explains the views of various medical sects regarding how the medical art should be conceptualized, taught, and practiced. In explaining the name of the group *Empirici*, he makes it clear that *experientia* is his translation of ἐμπειρία: *ii qui se Empiricos ab experientia nominant* ("Those who call themselves Empiricii from *experientia*," 1.pr.27). *Experimentum* appears ten times in the preface, and another nine times in books 5, 6, and 7. Like *experientia, experimentum* in the preface is used narrowly to describe the views of the Empiricists and to contrast those views with what other medical sects believe. In subsequent uses, however, *experimentum* acquires a broader function and describes generally the role of firsthand observation in diagnosis and in the determination of appropriate treatment. In this sense, it often appears as an ablative with, or as the subject of, verbs of showing or knowing, such as *adprobare* (4.2.8), *testari* (4.11.7), *credere* (4.26.4), *scire* (5.28.2), *cognoscere* (5.28.7, 6.9.7, and 7.4.3), and, in its figurative sense, *colligere* (5.28.19). *Experimentum*, then, provides this means of knowing. The relatively circumscribed use of both *experientia* and *experimentum*, especially in the preface's discussion of schools of medicine, suggests that we should consider them as technical terms, employed with a meaning that is closely linked to the ἐμπειρία—broadly, firsthand experience in seeing patients—of the Greek Empiricist physicians.[14]

To understand Celsus' views on experience in medicine, we must look to the conceptually related word *usus*, which appears far more frequently (approximately 50 times) than *experientia* or *experimentum*. In contrast to those words, which Celsus typically employs in a specific way, *usus* carries a broader meaning. It can signify "employment" or "use" of a drug or method (3.21.17, 3.22.6, 4.5.6, 4.6.6), as well as the physician's day-to-day practice of "applying" and "expanding upon" what he has learned through the process of seeing and treating patients. But most often, Celsus uses the word in one of its ordinary senses to denote both "experience"—in a medical context, acquired through a physician's daily, repeated efforts to identify and treat illnesses—and the moment, repeated anew for each patient, of observing and trying to heal. In this meaning, Celsus prefers the more familiar *usus* to *experientia* and *experimentum* throughout his work.

This kind of experience is instructive, and Celsus often pairs verbs such as *ostendere* or *docere* with *usus* (for *ostendere*, 1.pr.17, 2.10.2, 7.4.3, and 8.3.6; for *docere*, 2.10.14 and 5.27.4; for *monstrare*, 1.pr.75). *Usus* shares this feature with *experimentum*, but Celsus writes of *usus* more often. In pairing *usus* with verbs of instruction or demonstration, he is not alone: writers as early as Varro and Cicero, as well as Celsus' younger contemporaries Columella and Seneca, all describe how *usus* instructs, showing the appropriate course for various situations.[15] Though writing half a century later than Celsus, Pliny the Younger neatly describes the idea of *usus* as a teacher in one of his letters (1.20). Explaining to Tacitus why he believes a longer speech is better than a shorter one, he writes:

> *adiciam quod me **docuit usus, magister egregius**. Frequenter egi, frequenter iudicavi, frequenter in consilio fui: aliud alios movet, ac plerumque parvae res maximas trahunt. **Varia sunt hominum iudicia, variae voluntates. Inde qui eandem causam simul audierunt, saepe diversum, interdum idem sed ex diversis animi motibus sentiunt.***

> Let me add what **experience, the best of all instructors, has taught me**. On the many occasions when I have been counsel, judge or assessor, I have found that people are influenced in different ways, and that small points often have important consequences. **Men's powers of judgment vary with their temperaments; thus they can listen to the same case but reach different conclusions, or perhaps the same one by a different emotional reaction.**

Pliny's comments are relevant to our purposes for several reasons. First, he employs *usus* in a way that sheds light on Celsus' use of the term, that of *usus* as a *magister* that *docet*. Second, he emphasizes that this *usus* has shown him the variability of human nature and the possibility that one's best efforts can be thwarted by such variability and its attendant ambiguity. He uses corporeal imagery to make his point:

> *Praeterea suae quisque inventioni favet, et quasi fortissimum amplectitur, cum ab alio dictum est quod ipse praevidit. Omnibus ergo dandum est aliquid*

25

quod teneant, quod agnoscant. Dixit aliquando mihi Regulus, cum simul adessemus: "Tu omnia quae sunt in causa putas exsequenda; ego iugulum statim video, hunc premo." Premit sane quod elegit, sed in eligendo frequenter errat. Respondi posse fieri, ut genu esset aut talus, ubi ille iugulum putaret. At ego, inquam, qui iugulum perspicere non possum, omnia pertempto, omnia experior, πάντα denique λίθον κινῶ.

Moreover, everyone is prejudiced in favor of his own powers of discernment, and he will always find an argument most convincing if it leads to the conclusion he has reached for himself; everyone must then be given something he can grasp and recognize as his own idea. Regulus once said to me when we were appearing in the same case: "You think you should follow up every point in a case, but I make straight for the throat and hang on to that." (He certainly hangs on to whatever he seizes, but he often misses the right place.) I pointed out that it might be the knee or the heel he seized when he thought he had the throat. "I can't see the throat," I said, "so my method is to feel my way and try everything—in fact I 'leave no stone unturned.'"

Pliny's point is that, in the setting of a limited ability to observe the whole picture (or the whole body), a person does not know exactly what part he perceives. To prevent the misinterpretation that results from a decision based on limited information, Pliny prefers that *omnia experiri*: or, to extend his metaphor, that one become aware of the entire body and its constituent parts before deciding what part is what. Moreover, Pliny writes, a person delivering a speech in a court does not know what will move each of his listeners to agree with him, since men's temperaments and motivations are *varius* and *diversus*. Similarly, a physician cannot know that a treatment that has worked on most patients with a given set of symptoms will work on the next patient with the same symptoms. *Usus*, the day-to-day practice of applying acquired experience, is what helps both a doctor and a lawyer to know how best to deploy their skills.[16]

Within *De Medicina*, three appearances of *usus* are important for understanding how Celsus sees "experience" as a solution to the problems raised by the inherent ambiguity of medicine. The first two appear in the preface and are connected with *experientia* and *experimentum*, respectively:

> *post quos Serapion, primus omnium nihil hanc*
> *rationalem disciplinam pertinere ad medicinam*
> *professus, in usu tantum et experimentis eam posuit.*
> (1.pr.10)

> After them Serapion, who was first of all to publicly
> declare that this theoretical way of thinking was not
> at all applicable to medicine, considered the art of
> medicine to lie within practice and experience.

Celsus is here describing the Empiricists, those who taught that knowledge of medicine should be acquired from direct observation, not from theorizing or searching for the "hidden causes" assumed to explain observations.[17] In the passage above, Celsus writes that Serapion[18] underscores the role of *usus* and *experimentum* in medicine in contrast to *cognitio naturae*, mentioned in the preceding sentence. *Usus*, linked this way to *experimentum*, carries with it a sense of firsthand observation and practice. Its relationship to *experientia* is similar, and here, Celsus uses the two terms together, along with *perpetuus*, to express the variability of medicine:

> *si vero quod propius est, vix ulla perpetua praecepta*
> *medicinalis ars recipit, idem sunt quod ii, quos*
> *experimenta sola sustinent . . . quid solutum teneat,*
> *si a ratione tractum est, rationalis est medicus; si, ut*

ei, qui se rationalem negat, confiteri necesse est, ab experientia, empiricus. ita apud eum morbi cognitio extra artem, medicina intra usum est. (1.pr.63–4)

But if—and this is nearer to the truth—the art of medicine admits of scarcely any universal precepts, (reasoners) are in the same position as those who maintain the importance of experience alone . . . But if (a remedy) that loosens a body braced up, or tightens a loosened body, has been deduced by a reasoning from theory, the practitioner is a reasoner; if, as the man who denies himself to be a reasoner must admit, he acts from experience, he is an Empiricist. Thus according to Themison, knowledge of a disease is outside the art, and medicine is confined to practice.

Celsus here highlights epistemological debates about the origins of medical knowledge and the proper ways for physicians to train, debates which led to the creation of medical sects based on these differences. The role of practical experience in medical education occupied a prominent place in these debates, and Celsus' diction related to this topic is important. The link between *usus* and *experientia/experimentum* also appears in Lucretius (5.1448–54), where both *usus* and *experientia* taught (*docuit*) men agriculture, law, road building, weaponry, poetry, painting, and sculpture. But *usus*, with its more frequent appearance in *De Medicina* relative to *experientia* and *experimentum*, conveys an element of repeated practice and, perhaps, the idea that this practice encourages a physician to confront the ambiguity he observes. One final quote, a continuation of an excerpt provided earlier, illustrates this point:

postea vero usus ostendit nihil in his esse perpetuum, aliasque potius observationes adhibendas esse, ad quas derigi curantis consilium. (2.10.2)

But *usus* later showed that nothing holds universally
in these cases, and that other observations are rather
to be made, to which the deliberation of the healer
ought to be directed.

As we have seen, medicine can and does deceive (*fallere*) experienced
and inexperienced practitioners alike. The variability of patients
means that, while some generally accepted precepts exist within the
medical art, hard-and-fast rules are scarcer than practitioners might
like. It is *usus* that bears witness to the scarcity of universal rules, and,
as repeated firsthand experience in facing uncertainty, also provides
guidance in how ambiguity might be confronted. Sometimes, *usus*
can resolve ambiguity, but even when it does not, it still, we might
say, increases a physician's tolerance of ambiguity.

4. Conclusions

Medicine will always involve ambiguity. In a modern medical
context, during a clinical encounter with a suffering patient, a
physician will probably ask the following question: "On a scale of
one to ten, with ten being the worst pain you've ever experienced in
your life, how would you rank your pain?" This question elicits what
might be considered both a sign and symptom (pain can be both,
depending on where it is located, its quality, and what elicits it) and
tries to make the answer seem objective by imposing a numerical
scale. Nevertheless, a symptomatic account of pain is still subjective
and depends, of course, upon the patient's most painful experience
as a point of reference. Even pain interpreted as a sign can lack the
objectivity a physician might want. Some signs require depressing
a particular point of the abdomen, for example, in order to reveal
them, but patients' underlying anatomy can be variable, especially in
the context of a problem, and physicians can use variable amounts of
force to depress patients' abdomens. On the pain scale, one patient's
five is another patient's ten. And, as the saying about horses and

zebras indicates, signs can be deceptive, and physicians play the odds—but cautiously, and with awareness of exceptions.

Using Latin to explain traditional Greek ideas about health and disease, Celsus draws his readers' attention to the ambiguity and uncertainty that affect all aspects of medicine: practical and theoretical approaches to the art, diagnosis, the physician-patient relationship, treatment, and prognosis. *Fallere* emphasizes the danger that ambiguity poses for physicians who may think they are certain in their interpretation of signs and symptoms—only to learn that they judged incorrectly. Words of doubt highlight sections of text where Celsus provides methods for limiting these misjudgments. However, as close study of *perpetuus* and cognates of *dubius* shows, no categorization system or algorithm for decision making is universally applicable. Only *usus* can teach a physician what to do when he encounters the unknowns of the patient's body and the disease from which the patient is suffering. Celsus emphasizes that a physician should focus on acquiring varied practical experience, and that the focus of his professional efforts should be the ever-changing patient. In this sense, he advises physicians to accept ambiguity as an essential part of their practice, and, perhaps, as part of the "uncertainty that pertains not alone to our science, but to the very hopes and fears that make us men."

* * *

Celsus' admonitions to awareness, emerging from text written two thousand years ago, call to mind Reggie's words, frequently ringing off the walls of the cafeteria in the Scuola del Divino Amore in the hot Roman afternoon: "Listen, friends, listen! Listen! The Romans are speaking to you, friends." Thank you, Reggie, for helping me to hear the people beyond the pages, and for showing me how to teach others to hear them, too.

BIBLIOGRAPHY

Bailey, C. 1963. *Lucretius' De Rerum Natura*. Oxford: Oxford University Press.

Caulfield, M., K. Andolsek, D. Grbic, and L. Roskovensky. 2014. "Ambiguity Tolerance of Students Matriculating to U.S. Medical Schools." *Academic Medicine* 89:1526–1532.

Celsus, *De Medicina I–VIII*. Edition: Marx, F., ed. 1915. A. Cornelii Celsi quae supersunt. Leipzig/Berlin: Teubner.

Clackson, J., ed. 2011. *The Blackwell Companion to the Latin Language*. Mauldin, MA: Blackwell.

Craik, E. 2014. *The 'Hippocratic Corpus': Content and Context*. New York: Routledge.

Dodds, E. R. 1959. *Plato's Gorgias: A Revised Text with Introduction and Commentary*. Oxford: Clarendon.

Deichgräber, K. 1965. *Die griechische Empirikerschule* (2nd ed.). Berlin: Druckerei Hildebrand.

Evans, L. and D. R. Trotter. 2009. "Epistemology and Uncertainty in Primary Care: An Exploratory Study." *Family Medicine* 41:319–326.

Evans, L. et al. 2012. "Epistemology and Uncertainty: A Follow-up Study with Third-year Medical Students." *Family Medicine* 44:14–21.

Fögen, T. 2000. *"Patrii sermonis egestas": Einstellungen lateinischer Autoren zu ihrer Muttersprache. Ein Beitrag zum Sprachbewußtsein in der römischen Antike*. Munich and Leipzig: Saur.

———. 2009. *Wissen, Kommunikation und Selbstdarstellung: Zur Struktur und Charakteristik römischer Fachtexte der frühen Kaiserzeit*. Munich: C. H. Beck.

———. 2011. "Latin as a Technical and Scientific Language." In *The Blackwell Companion to the Latin Language*, ed. J. Clackson, 445–463. Maulden, MA: Blackwell.

Hankinson, R. J. 1987. "Causes and Empiricism: A Problem of Interpretation of Late Greek Medical Method." *Phronesis* 32:329–348.

————. 1995. "The Growth of Medical Empiricism." In *Knowledge and the Scholarly Medical Traditions*, ed. Don Bates, 60–83. Cambridge: Cambridge University Press.

Hohl, E. 1927. *Scriptores historiae Augustae*. Leipzig: Teubner.

Langholf, V. 1990. *Medical Theories in Hippocrates: Early Texts and the 'Epidemics.'* Berlin: Walter de Gruyter.

Langslow, David. 1989. "Latin Technical Language: Synonyms and Greek Words in Latin Medical Terminology." *Transactions of the Philological Society* 87:33–53.

————. 1994. "The Development of Latin Medical Terminology: Some Working Hypotheses." *Proceedings of the Cambridge Philological Society* 37:106–30.

————. 2000. *Medical Latin the Roman Empire*. Oxford: Oxford University Press.

Luther, V. P., and S. J. Crandell. 2011. "Ambiguity and Uncertainty: Neglecting Elements of Medical Education Curricula?" *Academic Medicine* 86:799–800.

Mynors, R. A. B., ed. 1963. *C. Plini Caecili Secundi: Epistularum libri decem*. Oxford: Oxford University Press.

Nutton, V. 2013. *Ancient Medicine* (2nd ed.). New York, Routledge.

Osler, W. 1995. "Aequinamitas." In *On Doctoring: Stories, Poems, Essays*, ed. R. Reynolds and J. Stone. New York: Simon and Schuster.

Radice, B., trans. 1969. *Pliny the Younger. Letters*, vol. I: books 1–7. Cambridge: Harvard University Press.

Sabbah, G., and P. Mudry, eds. 1994. *La Médicine de Celse*. Saint-Étienne: Publications de l'Université de Saint-Étienne.

Spencer, W. G., trans. 1935. *Celsus. On Medicine*, vols. I–III. Cambridge: Harvard University Press.

————. 1994. "*Media quodammodo diuersas inter sententias*: Celsus, the 'rationalists', and Erasistratus." In *La Médicine de Celse*, ed. G. Sabbah and P. Mudry, 77–101. Saint-Étienne: Publications de l'Université de Saint-Étienne.

————. 1989. *Herophilus: The Art of Medicine in Early Alexandria*. New York: Cambridge University Press.

Von Staden, H. 1975. "Experiment and Experience in Hellenistic Medicine." *Bulletin of the Institute of Classical Studies of the University of London* 22:178–199.

Walzer, R., and M. Frede. 1985. *Galen's Three Treatises on the Nature of Science.* Indianapolis: Hackett.

Wayne, S., et al. 2011. "The Association between Intolerance of Ambiguity and Decline in Medical Students' Attitudes toward the Underserved." *Academic Medicine* 86:877–882.

ENDNOTES

I would like to thank the editors, as well as James L. Zainaldin, for their insightful comments and suggestions. Their gracious efforts clarified my arguments, and the responsibility for any remaining ambiguity rests with me.

[1] Osler 1995.

[2] For examples of such studies, see Wayne 2011, Evans 2009 and 2012, Caulfield 2014, and Luther 2011.

[3] For examples of a Hippocratic author explaining his experience and observations so that physicians can avoid uncertainty and error, see *Joints* 10 and 47. For more about the Hippocratic Corpus and the motivations of its authors, see Craik 2014.

[4] This and subsequent translations are my own unless otherwise noted.

[5] Nutton 2013 provides a useful overview of these debates.

[6] See, for example, Von Staden 1989, 262ff., and Nutton 2013, 127–8, 243–4, and 351n29 for overviews.

[7] In modern parlance, this phenomenon is called "white coat hypertension."

[8] For discussion of different schools of medical thought and their views of hidden causes, see Walzer and Frede 1985, especially the introduction, and Galen's *On the Sects for Beginners*.

[9] Langholf 1990, 79–135.

[10] "Critical" in the ancient sense (a point of decision), generally not in the modern medical sense of "acute" or "nearing death"—although the latter meaning can be implied, since acute moments in a disease course often necessitate a decision. See Langholf 1990, 79–135.

11   Schiefsky 2005, 14ff., and especially 193ff. on the idea of the μέτρον: "The term μέτρον . . . turns out also to have the sense of criterion or measuring tool . . . The passage [Ancient Medicine 9.3] expresses two thoughts that the author does not clearly distinguish: first, that there is no fixed prescription specifiable in terms of measure, number, and weight to which one can appeal to determine what is suitable for a particular patient, and second, that there is no criterion or tool that the doctor can use to determine the correct therapy except the patient's αἴσθησις (i.e., "subjective" symptoms)."

12   Much has been written on the topic of ἐμπειρία. For overviews, see Nutton 2013, von Staden 1975, Hankinson 1987 and 1995, and Walzer and Frede 1985.

13   Von Staden 1994, 81 and 85; Von Staden 1975.

14   For additional discussion of the characteristics of technical language, see Fögen 2011.

15   *TLL* 5/1.1740.57–79 (Bulhart).

16   Here Pliny is working with a long tradition of comparisons between rhetoric and medicine. See especially Plato's *Gorgias* 464–468 for an early example.

17   See n. 12 for more on the Empiricists.

18   A prominent Alexandrian Empiricist physician of the late third century BCE who emphasized the role of ἐμπειρία in medical practice. See Deichgräber 1965 for the few fragments that mention him.

Purveying Rhetoric: Quintilian *Insti(tu)tor*

Curtis Dozier

The works of Quintilian, who is known as a dutiful, if not particularly original, compiler of rhetorical theory—one scholar has described him as "invariably manly, honourable, and *straightforward*" (Peterson 1891, xi; my emphasis)—may seem at first glance to be an unlikely place to look for interesting ambiguities. But they can be found, even without looking beyond the limited category of *ambiguitas* that was available to ancient critics.[1] Quintilian himself recognized that grammatical cases could produce indeterminacy (*Inst.* 7.9.6–8), and we find something like an instance in one of his early passages, where he is giving advice on correcting students' compositions. Especially with young students, he says, it is important not to stifle their love of learning through overly severe correction. Instead, the teacher should "praise some things, tolerate others, suggest changes (always giving reasons for them), and brighten up passages by putting in something of his own" (*interponendo aliquid sui*, 2.4.12). Russell's translation[2] occludes an ambiguity in this last phrase: the genitive *sui*, if it is an adjective, means what Russell says it does ("of his own [material]"), but it can also be read as a genitive pronoun, creating the possibility that this phrase can also mean "something of himself." "Something of his own material" has Quintilian providing a model for what a good composition should look like.[3] The second, more personal reading

189

has Quintilian making himself the model. This is something that great teachers know almost instinctively: teaching is not just about conveying information, it's a performance. And Quintilian, as we shall see, understands this very well.

The ambiguity of *aliquid sui* is in fact paradigmatic for an ambiguity that runs throughout the whole *Institutio Oratoria*, because both interpretations describe Quintilian's own practice in composing his treatise. Martin Luther praised Quintilian because he "educates and at the same time demonstrates eloquence" (quoted by Kennedy 1969, 150), and many scholars have identified places where Quintilian employs the same rhetorical techniques he teaches (Zundel 1981, Gunderson 2009, Dozier 2014), thus exemplifying for his students how those techniques should be used. It is not difficult to find examples throughout the *Institutio* of many of the techniques Quintilian quotes from Cicero's list of the ideal orator's skills at *Inst.* 9.1.42–45 (= Cic. *Or.* 137–139), examples used to define and defend his conception of the art of rhetoric and the ideal orator. At the same time, Quintilian puts himself into his teaching with a series of autobiographical passages that call attention to the performative dimension of his work, particularly in the prefaces to the books of the treatise. The most memorable is his extended lament, in the preface to book six, for his wife and two sons, who, he tells us, died in quick succession, a catastrophe that nearly drove him to abandon work on the *Institutio* itself. This preface has been called "one of the saddest things in all Latin literature" (Austin 1948, x), but as Matthew Leigh (2004, 122) has observed, Quintilian creates this powerful emotional effect by using the very techniques for arousing emotions that he explicates in the two chapters immediately following the lament (*Inst.* 6.1–2). This is but one example of how Quintilian has taken his own advice to "insert himself" into his teaching: the *Institutio Oratoria* is not just a textbook of rhetoric, but a performance of it.

I call this state of affairs "ambiguous" because Quintilian's display of his mastery of rhetorical techniques, both in autobiographical passages and elsewhere in the treatise, can be seen as serving multiple and even contradictory goals, depending on what audience we imagine for them. On the one hand, this display can be understood as an advertisement for Quintilian's excellence as a teacher of rhetoric. In all likelihood, Quintilian made a living by charging students for his instruction, students whom he had to attract in what must have been a competitive marketplace of teachers. Quintilian himself acknowledges this professional necessity when he says he is attempting to "add some touch of elegance" (*aliquid nitoris*) to the *Institutio* in order "to lure young people into learning what I regard as necessary for their studies" (3.1.3). But to those who have already committed themselves to studying with Quintilian, these passages become, at least implicitly, models for imitation. Although the pragmatic, economic side of his performance is not often noted, it should not be surprising that a teacher might speak both to prospective and current students. What complicates the picture, however, is that a teacher of rhetoric such as Quintilian is in a different position from that of teachers of other "arts," who use rhetoric to attract students to learn something else. Quintilian, by contrast, is the salesman who teaches his customers to use the same techniques he used to attract them in the first place. I argue here that the theory of rhetoric that Quintilian teaches his students, when applied to his own persuasive displays, should undermine our confidence in his ability as a rhetorician and so discredit him as a model of oratorical excellence. It is in confronting this ambiguous self-contradiction, however, that we can recognize that the *Institutio Oratoria* offers its readers something more than instruction in how to use rhetorical techniques well. It offers a revelation of the artificiality of the rhetorical constructs that those in power, whether teachers or emperors, use to maintain it.

Although Quintilian makes his presence as author and rhetorician known most obviously in autobiographical passages, the extent to which he employs rhetorical techniques throughout the whole *Institutio* should prompt us to watch closely for places where he may be hiding, as it were, in plain sight. One such passage is his description of the speaker who, like Quintilian, advertises his rhetorical skill. Quintilian calls this speaker the *institor eloquentiae*, the "salesman of eloquence." Such a speaker "openly displays all the arts of speech and puts its ornament on view," and "will allow the customer to see and almost to handle all his most attractive maxims, all his brilliant words, all his pretty figures, grand metaphors, and studied composition" (8.3.11–12). Quintilian makes no reference to himself in this description, which comes in a passage discussing epideictic ("display") oratory as one of many possible styles, yet what this "salesman of eloquence" does corresponds to a high degree with what Quintilian has done in the preface to book six, where the "arts of speech" that Quintilian used to produce emotions in the preface are rendered obvious by their close juxtaposition with the analysis of them in the ensuing chapters. Quintilian indicates that such obviousness is a good thing, because oratory that displays its technical mastery is the most powerful oratory of all: such an orator "is fighting with weapons that are not only effective, but polished and gleaming" (8.3.2). Thus if Quintilian means for us to recognize him as an *institor eloquentiae*, his open use of rhetoric redounds to his credit. But playing this role also, as I have said, was a necessity for him: as any enrollment-conscious teacher of Latin knows, if you want to be an *institutor* you have to be an *institor*.

This self-identification by Quintilian of the *institutor* as an *institor* plays on a lexical ambiguity that arises from "omitting a syllable," which Quintilian calls a barbarism at 1.5.10 but sanctions on metrical grounds at 9.4.59. The ambiguity is common enough that the two words are often confused in Latin manuscripts (according to *TLL* 7.1.1986.3 s.v. *institor*). Gregory the Great can even argue, in his commentary on the Book of Job, that where Jerome's text has *institorum* (*Iob* 28:8) we should understand *institutorum* (*Moralia in Iob* 18.35). But the lexical ambiguity that Quintilian introduces here also aligns with the ambiguity with which I began my discussion: that in a text on rhetoric written by a rhetorician who uses rhetoric we cannot always be sure whether we are listening to the *institutor* (who wants us to learn rhetoric) or the *institor* (who wants us to pay him).

If this reference to the *institor eloquentiae* introduces a tension between these two identities, a later but very different reference to the same figure drives a wedge between them. The *institor eloquentiae* reappears in a passage where Quintilian attempts to define how much display of rhetorical technique is appropriate for different kinds of cases. His general argument is that many speech contexts require the speaker to avoid too much rhetorical display because an audience may regard such showiness as inappropriate for serious cases. "Would anyone be moved," asks Quintilian, "by the plight of a man whom he perceived to be a puffed up self-advertiser, ostentatiously marketing his eloquence (*iactantem et ambitiosum institorem eloquentiae*) when his fate was in the balance?" (11.1.50). The shift in tone of Russell's translation from the passage in book eight, where *institor eloquentiae* was a "salesman of eloquence," to this passage, where the same figure is an "ostentatious self-advertiser," captures well the shift in Quintilian's treatment of the figure, a shift to which the repetition of the phrase *institor eloquentiae* calls attention. It is surprising to find Quintilian dismissing as unpersuasive and, indeed, unprofessional a figure with whom he had implicitly aligned himself earlier in his work.

Even more surprising, however, is that Quintilian goes out of his way to connect himself with this second version of the *institor*. He does so by citing a situation in which his readers know he himself has delivered a speech as an example of when the self-advertising speaker will be ineffective: "Suppose a father has to speak of his son's death" (11.1.53). Russell comments, "It is natural to recall Quintilian's emotional account of his own bereavements," and so it is; Quintilian clearly wants to connect his discussion here with his performance in the preface to book six. But this connection undermines Quintilian's claim to be a master practitioner of rhetoric, because here, in book eleven, he argues that an "unemotional observance of textbook rules" (*secura observatio artium,* 11.1.54) obliterates the effectiveness of the speech, because it is at odds with the authentic emotions that the occasion requires. The preface to book six is hardly "unemotional," but it is nevertheless marked by a thoroughgoing observance of the advice to be found not just in any textbook but in Quintilian's own textbook of rhetoric, and not just anywhere in that textbook but in the passages immediately following his observance of those rules in his preface. Just as in book eight, it is hard to avoid the conclusion that Quintilian intends for us to recognize him in the *institor*. But here the recognition forces us to question, on the basis of his own criticism of that figure, whether Quintilian may, in fact, not be the *institutor* we need if we hope to become skilled rhetoricians by reading his treatise.

The problem of apparent self-criticism raised by these two references to the *institor* turns out to extend far beyond this specific context, because the *ostentatio* ("display") that marks the epideictic oratory of the *institor eloquentiae* (8.3.11) is a source of ambivalence that pervades Quintilian's entire treatise.[4] The few passages in which Quintilian seems to praise such showiness—for example when he says (not without pride) that the Romans, unlike the Greeks, have "found a place for [epideictic] in practical business" (*negotia*, 3.7.2)—are more than counterbalanced by a whole series of references to *ostentatio* that mark it as something Quintilian avoids as a matter of principle. In the opening passage of the *Institutio*, Quintilian criticizes the authors of other manuals of rhetoric for neglecting the elementary stages of instruction "because they had no hope for winning favor for their talents by dealing with subjects which, however necessary, are very far from being showy" (*procul ab ostentatione positae*, 1.pr.4). This attitude recurs in Quintilian's own treatment of these rudiments when he praises grammar as "perhaps the only branch of study that has more substance (*opus*) than show" (*ostentatio*, 1.4.5). Thus Quintilian suggests at a very early stage of his discussion that there is more to rhetoric than "display" and, further, that his particular contribution to the study of rhetoric is to deemphasize such ostentation in favor of substance. As for his students, Quintilian warns them to "remember that the orator should not follow the poet in everything, neither in his freedom of vocabulary nor in his license to develop figures, and that poetry is designed for display" (10.1.28). This last phrase, *genus ostentationi comparatum*, is almost identical to Quintilian's description of epideictic (cited above, *genus ostentationi compositum*, 8.3.11), thus indicating that the problem with a poetic style is that it is too epideictic. It is hard to reconcile either attitude with Quintilian's self-identification as an intentionally ostentatious *institor*.

Equally problematic is that a speaker who advertises his rhetoric in the manner of the *institor* violates one of the oldest axioms of Greco-Roman rhetorical theory, that the highest art is to appear artless.[5] Despite his obvious use of rhetoric, Quintilian cites this idea several times with approval, in relation both to delivery and gesture (1.11.3: "If speakers do possess an art of these things, its first rule is not to seem to be art.") and to figures of thought and speech (9.3.102: "Wherever art is put on show [*ostentatur*], truth seems to be absent."). In keeping with this tradition of concealed eloquence, Quintilian treats *ostentatio* as a major cause of the decadence of his age.[6] In a discussion of the proper style for narrating the facts of a case, he contrasts "the days when every speech was designed for use (*utilitas*) rather than for show (*ostentatio*) and the courts had stricter principles" with "now, when pleasure has forced its way in even where life or fortune is in jeopardy" (4.2.122). He complains that speakers have made display, and the pleasure it provides, their only goal, to the detriment of serious oratory.[7] His own view is that "everything must seem to come from the case, and not from the orator . . . the truth is that [art] ceases to be art once it is detected" (4.2.126), while his summary of his contemporaries' position is that "we find this intolerable, and we think our art is wasted unless it can be seen!" Yet Quintilian's use of "we" in "we find this intolerable" (*hoc pati non possumus*) breaks down the very distinction he has set up between his more traditional view and the decadence of his own time. Quintilian's own practice seems to align him more with those he criticizes—the "we"—than with the position he claims to hold: he actually does seem to "find it intolerable" to conceal his use of rhetorical skill. And the depth of this self-contradiction is driven home by Quintilian's explanation for why speakers continue to display their artistry even in the knowledge of this advice: "We are addicted to applause (*laus*) and think it the goal of all our labor" (4.2.127). Again that "we," which Quintilian seems to be applying to those whose position he rejects, can at least potentially include Quintilian, who describes the epideictic rhetorical style of his alter ego, the *institor eloquentiae*, as one that "does not lay traps or plan to win a case but addresses itself solely to the end of praise (*laus*) and glory" (8.3.11). If Quintilian intended his demonstration of rhetorical skill to win him the admiration of students and to serve as a model for them to emulate, it is hard to see why he keeps digging himself deeper and deeper into this hole, fueling our suspicion that our revered teacher of rhetoric is at best a hypocrite or, at worst, incompetent.

Yet still he digs, by declaring in a section on the "duties" (*officia*) of the orator that "above all, he should never, as so many do, let his desire for praise (*cupido laudis*) distract him from the practical needs (*utilitas*) of the case" (12.9.2). "Desire for applause" leads orators to adopt a style that "will deploy its whole strength with popular approval" (*totas vires populariter explicabit*). Quintilian's use of *explicare* highlights the revelatory aspect of the style, which "displays" all its strength in a way intended, according to Quintilian's *populariter*, to impress as broad an audience as possible. This advice could hardly be more at odds with Quintilian's own practice throughout the *Institutio Oratoria*, where he has been at pains to display "all the strength" of his rhetoric, which by his own analysis signals his "desire for praise." Quintilian goes on to dismiss the showy orator as no better than a general who only knows how to lead his army through "level, pleasant country"; just as commanders must rely on more sophisticated skills in real conflicts, the orator who wants to do more than impress the populace will need a more sophisticated form of oratory, one that relies on "secret skills" (*occultae artes*, 12.9.3). The reader hoping to develop these skills may feel that Quintilian has in fact put praise ahead of the *utilitas* of the *Institutio* as a teaching tool, because he has only modeled the form of oratory that he himself is always denigrating as lightweight and inappropriate for any matter of significance. Our schoolmaster seems to be an *institor* first, and an *institutor* second.

This contradiction is made all the more acute by the forcefulness with which Quintilian affirms the ideals of rigorous judicial and deliberative oratory over and above the epideictic bluster that he himself seems to practice. His disdain for oratory that seeks popular approval is palpable when he pivots from arguing that orators should place *utilitas* above *laus* to an attempt to define the kind of praise orators should seek. Of the "secret skills" that are the hallmark of proper oratory, he remarks "these things are never praised (*laudantur*) while they are being done, but only afterwards; and thus even the most ambitious for renown will find greater reward here" (12.9.4). This remark distinguishes the kind of praise the epideictic orator seeks—what in the next sentence he calls the "preconcerted applause" that "perverse displays of oratory" win—from a different kind of praise, one which pointedly comes not from the popular audience for a speech but from a more specialized group: "the judges do not conceal (*non dissimulant*) what it was that moved them, and well-informed critics are believed (*doctis creditur*). There is no true praise (*vera laus*) for a speech till after it has finished" (12.9.4). This is the kind of argument we expect from Quintilian, purveyor of a form of knowledge deeply implicated in the formation of elite identity in Rome (see, e.g., Corbeill 2007): that the orator should disdain popular approval in favor of the "true praise" that only a more specialized, elite audience, can confer. His authority to give such advice, however, is undermined by his own apparent commitment to revealing his oratorical skill in ways characteristic of ostentatious speakers.

Quintilian's own discussion, however, leaves this evaluation to the *docti* who wait until the end of a speech to assess it. Translators and editors are divided over the identification of this group. Several, including Russell, regard them as specialist critics whose praise carries more weight than that of the crowd; others take the *docti* as the speakers themselves (Watson: "respect will be paid to the truly learned"). I prefer to highlight Quintilian's granting of a privileged right of assessment to those who "have been taught," the literal meaning of *docti* and a connotation more likely to be felt in an educational context such as the *Institutio Oratoria*. And while for a courtroom speech the *docti* might consist of Russell's "well-informed critics," at the end of the *Institutio Oratoria* the audience of those "who have been taught" must consist of Quintilian's readers themselves, who, if Quintilian has done his job in "training the young" (*erudiendis iuvenibus*, 1.pr.1), will have become *docti* in the art of rhetoric from reading the *Institutio Oratoria*, and thus be in a position to dispense "true praise."

What do these *docti* find at the end of the *Institutio*? A passage into which Quintilian has again inserted himself. The very last section of the work (12.11) begins with a description of the retirement of the ideal orator, which Quintilian says may be devoted to producing a history (*monumenta*) for those who come later (*posteris*), to making judgments about laws (*iura reddet*), to composing a treatise on oratory (*eloquentiae artem componet*), or to "giving fitting expression to the noblest precepts of morality" (*pulcherrimis vitae praeceptis dignum os dabit*, 12.11.4–5). Scholars, most recently Winterbottom (2005), have argued that this is not just an ideal for the general reader but, on the basis of several allusions to a discussion of retirement from public life in Cicero's *De Oratore,* a description of what Cicero's retirement would have looked like had he lived to see it. Winterbottom is on the right track in seeing a specific referent in what had traditionally been understood as a generalized portrait, but he does not pursue his observation that Quintilian begins the *Institutio Oratoria* with the announcement that the treatise is the work of his retirement. Furthermore, the *Institutio Oratoria* conforms in varying degrees to all the different kinds of work that Quintilian says the ideal orator will pursue after finishing his career. It is unmistakably an *ars eloquentiae*, a treatise on oratory; Quintilian's reputation as a moralist speaks to how much of it is devoted to teaching the *pulcherrima praecepta* of the virtuous life; legal historians' use of the *Institutio* as a source for Roman law signals how much of it is devoted to legal judgments; and while Quintilian nowhere describes his work as a *monumentum posteris*, he does describe it as a *patrimonium*, "legacy," that he is "leaving for others" (6.pr.16). The *optimi iuvenes* who Quintilian says will "frequent [the retired orator's] house, as in the old days, and learn the road to true oratory from him as from an oracle" sound very much like the *boni iuvenes* who, in their zeal for Quintilian's oratorical wisdom, circulated notes from his lectures without his permission (1.pr.7). The retired orator that Quintilian describes also turns out to be an educator: when Quintilian says that he will "shape (*formabit*) those young men who visit him," he uses the same verb that describes his own training of orators (e.g., 1.pr.4, 1.pr.22). Once again, the ideal orator's retirement looks uncannily like Quintilian's own, and what's more, a declaration that Quintilian is not only a practitioner of rhetoric but actually the ideal orator he has been describing all along. This is a bold claim for Quintilian to make, because it accentuates the contradiction between Quintilian's stated vision for oratory and his own practice. The ideal orator that Quintilian has described throughout the *Institutio* is not an epideictic *institor*. To those who have observed Quintilian's continuous advertisement of his rhetorical skill throughout the *Institutio*, it should seem very unclear whether his (self-)praise in declaring himself the ideal orator at the end of his work should qualify as the "true praise" he urged his orators to seek.

So is Quintilian trying to teach rhetoric or just to show off? We can make sense of this apparent duality by embracing it as an essential feature of his text. Quintilian has in fact given us clues for how we might do this in another implicitly self-referential passage. His introduction in 12.9 of the *docti* qualified to make judgments on his text is not the first time Quintilian has argued that speeches can only be properly evaluated after they have been completed. A few books earlier, in his discussion of what the aspiring orator should read, he gives advice on how to read oratory: "We must do more than examine everything bit by bit. Once read, the book must be taken up again from the beginning, especially if it is a speech, the virtues of which are often deliberately concealed" (10.1.20). Oratory in particular requires this kind of re-reading because "the orator often prepares his way, dissembles, lays traps, and says things in the first part of the speech that will prove their value at the end, and are accordingly less striking in their original context, because we do not as yet know why they are said, and therefore have to go back over them when we know the whole text" (10.1.21). Those evaluating a speech—or a treatise-cum-rhetorical performance—must do more, Quintilian says, than wait until the end to form their judgments. They must look back over the speech or treatise and consider the order in which the orator said things, what effect that order had when it was first encountered, and what effect it has when the whole arc of the speech is understood. When we do this for the *Institutio Oratoria*, the contradictions that Quintilian has built up around himself do not disappear, but they collectively signal that the education Quintilian offers encompasses more than a training in how to use rhetoric.

Quintilian's flaw, as an orator and therefore as a teacher of oratory, is that his deployment of rhetoric is too obvious. His instructions on how to use rhetoric pull back the veil from his own deployment of those techniques in a way characteristic of the kinds of epideictic orators that Quintilian himself condemns. But the advice to consider the order in which a speaker moves through his case prompts us to recognize that Quintilian has arranged his deployment and exposition of rhetoric so that display precedes analysis. The preface to book six, that virtuoso display of all the techniques for arousing emotions, is followed by his discussion of those techniques. The discussion of what techniques to use in a preface (4.1) comes after Quintilian has presented his reader with two formal prefaces (1.pr and 4.pr). The techniques of argumentation in book three come after Quintilian has employed many of them in his defense of rhetoric in the second half of book two. This order seems designed to let his readers experience the rhetorical power of "concealed" techniques (for example, by making them (us?) weep at the deaths of Quintilian's wife and sons) before giving them the tools to see through that concealment and recognize what has been done to them. Again and again, Quintilian first presents himself as a master rhetorician in action before revealing the machinery behind his effects.

To be sure, as the work progresses, the *institutor* looks more and more like an *institor*, and Quintilian's power of persuasion looks more and more like a rote performance of textbook rules. But many of the passages that call attention to this aspect of Quintilian's performance—his references to the *institor eloquentiae* in books eight and eleven, his quotation in book nine of Cicero's list of figures the ideal orator should use, and ultimately his insinuation that he is the ideal orator in his final chapter—come relatively late in the work. By the end, his readers can see Quintilian's rhetoric for what it is.

But perhaps this is as it should be, because at the end of the treatise it is time for his reader to leave the schoolroom and make his way in the world as a rhetorician in his own right. When Quintilian tendentiously, even unpersuasively, declares his oratorical supremacy at the end of his work, his reader has already been trained to recognize the limitations of that claim.

In the second section of book ten, Quintilian discusses the likelihood that a speaker might achieve his oratorical ideal. "It would be perfectly appropriate that he should come to perfection in our time, when there are so many more models of good oratory to be found than were available to those who were the great masters of the past" (10.2.28). Knowing as we do that Quintilian ends his treatise by identifying himself with the ideal orator, it is hard not to see in this prediction a reference to himself as the culmination of oratorical history. But he goes on to say that those who went before "will acquire another glory (*laus*) too: that of being said to have surpassed their predecessors and taught their successors" (*priores superasse, posteros docuisse*). This remark may help define the kind of praise Quintilian can expect at the end of his treatise. Because his oratory reveals the way it works, not just to the *docti* but to *discipuli,* he is not really eligible for the "true praise" that only the *docti* can give, the praise for an effective but well-concealed deployment of technique. But he may well be eligible for the *laus* that comes from producing the next generation of rhetoricians, one that he may hope will surpass their master just as he believes he has surpassed his. But Quintilian also understood, I believe, that success in rhetoric means more than finding ever more sophisticated ways to conceal its operation. It means being able to see the ambiguities and limitations inherent in any rhetorical project, ambiguities that undermine the certainty of the worldview that most rhetoricians, including Quintilian in his self-advertisements, seek to impose on their audiences.

Quintilian gives his students not only a traditional education in rhetoric but also shows them his own limitations as an orator: his self-contradictions, his blind spots, his penchant for special pleading, his addiction to easy applause. Indeed, these are the traps into which

201

any accomplished practitioner of rhetoric, even Cicero, as Quintilian himself reports (*Inst.* 12.10.12–13), may fall. Those who recognize the hollowness of Quintilian's promotion of himself as the ideal orator develop a skepticism about other claims of authority that may turn out to rest on similarly shaky foundations. This is a skill with utility stretching far beyond making counterarguments in court. The world in which Quintilian and his students lived was one ruled by what most historians regard as an oppressive autocracy. To survive, let alone advance, they needed to know not only how to use rhetoric, but to recognize when, and how, it was being used on and against them.

*　*　*

It is an honor to be able to offer this reading in a volume dedicated to Reginald, whom I have heard more than once remarking that too few people read Quintilian. It was in his classroom in the summer of 1999 that I heard the name "Quintilian" for the first time. For that and for all the other gifts I took away from that experience, I offer this essay with heartfelt gratitude.

BIBLIOGRAPHY

Atherton, Catherine. 1993. *The Stoics on Ambiguity*. Cambridge: Cambridge University Press.

Austin, R. G., ed. 1948. *Quintiliani Institutionis Oratoriae Liber XII*. Oxford: Clarendon Press.

Bahti, Timothy. 1986. "Ambiguity and Indeterminacy: The Juncture." *Comparative Literature* 38(3):209–23.

Caplan, Harry, ed. 1954. *Ad C. Herennium de Ratione Dicendi (Rhetorica Ad Herennium)*. Cambridge: Harvard University Press.

Corbeill, A. 2007. "Rhetorical Education and Social Reproduction." In *A Companion to Roman Rhetoric*, ed. William J. Dominik and Jon Hall, 69–82. Malden, MA: Blackwell.

Dozier, Curtis. 2012. "Poetry, Politics, and Pleasure in Quintilian." In *Aesthetic Value in Classical Antiquity*, ed. R. M. Rosen and I. Sluiter, 345–63. Leiden: Brill.

———. 2014. "Quintilian's Ratio Discendi (Institutio 12.8) and the Rhetorical Dimension of the Institutio Oratoria." *Arethusa* 47(1):71–88.

Gunderson, Erik T. 2000. *Staging Masculinity : The Rhetoric of Performance in the Roman World*. Ann Arbor: University of Michigan Press.

———. 2009. "The Rhetoric of Rhetorical Theory." In *The Cambridge Companion to Ancient Rhetoric*, ed. Erik T. Gunderson, 109–25. Cambridge: Cambridge University Press.

Kennedy, George Alexander. 1969. *Quintilian*. New York: Twayne Publishers.

Leigh, Matthew. 2004. "Quintilian on the Emotions (*Institutio Oratoria* 6, Preface and 1–2)." *The Journal of Roman Studies* 94:122–40.

Peterson, W., ed. 1891. *M. Fabi Quintiliani Institutionis Oratoriae Liber Decimus*. Oxford: Clarendon.

Russell, D. A., ed. 2001. *Quintilian: The Orator's Education*. 5 vols. Cambridge, Mass.: Harvard University Press.

Stanford, William Bedell. 1939. *Ambiguity in Greek Literature, Studies in Theory and Practice*. Oxford: B. Blackwell.

Winterbottom, Michael. 1983. "Quintilian and Declamation." In *Hommages À Jean Cousin: Rencontres Avec l'Antiquité Classique*, 225–35. Institut Félix Gaffiot.

———. 2005. "Approaching the End : Quintilian 12.11." *Acta Classica* 48:175–83.

Zinsmaier, Thomas. 2003. "Quintilian Als Deklamator : Die Topik Des « Parens Superstes » Im Proömium Zu Buch VI Der « Institutio Oratoria »." In *Studium Declamatorium*, edd. B.-J. and J.-P. Schröder, 153–67. Munich: Saur.

Zundel, Eckart. 1981. *Lehrstil und rhetorischer Stil in Quintilians Institutio oratoria. Untersuchungen zur Form eines Lehrbuchs*. Frankfurt: Haag & Herchen.

ENDNOTES

1   Stanford (1939, 11) called ancient theories of ambiguity "disappointingly inadequate" because, as Atherton (1993, 500–1) puts it in a much later study, they leave "little room for ambiguity as a manifestation of the creativity of language and its users." Bahti 1986 is one convenient summary of the capaciousness of modern (and indeed postmodern) approaches to the phenomenon.

2   Throughout this essay I have quoted Russell's excellent translation of Quintilian for the Loeb Classical Library (2001). With such an outstanding translation readily available, there was little need to provide my own, except when I needed to make specific points about Quintilian's Latin. I have also taken the liberty of replacing Russell's "cause" with "case" for Quintilian's *causa* when it refers to a legal action undertaken by a pleader.

3   If Quintilian had wanted to say "something of his own material" unambiguously, he could have used *aliquid suum*, as is found at *Rhet. Her.* 4.4 in a similar context.

4   It was also, to judge from Quintilian's instructions, a source of ambivalence for all Roman men attempting to be orators. See Gunderson 2000, chs. 3–4.

5   Apparently first articulated by Aristotle at *Rhet.* 3.2.4, 1404b, and traced throughout antiquity in Caplan's (1954) note on *Rhet. Her.* 4.10.

6   Epideictic oratory and declamation, the other source of decline that Quintilian repeatedly cites, are closely related. Declamation is itself, like *ostentatio*, a source of deep ambivalence for Quintilian, as Winterbottom 1983 has shown. At the same time, Quintilian himself writes like a declaimer (Zinsmaier 2003).

7   Pleasure itself is (yet another) a source of ambivalence for Quintilian. See Dozier 2012.

The Ethics of Ambiguity in Quintilian

Charles McNamara

I n a list of twelve stylistic and grammatical errors of oratory, the fourth-century grammarian Donatus includes the fault of *amphibolia*, a transliteration of a Greek word that Donatus further defines as an *ambiguitas dictionis*.[1] This understanding of *ambiguitas dictionis* as a flaw in composition is unique neither to the texts of late antiquity nor to technical grammatical treatises, and one can find ample cautioning against it in pedagogical texts both before and after Donatus.[2] In his first-century *Institutio Oratoria*, for instance, Quintilian similarly cautions against writing ambiguous language and encourages his students to compose lucid and straightforward Latin, particularly in regard to syntax. As part of his manual for the instruction of the ideal orator, Quintilian advises that

> *vitanda in primis ambiguitas, non haec solum, de cuius genere supra dictum est, quae incertum intellectum facit, ut 'Chremetem audivi percussisse Demean,' sed illa quoque, quae etiam si turbare non potest sensum in idem tamen verborum vitium incidit, ut si quis dicat visum a se hominem librum scribentem. nam etiam si librum ab homine scribi patet, male tamen composuerit, feceritque ambiguum quantum in ipso fuit.* (8.2.16)

Above all, ambiguity is to be avoided, not only ambiguity of the kind discussed above, which makes understanding uncertain—"I heard that Chremes Demea struck"—but also that which, although it cannot confuse the sense, falls into the same verbal fault. So if you were to say, for example, "I saw a man a book writing," although it is obvious that the man is writing the book, it would be a bad piece of composition, and you will have made it as ambiguous as you could.

Like Donatus, Quintilian shows that the use of two accusatives with a transitive verb in indirect statement merits special pedagogical reproach, and such syntactical *ambiguitas*, our oratorical instructor cautions, should be avoided even when a sensible audience can reliably deduce the correct meaning. In an earlier discussion, too, Quintilian uses the term *amphibolia* to describe a similar syntactical ambiguity, where "the ambiguity (*amphibolia*) resulting from two accusatives is remedied by using the ablative" (*accusativi geminatione facta amphibolia solvitur ablativo, ut illud 'Lachetem audivi percussisse Demean' fiat 'a Lachete percussum Demean,'* 7.9.10). Both of these monuments of ancient pedagogy, then, show a consistent disapproval of ambiguity, both as *amphibolia* and as *ambiguitas*, particularly as it bears on syntax. By cautioning so strongly against these ambiguous constructions, Quintilian and Donatus make at least this one lesson crystal clear: *ambiguitas delenda est*.

But unlike Donatus' litany of compositional vices, Quintilian's work aims to achieve more than simply teaching students the pitfalls of Latin grammar. It attempts to train a *vir bonus dicendi peritus*, a "good man skilled in speaking," one who is "perfect not only in morals, but also in knowledge" (*nec moribus modo perfectus . . . sed etiam scientia et omni facultate dicendi*, 1.pr.18). In service to these broader ethical aspirations, the *Institutio* revisits the concept of *ambiguitas* throughout its several books, positioning the topic of ambiguity not just within the guidelines of grammar and syntax, but also within its recommendations for forming ethically good orators, those who are able to plead the right cases in the courtroom with the right arguments. As Quintilian explains in his final book, such cases often rest on questions of *ambiguitas*, an issue that "at some point or another involves the discussion of equity and goodness" (*nulla fere dici potest cuius non parte in aliqua tractatus aequi ac boni reperiatur*, 12.2.15). He thus transposes pedantic lessons of syntax and composition into matters of jurisprudence and morality. By showing how recognizing, resolving, and leveraging ambiguity is a matter of ethical concern and not merely a lesson in grammar and composition, Quintilian recasts ambiguity as a topic that the "good man skilled in speaking" must master, not avoid. In fact, one's ability to interpret ambiguous laws—a task that requires both technical knowledge and a well-developed sense of "equity" or *aequitas*—constitutes the foundation of Quintilian's moral thinking. Rather than defining ethics as adherence to the doctrines of Epicurus or the Stoic Sage, Quintilian instead argues that ethical training above all must refine the orator's ability to grapple with the ambiguity of statutes.

Before turning to these explicitly ethical considerations at the end of the *Instiutio*, it is helpful to view Quintilian's earlier elaboration of *ambiguitas* as a topic of rhetorical invention: not yet a meditation on moral philosophy, but nevertheless a fundamental recasting of ambiguity as a concern of interpretation rather than of composition. After surveying matters of early childhood education and philosophical issues surrounding rhetoric's status as an art, Quintilian turns to the methods for devising and shaping arguments (*inventio*).[3] Like many rhetorical theorists before him, including Cicero and the author of the *Rhetorica ad Herennium*, Quintilian grounds much of his approach to *inventio* in status theory, a framework of invention that heavily influenced Roman rhetorical thought and its practitioners.[4] First elaborated in the now-lost writings of Hermagoras of Temnos in the second century BCE, status theory attempts to articulate the central issue (*status*) of a forensic dispute by asking three progressively specific questions: whether something happened (the "conjectural" issue, often rendered *an sit?*), what happened ("definitional," *quid sit?*), and what kind of thing happened ("qualitative," *quale sit?*). Quintilian himself illustrates the application of this framework with several examples, and for the issues of definition and quality, for instance, he sets out a hypothetical accusation of murder:

> *sit enim accusatoris intentio: 'hominem occidisti': si negat reus, faciat statum qui negat. quid si confitetur, sed iure a se adulterum dicit occisum (nempe legem esse certum est quae permittat)? nisi aliquid accusator respondet, nulla lis est. 'non fuit' inquit 'adulter': ergo depulsio incipit esse actoris, ille statum faciet.* (3.6.17)

> Let us suppose the charge made by the accuser is "You killed the man." If the defendant denies it, it is he who produces the issue. But suppose he admits the fact, but says the adulterer was justifiably killed by him. (It is of course established that there is a law permitting this.) Unless the accuser makes a reply, there is no dispute. If he says, "He was not an adulterer," then the rebuttal of the charge is now the prosecutor's business, and he will produce the issue.

In this trial, the case progresses from the definitional issue of what the defendant did to the qualitative issue of what kind of thing was done. (The conjectural question of whether something happened, we can assume, has been settled affirmatively.) While the two parties agree that the defendant did kill another man, they disagree on the existence of mitigating conditions, since the circumstance of adultery would exonerate the defendant. The two sides, then, would focus on the kind of homicide that had taken place.

While discussions of status theory most often center around these three *status rationales*—conjecture, definition, and quality—several rhetorical theorists, including Quintilian, add a second collection of issues that situate this framework more specifically in the context of forensic disputes.[5] In Quintilian's account, this second category includes four *status legales*, issues that concern the application of legal codes: letter and spirit (*scriptum et voluntas*), inference (*syllogismos*), conflicting laws (*leges contrariae*), and ambiguity (*amphibolia* or *ambiguitas*).[6] Quintilian notes that the *status legales* are more complex than three *status rationales*, for in logical issues

> *itaque in eo satis est ostendisse coniecturam finitionem qualitatem. legalium plures sint species necesse est, propterea quod multae sunt leges et varia habent formas. alia est cuius verbis nitimur, alia cuius voluntate: alias nobis, cum ipsi nullam habeamus, adiungimus, alias inter se comparamus, alias in diversum interpretamur.*
> (3.6.86–87)

> it is enough to point to conjecture, definition, and quality. Of legal issues there are inevitably more varieties, because there are many laws and they have many forms. We rely on the letter of one, on the intention of another; others we harness to our cause, though we have no law really on our side; sometimes we compare one law with another, sometimes we give different interpretations.

In this explanation of the four varieties of *status legales* through the activities of the orator, Quintilian shows that *ambiguitas* bears on the rhetorician's interpretation of laws that might be variously construed (*alias in diversum interpretamur*).[7] No longer a mere warning to students about composing sentences, *amphibolia* and *ambiguitas* now point to a lack of clarity in legal codes and their attendant interpretive difficulties.

Surviving declamatory speeches from the early Roman Empire show that Quintilian is not alone in understanding *ambiguitas* as a central concern of rhetorical invention. We find a particularly helpful example in the sixth of the *Declamationes Maiores* of

Pseudo-Quintilian. Like many of the cases presented in these nineteen speeches, long attributed to the author of the *Institutio* itself, the sixth declamation includes at its outset the applicable statute: "Whoever deserts his parents in a state of disaster shall be thrown out without burial" (*qui in calamitate parentes deseruerit, insepultus abiciatur,* 6.pr).[8] The author then summarizes the controversy at hand, highlighting how statutory interpretation can serve as the central issue in the courtroom:

> *qui habebat uxorem et filium, captus a piratis scripsit domum de redemptione. uxor flendo oculos amisit. Filius retinente matre profectus vicariis manibus redemit patrem. idem in vinculis decessit. abiectus in mare et appulsus ad litus patrium est eiectus. vult illum sepelire pater, mater prohibet.* (6.pr.)

A man who had a wife and a son was captured by pirates and wrote home for his rescue. The wife lost her eyesight from crying. Even though the mother tried to restrain him, the son set out and freed his father by offering to take his father's place. During his captivity, the son died. He was thrown into the sea, and he later drifted to his father's homeland and washed ashore. The father wishes to bury the son. The mother prohibits it.

In the remainder of the text, the father argues for the son's burial on the grounds that the son has not transgressed the statute, grounding his case in the law's intent (*voluntas*) rather than a more pedantic understanding of its literal meaning (*scriptum*). Crucially for our purposes, the father forthrightly explains that the case "concerns the letter and the meaning of the law, whether one should rely on the ambiguity of the words or the adherence to its intent" (*omnis nobis in hac†prius causa, iudices, de scripto et intellectu legis contentio est, utrum verborum ambiguitate an voluntatis fide standum sit,* 6.11), thus aligning *ambiguitas* with the letter of the law (*scriptum*), and the meaning found through interpretation (*intellectum*) with the law's intent (*voluntas*).[9]

Almost paradoxically, the father argues that the apparent *ambiguitas* of the law can be circumvented if one simply interprets the text appropriately and avoids a slavishly literal (and therefore distorting) reading. While the mother, he argues, grounds her argument in an implausible interpretation of the law, the father explains how the intent of the law, itself unambiguous, disallows her literal understanding:

> *pars enim diversa id nititur parentem fuisse in calamitate eam, quae deserta sit; cuius rei poena est abici insepultum. quid tum fuerit in causa, quid sit postea consecutum, quomodo legem intellegere conveniat, subterfugit dicere, neque a vestigio scripti recedit, sed nuda recitatione contenta est. nos neque omnibus personis neque omnibus causis scriptam esse legem, et iuveni iustas ac necessarias recedendi causas, et, cui rei semper ius satis plenum est, contendimus, atque eo causam demittimus, ut non sit absolvendus nisi etiam laudandus. qui autem dubitat, an scripti voluntatem sequi conveniat, is mihi videtur quaestionem temptare†incertus.* (6.12)

One side of the case contends this: that she was a parent in a distress, and she was abandoned; that the punishment for this crime is to be denied burial. But she dodges having to say what the motive was at that time, what happened afterward, and how one should interpret the law. And she does not step from the footprint of the law, but instead she is content with an unsophisticated reading. We maintain, however, that the law was not written for all people and all cases, and that the boy's motives for leaving were just and

necessary, and that his intentions were good (a factor
the law is very generous about), and finally, that he did
not commit desertion. And we settle her case for this
reason as well: the boy does not deserve acquittal, but
actually praise. Whoever doubts whether one should
follow the intent of the law, in fact, seems to be unsure
of how run an investigation.

Returning to the vocabulary of interpretation (*intellegere*) and
intent (*voluntas*), the father clarifies that the mother relies on "an
unsophisticated reading" (*nuda recitatio*) and neglects to interpret the
law sensibly. She refuses to consider interpretive questions underlying
the case: What does it mean to leave one's parents *in calamitate*?
Does abandonment (*deserere*) require malicious motives? Unlike the
compositional focus on ambiguous syntax, the *ambiguitas* of the
status legales centers on the multiple approaches that one can take
to a law, here tightly bound to the well-known opposition between
the law's letter and spirit (itself another of the *status legales* in the
Institutio): while the mother argues for a literal understanding of the
law's *scriptum*, the father argues against the *ambiguitas* afforded by
this strict reading and instead supports an adherence to the evident
voluntas found through fair-minded interpretation.[10] This case thus
illustrates how *ambiguitas* extends far beyond Donatus' purely
grammatical concerns. The problem of ambiguity requires litigants
to read statutes sensitively, since their words often admit multiple
meanings, even when the syntax is clear.

Like Pseudo-Quintilian's declamatory exercise, Quintilian's
Institutio also understands ambiguity as a concern for the excavation
of statutory *voluntas*. As part of a discussion of the *status legales*
within his treatment of oratorical *dispositio* in Book 7, Quintilian's
manual again turns its attention to *ambiguitas* and explains how
two kinds of ambiguity (or at least two attitudes toward ambiguity)
bear on rhetorical education. First, he cautions his students that one
should not aim to resolve an ambiguous expression conclusively: "It
is therefore futile to recommend that, in this case, we should try to

turn the ambiguous expression itself to our advantage, because if that can be done, there is no ambiguity in the first place" (*ideoque frustra praecipitur ut in hoc statu vocem ipsam ad nostram partem conemur vertere: nam si id fieri potest amphibolia non est*, 7.9.14). Quintilian here perhaps has in mind the unresolvable ambiguity of two accusatives in indirect statement. To return to his earlier example, the sentence *Chremetem audivi percussisse Demean* offers two interpretations, neither of which is conclusively or obviously better than the other.

Immediately following this pessimistic outlook for one's ability to resolve ambiguity, however, Quintilian suggests that *ambiguitas* often requires the orator to seek out the *voluntas* of the law and its most equitable interpretation, again recasting the problem of *ambiguitas* as a conflict between the letter and the spirit of the law. Not merely an irreconcilable debate of unclear syntax, this second kind of ambiguity "rests sometimes on which is the more natural interpretation, but always on which is the more equitable interpretation and which the writer or speaker intended" (*amphiboliae autem omnis erit in his quaestio: aliquando uter sit secundum naturam magis sermo, semper utrum si aequius, utrum is qui scripsit ac dixit voluerit*, 7.9.15). In the vein of his earlier discussion of interpreting ambiguous language as a strategy of rhetorical *inventio* (*in diversum interpretamur*, 3.6.87), Quintilian again underscores in this treatment of *dispositio* that the orator should consider both "natural interpretation" as well as equitable interpretations of the speaker's intent (*voluerit*). Hardly without resolution or opportunities for securing an advantage in the courtroom, then, this second attitude toward ambiguity invites the rhetorician to use his interpretive acumen to find the most sensible or convincing reading of the law.

The role of *ambiguitas* in this process of equitable interpretation is bound up, moreover, with the other *status legales*, for "it is well-known that this treatment according to *ius* and *aequitas* is merely a general manifestation of the detailed doctrine of [these four issues]."[11] And Quintilian's reference here to *aequitas*—the "equity" one needs to interpret ambiguous language fairly and correctly—signals an important shift into the territory of ethical training. Not only do the *status legales* require interpretive skill; they also require the moral disposition of the orator who is *aequus*. In the final book of the *Institutio*, as we shall now see, Quintilian cements this link between *ambiguitas* and ethics in his meditations on the philosophical training of the ideal orator. For without ethical training, he argues, the orator will be a poor reader, poor interpreter, and thus poor courtroom advocate. When Quintilian defines *aequitas* as the indispensable foundation of the rhetorician's ability to grapple with ambiguous language, therefore, he advances a key justification for one of the most important but least intuitive claims of his entire manual: that unless one is a morally good man, one can never be a skillfully good orator.

In the final book of the *Institutio*, Quintilian takes a more general approach to the aims and activities of oratory.[12] As part of this culminating discussion, he investigates the relationship between philosophical learning and the practice of the orator, most importantly in matters of moral philosophy: "the orator must above all else develop his moral character by study, and undergo a thorough training in the honorable and the just, because without this no one can be either a good man or a skilled speaker" (*mores ante omnia oratori studiis erunt excolendi atque omnis honesti iustique disciplina pertractanda, sine qua nemo nec vir bonus esse nec dicendi peritus potest*, 12.2.1). Here Quintilian alludes to his requirement that no one can be an orator unless he is a good man, an utterly surprising claim when one considers that both modern and premodern eras are rife with examples of talented but depraved speakers.[13] Apparently aware of how unintuitive his claim is, Quintilian devotes the whole first chapter of book 12 to defending it, and even in the second chapter, in which he turns his attention to the philosophical training of the rhetorician, he often returns to a defense of this major thesis. And it is in this second discussion that Quintilian explores the foundational role that one's facility with *ambiguitas* has in developing this necessary ethical character.

As Quintilian surveys the various areas of philosophical training— logic, ethics, and natural philosophy—that one needs to achieve oratorical excellence, he underscores the importance of developing a facility with *ambiguitas*, first as a matter of logical precision and second as a matter of moral disposition. First turning his attention to training in logic, Quintilian explains how the orator must be able to "know the properties of every word, clear up ambiguities, unravel perplexities, judge falsehoods, and produce whatever inferences and refutations we wish" (*proprietates vocis cuiusque nosse et ambigua aperire et perplexa discernere et de falsis iudicare et colligere ac resolvere quae velis oratorum est*, 12.2.10).[14] It is unsurprising that ambiguity would arise in this discussion of the orator's logical training. Without the ability to evaluate the truthfulness of courtroom statements and make inferences from evidence, the orator would lack the crucial skills of the dialectician that—as Aristotle notes in the first sentence of his *Rhetoric*—are central to rhetorical practice.[15]

Although Quintilian includes *ambiguitas* in his discussion of the orator's logical training, he also firmly positions facility with interpreting ambiguous language within ethical education, the second branch of the rhetorician's philosophical learning. Returning to the language of status theory, Quintilian almost immediately pivots in his discussion of ethical training to the *status rationales* and the *status legales* elaborated in books 3 and 7:

> *iam quidem pars illa moralis quae dicitur ethice certe tota oratori est accommodata. nam in tanta causarum sicut superioribus libris diximus varietate, cum alia coniectura quaerantur, alia finitionibus concludantur, alia iura summoveantur vel transferantur, alia colligantur vel ipsa inter se concurrant vel in diversum ambiguitate ducantur.* (12.2.15)

Moral philosophy, or ethics as it is called, is surely wholly appropriate to the orator. As I have shown in previous books, there is a huge variety of cases. We have issues of conjecture, conclusions reached by definition, cases dismissed on legal grounds, questions of competence, cases based on inference, contrary laws, or ambiguities.

As he explains in the sentence that immediately follows this passage, Quintilian understands how these *status rationales* and *status legales* all involve matters of "equity and goodness" (*tractatus aequi ac boni*, 12.2.15). In fact, he underscores the central place of statutory interpretation in moral philosophy more generally: "Does not every question of law rest upon the correct sense of words or on a point of equity or on a conjecture about intention?" (*non quaestio iuris omnis aut verborum proprietate aut aequi disputatione aut voluntatis coniectura continetur?* 12.2.19). Not describing the rhetorician's ethical training through the maxims of a particular philosophical school or an ethical authority—there is no explicit mention of Stoic *ratio* or Aristotelian deliberation here—Quintilian instead frames it as facility with a Hellenistic technique of rhetorical invention and sensitivity to ambiguous language. Without a sense of *aequitas*, the fairness needed to resolve interpretive ambiguity, and without the related ability to discover the spirit of the law (*voluntas*), the orator will come up short in the courtroom and lose his cases.[16] In fact, when the orator lacks these hermeneutic and inventional skills, his practice will devolve into simple "loquaciousness" (*loquacitas*, 12.2.20), a symptom of language that "has either no guides to follow or false ones" (*vel nullos vel falsos duces habeat*, 12.2.20).

Quintilian elaborates the proposed relationship between ethics and interpretation in a later discussion of the orator's knowledge of civil laws. Admitting that some points of the law are "certain" because they "stand firm in either writing or custom" (*omne ius, quod est certum, aut scripto aut moribus constat*, 12.3.6), Quintilian explains that what is "doubtful" in the law must be understood by the standard of equity (*dubium aequitatis regula examinandum est*, 12.3.6). While an investigation of the former kind of "certain law" requires "knowledge, not invention" (*cognitionis sunt enim, non inventionis*, 12.3.7), because presumably there are no controversies surrounding these plainly understood statutes, "doubtful" points invite multiple interpretations and demand careful invention and argument. As Quintilian explains in the sentences that follow, the ability to wrestle with these interpretive controversies stems from the equity one develops through moral training:

> at quae consultorum responsis explicantur aut in verborum interpretatione sunt posita aut in recti pravique discrimine. vim cuiusque vocis intellegere aut commune prudentium est aut proprium oratoris, aequitas optimo cuique notissima. nos porro et bonum virum et prudentem in primis oratorem putamus. (12.3.7–8)

> Points explained in the responses of legal consultants rest either on the interpretation of words or on the distinction between right and wrong. To understand the meaning of each word is either common ground to sensible men, or peculiar to the orator; equity is perfectly familiar to all good men. We believe, in fact, that the orator is first and foremost a good and prudent man.

Here Quintilian treats the "interpretation of words" and "the distinction between right and wrong" as parallel concerns, and he suggests that without the *aequitas* of the good man, one cannot "understand the meaning of each word." (To return to our declamatory example from Pseudo-Quintilian for a moment, the *Institutio* here implies that the father's ability to correctly interpret the concepts of "desertion" and "calamity" stems from his equity.) Quintilian's discussion of ethical education in book 12, then, shows a certain internal consistency surrounding the place of morality in oratorical skill. Unlike the *ambiguitas* of composition, the *ambiguitas* of the *status legales* presents an interpretive challenge. Only with the correct ethical training and a refined *aequitas* will the orator have the "guides" (*duces*, 12.2.20) he needs to grapple with ambiguity and to avoid the likelihood of courtroom defeat. Or as Quintilian lays out in the first sentences of this final book, the orator cannot be successful unless he is a good, equitable man.

By way of conclusion, I offer a third consideration of the role of ambiguity in rhetorical education as it relates to decorum and humor, topics adjacent to both morality and invention. In a discussion of sources of laughter, Quintilian explains that "*ambigitas* undoubtedly gives the most frequent opportunities" (*cui sine dubio frequentissimam dat ocasionem ambiguitas*, 6.3.87) for inspiring comedic responses in one's audience, and he goes on to explain that "all witty speech consists in expressing things in a way other than the direct and truthful one" (*omnis salse dicendi ratio in eo est, ut aliter quam est rectum verumque dicatur*, 6.3.89). This understanding of ambiguity as a source of urbane comedy is not Quintilian's own creation: earlier rhetorical texts including the *Rhetorica ad Herennium* consider "ambiguities as deliberate stylistic flourishes, when the intended double or triple meaning was seen as witty and entertaining, a flattering challenge to the audience's intelligence, rather than an obstacle to their understanding."[17]

Not all kinds of ambiguity, however, result in appropriate or acceptable humor, and Quintilian is careful to include a cautionary note about the ethics of comedic propriety:

> *cum sint autem loci plures ex quibus dicta ridicula ducantur, repetendum est mihi non omnis eos oratoribus convenire, in primis ex amphibolia, neque illa obscura quae atellanio more captant, nec qualia vulgo iactantur a vilissimo quoque, conversa in maledictum fere ambiguitate.* (6.3.46–47)

Although there are many areas from which jokes may be drawn, I must emphasize again that they are not all suitable for orators: in particular any kind of *amphibolia*, either the obscure variety pursued in Atellan fashion, or the vulgar sort which the lowest of the low bandy about, and in which the *ambiguitas* commonly turns into abuse.

Here Quintilian underscores how *amphibolia* and *ambiguitas* lend themselves to comedy, but also how certain instances of such ambiguity are beneath the moral character of the ideal orator. Such "vulgar" kinds of ambiguity are used by the ethically compromised man (*vilissimus*), an adjective hardly befitting the *bonus homo* who epitomizes oratorical excellence in the *Institutio*'s final book.[18] Indeed, this debased kind of humor effects not the *urbanitas* of the learned rhetorician but the *maledictum* of the crass joker.

The role of *ambiguitas* in comedic decorum deserves a fuller treatment than it can be given here, but the term's appearance in Quintilian's discussion of humor and propriety exemplifies the schoolmaster's consistent and deep interest in the ethics of linguistic ambiguity. As Quintilian illustrates through his allusion to the *vilissimus* man who includes questionable comedy in his speeches, even these more ornamental considerations of *ambiguitas* can reveal the ethical character of the orator. Perhaps, then, Quintilian sees the ethical significance of ambiguity not merely in its interpretive dimension—whether one has the proper disposition to understand vague statutory language—but even in the compositional concerns with which this chapter begins. Incompetent in his handling of *ambiguitas*, the unskilled, unethical orator will fail in both his reading and his writing, both his laws and his punchlines.

BIBLIOGRAPHY

Atherton, Catherine. 2007. *The Stoics on Ambiguity*. Cambridge, UK: Cambridge University Press.

Austin, R. G., ed. and comm. 1948. *Quintilian Book XII*. Oxford: Oxford University Press.

Berti, Emanuele. 2015. "Law in Declamation: The *status legales* in Senecan *controversiae*." In *Law and Ethics in Greek and Roman*

Declamation, ed. Eugenio Amato, Francesco Citto, and Burt Huelsenbeck, 7–34. Berlin: De Gruyter.

Bernstein, Neil W. 2013. *Ethics, Identity, and Community in Later Roman Declamation*. Oxford: Oxford University Press.

Bobzien, Susanne. 2007. "Aristotle's *De Interpretatione* 8 is about Ambiguity." In *Maieusis: Essays in Ancient Philosophy in Honour of Myles Burnyeat*, ed. Dominic Scott, 301–321. Oxford: Oxford University Press.

Bonner, Stanley F. 1949. *Roman Declamation in the Late Republic and Early Empire*. Liverpool: University Press of Liverpool.

Brinton, Alan. 1983. "Quintilian, Plato, and the '*Vir Bonus*.'" *Philosophy & Rhetoric* 16 (3):167–184.

Dieter, Otto Alvin Loeb. 1950. "Stasis." *Communications Monographs* 17 (4):345–369.

Eden, Kathy. 2005. *Hermeneutics and the Rhetorical Tradition*. New Haven: Yale University Press.

Fantham, Elaine. 2011. *Beiträge zur Altertumskunde: Roman Readings: Roman Response to Greek Literature from Plautus to Statius and Quintilian*. Berlin: De Gruyter.

Hintikka, Jaakko. 1959. "Aristotle and the Ambiguity of Ambiguity." *Inquiry* 2:137–151.

Nadeau, Ray. 1959. "Classical Systems of *Stases* in Greek: Hermagoras to Hermogenes." *Greek, Roman and Byzantine Studies* 2 (1):361–424.

Sloan, Michael C. 2010. "Aristotle's *Nicomachean Ethics* as the Original Locus for the *Septem Circumstantiae*." *Classical Philology* 105 (3):236–251.

Walzer, Arthur E. 2003. "Quintilian's *Vir Bonus* and the Stoic Wise Man." *Rhetoric Society Quarterly* 33 (4):25–41.

Winterbottom, Michael, ed. and comm. 1984. *The Minor Declamations Ascribed to Quintilian*. Berlin and New York: de Gruyter.

———. 1964. "Quintilian and the *Vir Bonus*." *Journal of Roman Studies* 54:90–97.

ENDNOTES

1   *Ars Maior* III.3, *cum barbarismo et soloecismo vitia duodecim numerantur hoc modo: barbarismus, soloecismus, acrylogia, cacamphaton, pleonasmos, perissologia, macrologia, tautologia, eclipsis, tapinosis, cacosyntheton, amphibolia . . . amphibolia est ambiguitas dictionis.*

2   This pedagogical disapproval of ambiguity "was not seriously challenged until [the twentieth] century," as modern compositional textbooks illustrate (Atherton 1993, 483–484).

3   In the first book of the *Institutio*, Quintilian urges a father to begin the rhetorical training of his son "as soon as he is born" (*nato filio*, 1.1.1). For Quintilian's survey of philosophical debates surrounding the nature and purpose and rhetoric, see *Institutio* 2.11–21.

4   Status theory is a rhetorical framework in which parties in a forensic dispute come to "a standing still" (*status*) in their arguments. For a brief history of status theory (also called *stasis* theory), see Dieter 1950. For a history of the development of status theory, see Nadeau 1959. For a discussion of Aristotelian influence on status theory, particularly regarding the forensic framework of *circumstantiae*, see Sloan 2010. For examples of discussions of status theory in Roman rhetorical manuals, see Cicero *De Inventione* I.10–16 and *Rhetorica ad Herennium* I.18–19.

5   As Quintilian himself notes, status theory extends to matters outside the courtroom, even if its primary and original application is to forensic oratory. See, for example, his application of this framework to deliberative oratory at 3.8.4–6.

6   This four-part collection of Latin terminology can be found at 3.6.88, where *amphibolia* is used instead of *ambiguitas*. A similar list at 3.6.66 includes *ambiguitas* in place of *amphibolia*. The two terms seem interchangeable in Quintilian's text within the context of the *status legales*.

7   Compare with *Rhetorica ad Herennium* 1.20: *Ex ambiguo controversia nascitur cum scriptum duas aut plures sententias significat.*

8   One recent study of the *Declamationes Maiores* explains that they include "a group of nineteen declamations composed by multiple authors from the end of the first through the beginning of the third centuries CE ... [and] hardly fit Quintilian's stricture that the scenario [of a declamatory exercise] should be plausible" (Bernstein 2013, 4).

The *Declamationes Minores*, too, often attributed to Quintilian's own hand, are possibly written by another expert rhetorician: "whether the [author of the minor declamations] is Quintilian is a disputable matter, and not one, perhaps, of the highest importance. There is no doubt that, if he is not Quintilian, he is an avid reader of the *Institutio*" (Winterbottom 1984, xiv).

9   This sentence includes the only mention of the word *ambiguitas* in both the *Declamationes Maiores* and *Declamtiones Minores* of Pseudo-Quintilian.

10   For a similar treatment of statutory ambiguity in another ancient author, see Seneca the Elder *Controversiae* 1.2. In this declamatory exercise, Seneca's interest in the inevitable lexical ambiguities that arise from a law's compact composition parallels the desertion case from Pseudo-Quintilian's *Declamationes Maiores*. Instead of considering a dead son who may have deserted a grieving parent, this Senecan example looks to the problems surrounding an erstwhile virgin, captured by pirates and forced into prostitution, who later wishes to become a priestess. The law, however, dictates that "a priestess must be chaste and from chaste people, pure and of pure people" (*Sacerdos casta e castis, pura, e puris sit*, 1.2). Seneca includes one approach to the case that focuses on the ambiguity of the adjective *castus* (1.2.15). For recent work on the place of status theory more generally in the works of Seneca the Elder, see Berti 2015. For a discussion of Quintilian's consideration of *controversiae* in his own rhetorical treatise, see Fantham 2011, 320–330.

11   Bonner 1949, 47. Bonner also reports that "the origins of [the conflict between *ius* and *aequitas*] are at least as old as Aristotle and the *Rhetorica ad Alexandrum*, and were fully formulated by Hermagoras long before they appeared in Cicero's youthful *De Inventione*" (47). For another investigation of *aequitas* and its role in legal interpretation, see Eden 2005, 1–19. For an Aristotelian discussion of the relationship between equity and the interpretation of the law, see *Nicomachean Ethics* 5.10.

12   After the "protracted, laborious pursuit of systematic rhetorical learning with all its technicalities and precision" in the earlier books of the *Institutio*, "the preliminaries are finished, the boy has grown up, and the complete orator, the *vir bonus dicendi peritus*, is seen in action in the courts and councils of Rome" (Austin 1948, ix).

[13] For one formulation of Quintilian's claim, see 12.1.3: "Indeed, I do not only say this, that he who is an orator ought to be a good man, but rather that a man will not even be an orator unless he is a good man" (*neque enim tantum id dico, eum qui sit orator virum bonum esse oportere, sed ne futurum quidem oratorem nisi virum bonum*). For discussions of this confounding formulation and its roots in Stoic thought, see Brinton 1983, Walzer 2003, and Winterbottom 1964.

[14] For the meaning of *perplexus* related to "cryptic" or "baffling" language, see *OLD* 2b. For the meaning of *aperire* as "to make known or clear by words," see *OLD* 12. Compare Tacitus *Histories* 2.78, where *aperire* is used to interpret the unclear language of an oracle: *has ambages et statim exceperat fama et tunc aperiebat*.

[15] As Diogenes Laertius suggests in his account of the Stoic Wise Man's need for dialectic, "rhetoric is essential to the Wise Man's living the virtuous life," and rhetoric and dialectic should each be understood as both "a science and a virtue" (Walzer 2003, 30). For Aristotle's various views on ambiguity, particularly as it bears on dialectic, see Bobzein 2008 and Hintikka 1959.

[16] This facility with *ambiguitas* bears on the first branch of philosophical training, and Quintilian admits that this ethical training sounds similar to and overlaps with the logical training he has just prescribed in the previous paragraphs: "part of this set of problems overflows into logic, and part into ethics" (*quorum pars ad rationalem, pars ad moralem tractatum redundat*, 12.2.19).

[17] Atherton 1993, 484–485. In her discussion, Atherton points to the *Rhetorica ad Herennium* 4.67 as an example of this more positive view of humorous ambiguity in antiquity.

[18] For Quintilian's reference to the *vilissimi* as the worst authors, unfit even to be kept in a library, see 11.3.4–5.

Peter Damian and the Language of Friendship: The Polysemy of *Caritas*

Kathryn L. Jasper

I n the history of the eleventh-century reform of religious life often called the "Gregorian Reform," few figures are as well known as Peter Damian (1007–1072/73),[1] an ascetic, biographer, polemicist, theologian, Roman cardinal, and spiritual writer. Damian's life and work touch on practically every aspect of this dynamic century. I focus here on the impact Damian exerted through his campaign of letter writing before and after joining the papal curia in 1057. One hundred and eighty letters from Damian's hand survive, dating from the period between 1035 and 1072. They reveal Damian creating what has been called a "friendship network"[2] in Italy and over the Alps, decades before Pope Gregory VII would do the same. A key element of this project was the Christian virtue of *caritas*, a word whose mean can seem ambiguous, shifting from passage to passage even in a single text. This ambiguity is in part due to the inadequacy of modern concepts like "charity" and "love" to accommodate the semantic complexity of *caritas*. It also emerges because *caritas* was for Damian an inherently twofold ethical concept, both compulsory, because personal relationships failed without it, and voluntary, because it had to be sincere. The ambiguity of *caritas* rendered it sufficiently malleable to suit Damian's monastic reforms, which depended on "real" friendship and mutual aid. Still, as I argue, one overarching principle guided Damian's use of the term: *caritas* was the tie that binds. It joined the faithful together, and sealed and guaranteed relationships. Scholars have identified this particular meaning with the twelfth century and its intellectual movements, but Damian's letters show it was already present in the eleventh century.

The classical tradition couched friendship in an ambivalence between mutual obligation and sincere generosity.[3] Aristotle described three levels of friendship in the *Nicomachean Ethics* (8-9), of which the highest included mutual perfecting.[4] Many Roman authors (Cicero, Lucan, Seneca, and Plutarch) built on the earlier Greek philosophy of friendship, but it was Cicero's *De Amicitia* that most influenced Late Antique notions of friendship. The Church Fathers, in turn, drew on Cicero's description of an ethics of friendship, appropriated from Aristotle, in which good men mutually improved each other's virtue.[5] In spite of Roman social practices that created friendships predicated on a principle of strict reciprocity (*do ut des*), Cicero criticized hypocrisy in *amicitia* and described a more sincere form of friendship. Seneca also grounded friendship in mutual cooperation.[6] In sum, only men of virtue maintained "real" friendships.[7]

Augustine of Hippo provided a framework for understanding *amicitia* vis-à-vis love of God. Early Christian authors hesitated to accept completely the pagan interpretation of friendship, and complicated *amicitia* by linking it to the Christian notion of *caritas*. In fact, Saint Ambrose considered the two words nearly interchangeable.[8] In monastic circles, the Benedictine Rule had cautioned brothers against personal friendship and excluded it from monastic life.[9] By the eleventh century, however, a distinct language of friendship was emerging in monastic circles.[10] Though it would take a century for monks to speak of "friendship" (*amicitia*) with Christ, already in Peter Damian's letters we can see a link between Christ's love and the friendship implied in the term *caritas*.[11] Nevertheless, the concept is problematic for Damian. *Caritas* was already being used as a synonym for God as "Divine Love,"[12] yet Damian argues that *caritas* must be created, cultivated, and nurtured. He creates ambiguity in identifying a false kind of *caritas*—the most dangerous variety, because *caritas* should be sincere. More significantly, *caritas* represents at once both a virtue (and thus is voluntary) and a duty (*officium*).

Like classical *amicitia*, the natural manifestation of *caritas* was reciprocity. Damian represented *caritas* as mutual cooperation founded on love. This view of *caritas* was not unique to Damian, of course. The English Cistercian Abbot Aelred of Rievaulx, in his treatise *De Speculo Caritatis*, composed around 1142–43, was among the first to reconcile monastic friendship with Cicero's concept of *amicitia*. [13] Aelred described *amicitia* as a prelapsarian bond to which we all must return, whereas *caritas* served Christians in their fallen state.[14] Julian Haseldine states: "If *caritas* was now at the heart of the religious vocation, Aelred's *De Speculo Caritatis* (*The Mirror of Charity*) set friendship in turn at the heart of monastic *caritas*."[15] I would argue that Peter Damian accomplished the same feat much earlier, and certainly Damian was a far more influential writer than Aelred of Rievaulx. Although he never engaged with Cicero's *De Amicitia* as directly as Aelred, in the context of eleventh-century reform movements Damian also formulated innovative ways to reconcile *caritas* and Ciceronian *amicitia* while relying primarily on a Scriptural understanding of *amicitia*. Like Aelred, he also described the interdependence of *caritas* and *amicitia*, in spite of Benedictine suspicions of friendships.

The manner in which Damian deploys the term *caritas* in his letters serves his reform agenda in precise ways. He focuses on reform at the level of a single institution or even of an individual, and he puts *caritas* into practice in these relationships. Take, for instance, Damian's description of the relationship between the community and the individual, which corresponds to his overall understanding of the Church. Between 1048 and 1053 Damian sent one of his most well-known works, *Dominus vobiscum* (*Lord Be with You*), to a hermit at Fonte Avellana named Leo.[16] The text justifies why a solitary celebrant would use plural pronouns during the Mass, but it also defines Damian's ecclesiology, by which each member of the faithful is the whole church, and by extension the entire church lies within the soul of the individual; therefore, he is never alone.[17] The audience for this letter, a community of hermits, could take comfort in this defense for performing the Mass alone in a cell. As head of Fonte Avellana's congregation, Damian consideres the individual monk or hermit as fundamental to the whole and each monastery as a pillar supporting the overall structure. The *glutinum* (literally, "glue") holding it all together was *caritas*.

Damian often cites Jerome's Vulgate when discussing *caritas*. Early in this letter he references Romans 5:5: "Karitas enim Dei diffusa est in cordibus nostris per Spiritum sanctum, qui datus est nobis."[18] Scholarship has long understood *caritas* in this passage in the sense of "divine love." The word Jerome translates as *caritas* is *agape* (ἀγάπη) in the Greek original, a concept that refers particularly to brotherly love and even charity. Using this passage, Damian draws upon an Augustinian idea that the Holy Spirit imbues the hearts of the all the faithful with *caritas* and creates a common connection.[19] In later passages, he states that because *caritas* is shared, the Church will remain strong.[20]

Although Jerome's text provides Damian with a functional term, we must also look beyond Scripture to understand what Damian is trying to express. While *caritas* dwells in every man, it can be activated or deactivated by its host; that is, an individual acts on *caritas*, or actively ignores its presence, of his own free will. *Caritas* is often modified by *fraterna* in the corpus of Damian's letters, but the phrase first appears in this particular letter. For Damian, *caritas* alone fails to express adequately the notion of "brotherly" love. He writes that a priest must not only hold the precepts of the Mass in his heart, but should also demonstrate them in his external behavior, thereby affirming that he is united (*foederatus*) with the congregation in brotherly love (*fraterna caritas*).[21] Strangely, the solitary cell of the priest-hermit promotes brotherly love, transforming a man suffering from vices, because it prevents their manifestation, and even turning odious men into ascetics devoted to *fraterna caritas*.[22] Solitude naturally lends itself to silence and chastity, and it eliminates vanities.

Damian further develops this idea of activating *caritas* in a rather amusing letter that records an incident between Damian and an "urban" hermit named Teuzo. Teuzo had previously lived at the monastery of Saint Mary located in the center of Florence. After a dispute with his abbot, the situation proved unsatisfying and he abandoned his life at the monastery in favor of a hermit's cell. His abbot believed his decision in error and asked Peter Damian to set him straight. Damian accepted the request, not least of all because Teuzo had erected his cell in the middle of town, hardly an appropriate place for a hermit's wilderness. More problematic was Teuzo's presence in Florence as a radical ascetic. Although Damian himself had accepted the position of Cardinal Bishop of Ostia by 1057, he never argued that monks should live in the secular world.[23] His biting letter to Teuzo begins with a nod to *caritas* in his greeting, which he dispatches with *resuendae charitatis aculeum* ("a needle for sewing charity back together"), because the love between the two men required repair.[24] *Caritas* serves as the binding agent of the relationship. This greeting indicated that, for Damian, the relationship with Teuzo has lost *caritas*.

As the letter explains, Damian had previously met Teuzo in Florence, but the hermit had rejected his admonishments and forcibly expelled Damian from his cell, dragging him out by the cord of his robes. Damian regularly urged monastic reform at the individual and institutional levels, and he refused to give up on Teuzo. In the letter, Damian's line of reasoning hinges largely on *caritas* and reveals that he uses the word to express humility. Teuzo's primary transgression represented a lack of humility, which Damian addresses by articulating a correct view of *caritas*, reminding Teuzo that in a friendship between two individuals, one friend seemingly loves the other less if he excuses injury inflicted upon him by his friend. If this man refuses to speak on the matter under the pretense of understanding, he does his brother no favors and his *caritas* appears lessened (*imminuta*). Sincere *caritas* requires a brother to reprimand his friend; only by acknowledging his sin can the latter recover *caritas*. Damian personifies *caritas* as the judge of the situation. *Caritas* becomes responsible for preventing both men from sinning, one through feigned resignation and the other through giving offense.[25] *Caritas*, therefore, resting inside both men, must prevent the corruption of each through his own initiative and through self-denial; that is, each man must deny his self-serving behavior. The former should voice his complaint and the latter should seek forgiveness.

Once again, *caritas* must be activated. A monk performs an act driven by *caritas*, but, without action, *caritas* remains latent. In this case, mere "charity" or "love" falls short of characterizing the role of *caritas* in Damian's thinking; a combination of the two terms with the addition of the Benedictine understanding of humility would be more appropriate. While Damian regards *caritas* as innate in every man, he also makes it clear that it needs nurturing in order to function. That act requires both parties to humble themselves for reciprocal benefit. The Christian concept of charity understands the transaction between donor and recipient as reciprocal and mutually humbling. In the Gospel of Matthew (6:1–2), Jesus cautions that seeking recognition in giving alms essentially negates the act. The Benedictine interpretation links Christian humility to obedience and to the denial of self-will.[26] In this sense, Damian argued for submission (obedience) to *caritas*.

Damian also views *caritas* as more than the foundation of friendship. An act of *caritas* can repair the relationship. Damian had once entered Teuzo's cell to act as arbiter between the abbot and the former monk. He had focused his arguments on friendship, which he understood as an extension of *caritas*. At the time he received only an unkind rebuke as a reward for the offered *caritas*.[27] His subsequent letter gives numerous examples of ideal friendship (among those he deemed proper hermits, living in the wilderness) buoyed by a *caritas* consisting of humility and kindness. One anecdote Damian had heard well before his conversion to the eremitic life recounted the story of two men of Faenza. During an argument, one man blinded the other. The blind man then became a monk. Some time later, his assailant fell ill and also pondered the monastic life, but avoided the monastery in which his former victim resided. When the blind man overheard his brethren discussing the possibility of allowing this man to enter the community, he requested that his brothers receive him with complete *caritas* (*ut illum fratres cum omni charitate susciperent*).[28] He further asked to care for the man personally and to act as his servant (*custodem scilicet ac ministrum eius*).[29] The blind man performed his office guided by *caritas*, a charity anchored in humility. His sincere *caritas* was always voluntary and never imposed by an authority or required by an office.[30] The letter makes clear that the most alarming aspect of Teuzo's situation was the lack of humility, historically an essential feature of monastic life, which contributed directly to the failure of *caritas* in the friendship between Teuzo and Damian. Teuzo is in spiritual danger because his behavior displays the vice of pride rather than the virtue of humility. Living in the center of town, he makes an exhibition of his asceticism and inflates his arrogance. Damian advises Teuzo to reconcile himself with his brothers, to rebuild his friendships through patience and *caritas*, and to emulate the humility of Christ.

While *caritas* should be spontaneous and voluntary, it is also an essentially ambiguous virtue, since Damian obliges monks to exercise it. The performance of *caritas* appears in his letters sometimes as *officium caritatis*, which corresponds to the notion of responsibility imposed by monastic vows. But Damian uses this language even when communicating to bishops. In 1059, Damian asked two bishops to edit his writings for errors. At the close of the letter, he asks that his beloved friends honor their friendship (*veteris amicitie*) and fulfill this "obligation of friendship" (*officio caritatis*) even after Damian's death.[31] In the same year, Damian sent a very different letter to Archdeacon Hildebrand, also a member of the Roman curia, a former monk, and the future Pope Gregory VII. Hildebrand and Damian failed to see eye-to-eye on a number of issues, and Hildebrand received more than a few harsh words from his colleague. Indeed, Damian likes to refer to him as his "Holy Satan."[32] In this particular letter Damian expresses his displeasure at Hildebrand's support for a prominent Tuscan family's claim to the land on which he had founded the monastery of Acereta. According to Damian, retainers of the Guidi family had brought false evidence to the court, and Hildebrand had shown uncharacteristically poor judgment in supporting their case. After Damian expounds the merits of his own argument, he wishes Hildebrand God's forgiveness for his lapse in good judgment. He also tells the archdeacon that Hildebrand will be rewarded in heaven for his discharge of the "obligation of friendship" (*officium caritas*).[33] As in the previous letter, the word *officium* in this context carries a sense of duty, which conveys to Hildebrand that their relationship bound each man to act with kindness toward the other. The word allows Damian to express the desire for a favor while at the same time expressing an implied obligation.

For Damian, the root of the above-mentioned conflict with the Guidi retainers is avarice. Damian devotes many pages to the subject of avarice, as he did to *caritas*, because avarice represents its unqualified opposite. The Augustinian tradition also positions *cupiditas* against *caritas*.[34] In Patricia Ranft's study of Damian's letters, she identifies the core of his theology as the concept of witness. As Ranft writes, "[Witness] is an inclusive title used to express the totality of [the Apostles'] faith and their social responsibility. Here is the historical significance of witness. It mandates a relationship between the individual and the community. It is a relationship of communication and interdependence; to be saved one must save others."[35] The idea of witness is the foundation of Damian's theology as well as of his ecclesiology. He characterizes the foundation of the Church as the interdependence of the individual and the community. Avarice goes directly to the heart of the notion of witness because one's salvation depends on saving others. As Damian writes, the vice of avarice can drag the faithful away from fraternal charity.[36]

Damian's usage of the word *caritas* reveals something of a paradox, then. *Caritas* stands alongside humility and obedience as a core monastic virtue. On the one hand, it remains voluntary, as did all virtues. On the other hand, Damian makes it compulsory. Christianity had long accepted this ambiguity. While the sacraments were voluntary, performed and received with a willing heart, conversion absolutely demanded acceptance and action by the initiate. Even forced conversions in the early Middle Ages failed to be effective unless initiates voluntarily accepted baptism according to canon law, though the threat of death could render the idea of a voluntary baptism dubious. Likewise, the monastic life stipulated strict adherence to a rule (in this case, the Rule of St. Benedict), and failure to adhere to its principles and to maintain certain virtues could lead to excommunication.[37] Damian reasons that turning away from *fraterna caritas* made his brothers vulnerable to vices such as pride and greed.[38] He wrote to the schismatic canons of Fano in 1051 that even faith (*fides*) itself was no more important than *caritas*, for God and *caritas* were one and the same (I Corinthians 13). To retreat from *caritas* was to err in the faith. He calls *caritas* a law and therefore a divine commandment, and argues that if a man follows each divine law but abandons charity, then he has failed in all.[39]

In a later letter composed after 1067, Damian identifies a false *caritas* born of insincerity,[40] lacking both external and internal commitment to mutual love.[41] In 1067 Damian explained to Abbot Mainard of the monastery of Pomposa that *fraterna caritas* functions much like the Ark. As God commanded Noah to place pitch on both the inside and the outside of the Ark, so *caritas* must simultaneously live within and be expressed without, in complete sincerity. If a monk holds *caritas* in his heart for his brethren but remains at odds with them, he is no better than the monk who maintains false friendships while internally lacking sincere love for his brothers.[42] This passage evokes the brotherly love Damian sought to cultivate at Fonte Avellana.

Caritas takes on this meaning of reciprocity in the context of one of Damian's most important monastic reforms. In the tradition established by Saint Romuald, which recalled a far more ancient approach to monasticism, Peter Damian founded dual communities of monks and hermits. Unlike Romuald, however, Damian placed the houses at some distance from one another to ensure that the laxity of the monastery did not interfere with the stricter asceticism of the hermitage. This approach to monastic life contrasts sharply with the urban asceticism Damian criticized in his letter to Teuzo. Damian's hermits lived in individual huts, went barefoot throughout the year, and observed a regimen of prayer and fasting more rigorous than that of the monks, who followed the Benedictine Rule, a far gentler approach to monastic life. The congregation of Fonte Avellana included four hermitages and two monasteries.[43] Two of these hermitages held special relationships with nearby monasteries in the congregation. The hermitage of Fonte Avellana provided the monastery of Saint Bartholomew at Camporeggiano (near the city of Gubbio) with an example of ideal conversion and a place to "graduate" to a higher level of asceticism; in turn, the monastery cared for sick hermits when required.[44] The monastery of Saint John in Acereta (located in the Apennines near the modern town of Marradi) maintained a similar relationship with the hermitage of Saint Barnabas at Gamogna, roughly four kilometers distant. The two houses also held a common patrimony.

In a letter sent to his brother Stephen at Fonte Avellana in 1057, Damian revised his original rule for the hermits in the congregation. This second version of the rule indicates that the most important virtue in the community was mutual charity. When a brother died, for example, each hermit would accept a substantial penance that included fasting for seven days, performing seven hundred prostrations and seven self-flagellations with one thousand lashes each, chanting thirty psalters, and celebrating Mass for the deceased for thirty consecutive days.[45] The charters recording legal transactions at Fonte Avellana confirm that the monastery and the hermitage carried out these mutual obligations. In 1063 the abbot of Saint Bartholomew reconfirmed an earlier agreement (1057) between the monastery and the hermitage of Fonte Avellana that included a provision requiring the housing and care of sick hermits (*restaurandum*). Damian, present for the signing of the document, probably influenced its composition. The charter strategically employed the word *caritas* to describe the nature of the arrangement: "we have accepted with charity your monks who may remain at any time [at our monastery] to live or to recuperate."[46] A 1060 charter outlined a similar commitment on the part of the monastery at Acereta, which obligated the monks to receive sick hermits from Gamogna. In turn Gamogna would receive any monks coming from the monastery seeking the eremitic life.[47] This charter made no reference to an additional aspect of life in these dual communities that is recorded in Saint Bartholomew's 1057 charter, which had required the monks to share moveable goods with the hermits *cum caritate*.[48] The phrase implied travel between the two communities, and the sharing of property would have facilitated friendships, ideally grounded in *caritas*.[49] Damian once likened administration of property in a monastery to such examples in the Apocrypha as Nehemiah's sacrificing his own sheep to feed strangers at a feast (Esdras 5:14–19), and to Tobias, who shared what little he had (Tobias 2:19). These men, he wrote, exercised the duty and responsibility (*officium*) of *caritas*. He further said that a monastery should help outsiders (*extraneis*) whenever possible.[50] He thus legally mandated that the brothers of both houses extend favors and courtesies (*caritas*) to each other and to strangers.

The Roman paradigm of *amicitia* demanded reciprocity (*gratia*) for favors (*beneficia*).[51] Roman and Christian virtue intuited expressions of gratitude as voluntary and sincere, and at the same time mandatory. As a result, gift giving highlighted the paradox in *caritas*. Damian adamantly spoke against the exchange of material gifts as a requisite for friendship.[52] He believed that gift-giving could easily lead to bribery, and he urged bishops to avoid the corruption of avarice born of accepting gifts.[53] But he also recognized *caritas* in two separate interactions involving gifts. When Damian traveled to Milan in 1060 as papal legate, the abbot of the nearby monastery of Saint Simplicianus sent him a silver vase. Damian suspected the vase was a bribe and eventually met with the abbot in person. He asked if the abbot had any pending business with the Holy See. The abbot insisted he did not and claimed his gift represented only an offer of friendship. Damian responded that friendship among monks, unlike friendship among those in the world, should never carry a price.[54] Eventually he accepted the vase on behalf of two monasteries he had recently founded. He then returned to his cell at Fonte Avellana, where he was tormented by a remorse he likened to worms chewing his insides. Although Damian believed that the abbot's gift had been sincere and without obligation, he nevertheless felt defeated by his own avarice. He returned the vase.

Damian usually refused gifts. But a few years after he recounted the story of the silver vase, he willingly accepted another: two stoles from Archbishop Guido of Milan. What made this case different? A simple answer would be that refusing the archbishop's gifts could jeopardize the papacy's objectives in Milan. Damian undoubtedly had complicated motives, and we cannot know them all. He himself expressed confusion about his behavior, mentioning his past refusal of gifts and lamenting the danger of avarice. In the end he felt compelled by *caritas* to accept, writing that *caritas* inspired the gift and bound him to receive it.[55] *Caritas* in this case provided a mutual favor to both donor and recipient. Not only *caritas* but also the love of Christ moved the archbishop to relieve his servant of tattered clothes and to adorn him with priestly vestments.[56] The ambiguity emerges in Damian's statement that because he was not ungrateful (*non ingratus*) he had therefore *repaid* the archbishop (*vicissitudinem compensavi*) by inscribing his name in monasteries far and wide and including him in the prayers of his brothers. Possibly the bishop's name was inscribed in the *libri memoriales*, and that may have been the goal of the donation.[57] This reciprocity went beyond an exchange of *caritas* in an abstract sense. A material gift resulted in a reciprocal gift, complicating Damian's earlier argument to the abbot of Saint Simplicianus.

Damian rendered the bonds of *amicitae* akin to those of *caritas* when he wrote to the Florentines about their efforts to remove the alleged simoniac Bishop Peter Mezzabarba. Extending his observance of fraternal charity (*fraternae caritatis obsequium*) to the citizens of Florence, Damian proposed a mutual cooperation with the Florentines to reconcile the bishop with his see. To resolve the conflict would be to repair the severed bonds of friendship (*amicitiae, quae rescissa fuerat, foedera reformantes, in unum vos spiritum sequestra pace conflare*).[58] This passage brings Damian's letter to Teuzo to mind, with its request to restore *caritas* between the two men. As Damian wrote in a letter to the Burgundian monastery of Cluny, repairing the bonds of friendship with forgiveness mirrors the Divine remission of sins.[59] (Aelred of Rievaulx also saw a connection between friendship and salvation.) Ultimately Damian understood that friendship in the monastery existed to support the community. As Brian McGuire notes, it was not until Anselm of Canterbury that monastic discourses about friendship returned to Cicero and the reciprocity of virtue among individuals.[60]

Amicitia and *caritas* were not entirely identical in this context. Only a friendship (*amicitia*) grounded in *caritas* meliorated Benedictine misgivings of the concept. Moreover, a friendship without *caritas* would inevitably fail. *Amicitia* between the bishop and his congregation in Florence collapsed without *caritas*. That Damian's relationship with Teuzo could not continue until *caritas* had been mended underlines the active role of both parties maintaining it. As the letters make clear, acts of *caritas* demanded a sincere and willing heart.[61] But its presence was absolutely mandatory for friendship to exist. Paradoxically, one had simultaneously to manifest sincere *caritas* in friendship and witness it in action.

The word *caritas* appears many dozens of times in Damian's corpus, often repeatedly in a single letter, as well as in the charters of Fonte Avellana and its daughter houses. Damian himself wanted no misunderstandings or ambiguities, since *caritas* was the foundation of his reforms—not just at Fonte Avellana, but also in other communities and in other relationships. Nonetheless, he created a host of ambiguous meanings in describing this complex concept. *Caritas* had to be in earnest, and therefore had to be voluntary. At the same time, it was a monastic virtue: by definition, an office, a duty, and an obligation. This complex notion of *caritas* was paramount to Damian's reforms because it expressed perfectly the spirit of community. It stood for mutual cooperation, reciprocal aid, and sincere friendship. Damian never stopped short at an idea; he attempted to put his polemic into practice. At Fonte Avellana, we find observances unique to that congregation, such as the sharing of goods and resources, the travel of monks and hermits between communities, and care for for sick hermits at nearby monasteries. The idea of a congregation as a community united in *caritas* predominated in both Damian's communications and internal legislation. Damian put words into action outside the congregation as well. He advocated for *caritas* as the supreme monastic virtue in other communities, such as the monastery at Pomposa and the cathedral canons at Fano.

Damian's letter reveal that he spent most of his life trying to manifest *caritas* in action. The monastery of Acereta and the hermitage of Gamogna argued frequently over their shared patrimony. In 1060 Damian formally adjudicated a dispute between them and divided all properties held in common, but still mandated the care of sick hermits at the monastery.[62] Several years later, Damian similarly ended the practice of shared moveable goods in the congregation of Fonte Avellana. He mandated, under threat of excommunication, that after his death the brothers return any outside property to the monastery from which it came.[63] He wrote that while he hoped the same *caritas* that united them during his life would continue after his death, he ended the practice of shared goods to prevent disputes, lest their *caritas* cool (*ne frigescente forsitan caritate*). Here again he expresses his wish that *caritas* be both innate and self-generated.

During the contentious decades of the mid-eleventh century and the subsequent civil war between papal and imperial supporters, Damian's words carried enormous weight. His communications provide a persuasive argument for polygenesis in monastic reform; his reforms responded to local concerns. The inherent polysemy of *caritas* encapsulates the ideas that Damian most valued: cooperation, sincerity, humility, and love of God. The brokering of relationships contained in charters of Fonte Avellana show the tangible effects of his designs, realized within his own hermitage. Decades before Bernard of Clairvaux took his vows, Damian's initiatives anticipated the twelfth-century Cistercians, often celebrated as pioneers of the notion of a united congregation of monasteries. The founding of Cistercian governance was, in fact, recorded in a document called the *Carta Caritatis* (*Charter of Charity* or *Charter of Love*). But we should locate the origins of such reforms in the previous century, and especially among the monks and hermits of north-central Italy.[64]

* * *

In July 2008 I was studying Latin in Rome with Reginald Foster when he was called away for health reasons. A few of the more exceptional students organized to keep the course going in his absence. We met every single day at the appointed time and place and kept up our lessons, together. We frequently visited our beloved teacher, and when we told him what we had done his eyes welled with tears. He was and is a teacher who inspires such love, enthusiasm, and dedication to Latin that his students would carry on even in his absence. Over sixty people collectively decided to stay in Rome, despite the expense, to continue in a class that had lost its charismatic teacher. I studied with Reggie in 2003, 2004, and 2008, and he has been the single most important influence on my teaching. This essay is dedicated to him in the hope that he might see the fruition of his Latin lessons.

BIBLIOGRAPHY

Powell, J. G. F., ed. 2006. *M. Tulli Ciceronis De re publica; De legibus; Cato maior de senectute; Laelius de amicitia.* Oxford: Oxford University Press.

Bartlett, Robert C., and Susan D. Collins, eds. 2011. *Aristotle's Nicomachean Ethics.* Chicago: University of Chicago Press.

Blum, Owen J., ed. 1989–2005. *The Letters of Peter Damian.* Washington, DC: Catholic University Press.

Classen, Albrecht. 2010. "Friendship—The Quest for a Human Ideal and Value from Antiquity to Early Modern Time." In *Friendship in the Middle Ages and Early Modern Age: Explorations of a Fundamental Ethical Discourse,* ed. Albrecht Classen and Marilyn Sandidge, 1–183. Berlin: Walter de Gruyter.

Cariboni, Guido. 2008. "*Fraterna karitas utrumque in Christi amore connectat.* Ideali fondativi e dinamiche instituzionali presso i monasteri romagnoli legati a Pier Damiani." In *Pier Damiani e il monastero di San Gregorio in Conca nella Romagna del secolo XI*, Atti del Convegno di studio in occasione del primo millenario della nascita di Pier Damiani (1007–2007), ed. Nicolangelo D'Acunto, 105–118. Spoleto: Centro italiano di studi sull'alto medioevo.

Carosso, Marinella. 2009. "Le relazioni del dono. Chiavi di lettura recenti di un classic dell'antropologia. " In *Benefattori e beneficati: La relazione asimmetrica nel* beneficiis *di Seneca*, ed. Giusto Picone, Lucia Beltrami, and Licinia Ricottilli, 47–95. Palermo: Palumbo.

Cassidy, E. G. 1999. "'He who has friends can have no friend': Classical and Christian Perspectives on the Limits of Friendship." In *Friendship in Medieval Europe*, ed. Julian Haseldine, 45–67. Stroud, UK: Sutton Publishing.

D'Acunto, Nicolangelo. 2008. "Pier Damiani e gli esordi del monastero di S. Gregorio in Conca di Morciano." In *Pier Damiani e il monastero di San Gregorio in Conca nella Romagna del secolo XI*, Atti del Convegno di studio in occasione del primo millenario della nascita di Pier Damiani (1007–2007), ed. Nicolangelo D'Acunto, 119–146. Spoleto: Centro italiano di studi sull'alto medioevo.

Haseldine, Julian P. 2010. "Monastic Friendship in Theory and Action in the Twelfth Century." In *Friendship in the Middle Ages and Early Modern Age: Explorations of a Fundamental Ethical Discourse*, eds. Albrecht Classen and Marilyn Sandidge, 349–393. Berlin: Walter de Gruyter.

———. 2006. "Friends, Friendship and Networks in the Letters of Bernard of Clairvaux." Citeaux: *Commentarii Cistercienses* 57:243–279.

———. 1996. "Friendship, Equality, and Universal Harmony: The Universal and the Particular in Aelred of Rievaulx's *De Spiriutali Amicitia*." In *Friendship East and West: Philosophical Perspectives*, ed. Oliver Leaman, 192–214. Richmond, UK: Curzon.

———. 1994. "Understanding the language of amicitia. The criendship circle of Peter of Celle (c. 1115–1183)." *Journal of Medieval History* 20, 3:237–260.

Fitzgerald, John T. 1997. "Friendship in the Greek World Prior to Aristotle." In *Greco-Roman Perspectives on Friendship*, ed. John. T. Fitzgerald, 13–34. Atlanta, GA: Scholars Press.

Fry, Timothy, ed. 1981. *RB 1980: The Rule of St. Benedict in Latin and English*. Collegeville, Minn.: Liturgical Press.

Hoste, A., and C. H. Talbot, eds. 1971. *Aelredi Rievallensis Opera Omnia*, 1., *opera ascetica*, Corpus Christianorum Coninuatio Medievalis, 1, 2–161, 279–350. Turnhout: Brepols.

Howe, John. 2010. "Did St Peter Damian Die in 1073? A New Perspective on his Final Days." *Analecta Bollandiana* 128:67–86.

Jaeger, Stephen. 2010. "Friendship of Mutual Perfecting in Augustine's *Confessions* and the Failure of Classical *amicitia*." In *Friendship in the Middle Ages and Early Modern Age: Explorations of a Fundamental Ethical Discourse*, ed. Albrecht Classen and Marilyn Sandidge, 185–200. Berlin: Walter de Gruyter.

Jasper, K. L. 2012. "Reforming the Monastic Landscape: Peter Damian's Design for Personal and Communal Devotion." In *Rural Space in the Middle Ages and Early Modern Age: The Spatial Turn in Pre-modern Studies*, ed. Albrecht Classen, 193–207. Berlin: Walter de Gruyter.

Jestice, Phyllis G. 1997. *Wayward Monks and the Religious Revolution of the Eleventh Century* Leiden: Brill.

McAvoy, James. 1999. "The Theory of Friendship in the Latin Middle Ages: Hermeneutics, Contextualization and the Transmission and Reception of Ancient Texts and Ideas, from c. AD 350–c. 1500." In *Friendship in Medieval Europe*, ed. Julian Haseldine, 3–44. Stroud, UK: Sutton Publishing.

McDonie, R. Jacob. 2010. "Mysterious Friends in the *Prayers* and Letters of Anselm of Canterbury." In *Friendship in the Middle Ages and Early Modern Age: Explorations of a Fundamental Ethical Discourse*, ed. Albrecht Classen and Marilyn Sandidge, 309–348. Berlin: Walter de Gruyter.

McGuire, Brian Patrick. 1988. *Friendship and Community: The Monastic Experience, 350-1250.* Kalamazoo: Cistercian Publications, Inc.

Messina, Patrick A. 2011. "Love Lost and Found: The Ambiguities of *Amor, Caritas,* and *Concupiscentia* in St Thomas Aquinas' *Summa Theologiae.*" In *Confessions of Love: The Ambiguities of Greek* Eros *and Latin* Caritas, ed. Craig J. N. de Paulo, Bernhardt Blumenthal, Catherine Conroy de Paolo, Patrick A. Messina, and Leonid Rudnytzky, 55-73. New York: Peter Lang Publishing.

O'Donnel, James J., ed. 1992. *Augustine's Confessions.* Oxford: Oxford University Press.

O'Neil, Edward N. 1997. "Plutarch on Friendship." In *Greco-Roman Perspectives on Friendship,* ed. John. T. Fitzgerald, 105-122. Atlanta, GA: Scholars Press.

Pierucci, Celestino, and Alberto Polverari, eds. 1972. *Carte di Fonte Avellana, i Regesti degli anni 975-1139.* Rome: Edizioni di Storia e Letteratura.

Raccanelli, Renata. 2009. "Cambiare il dono: per una pragmatica delle relazioni nel *de beneficiis* senecano." In *Benefattori e beneficati: La relazione asimmetrica nel* de beneficiis *di Seneca,* ed. Giusto Picone, Lucia Beltrami, and Licinia Ricottilli, 303-356. Palermo: Palumbo.

―――. 1998. *L'amicitia nelle commedie di Plauto: Un'indagine antropologica.* Bari: Edipuglia.

Ranft, Patricia. 2011. *The Theology of Peter Damian: 'Let Your Life Always Serve as a Witness.'* Washington. D.C., Catholic University of America Press.

Reindel, Kurt, ed. 1983-1993. *Die Briefe des Petrus Damiani.* Munich: Monumenta Germaniae Historica.

Robinson, I. S. 1978. "The Friendship Network of Gregory VII." *History* 63:1-22.

Testard, M. 2001. *S. Ambrosii De Officiis Clericorum.* Corpus Christianorum Series Latina, 15. Turnholt: Brepols.

Van den Hout, M. P. J., M. Evans, J. Bauer, R. Vander Plaetse, S. D. Ruegg, M. V. O'Reilly, R.

Vander Plaetse, and C. Beukers, eds. 1969. *S. Augustini De Fide Rerum Invisibilium. Enchiridion ad Laurentium, de Fide, Spe, e Caritate.* Corpus Christianorum Series Latina, 46. Turnhout: Brepols.

Verboven, Koenraad. 2002. *The Economy of Friends. Economic Aspects of Amicitia and Patronage in the Late Republic.* Bruxelles: Éditions Latomus.

Wilcox, Amanda. 2012. *The Gift of Correspondence in Classical Rome: Friendship in Cicero's* Ad Familiares *and Seneca's* Moral Epistles. Madison, WI: University of Wisconsin Press.

ENDNOTES

[1] Howe 2010, 67–86.

[2] Robinson 1978, 1–22.

[3] For a good discussion on this subject, see Verboven 2002, 35–48, Fitzgerald 1997, 13–34, and O'Neil 1997, 105–122.

[4] Aristotle, *Nicomachean Ethics*, 9.12.3, 1172a.

[5] Cicero, *Laelius de Amicitia* 5.18.

[6] Raccanelli 2009, 303–356.

[7] Jaeger 2010, 187–189; McAvoy 1999, 6; Cassidy 1999.

[8] Ambrose, *De Officiis* III, xxi–xxii; McAvoy 1999, 32.

[9] *Regula Benedicti*, chapters 2, 54, 63, 69, 71; Haseldine 2010, 351n9; McGuire 1988, xiv.

[10] For a good overview see Classen 2010, 1–183.

[11] McGuire 1988, 208–209.

[12] Reindel 1983–1993, Letter 165, 230.

[13] Haseldine, 2010, 351. Both of Aelred's treatises on friendship, *De Speculo Caritatis* and *De Spirituali Amicitia*, appear in the same critical edition: A. Hoste and C. H. Talbot 1971, 2–161, 279–350.

[14] Haseldine, 2010, 352. See also Haseldine 1994, 237–260, Haseldine 1996, 192–214, Haseldine 2006, 243–279.

[15] Haseldine, 2010, 351.

[16] The English editions (Blum, 1989–2005) offer further details about the addressees of Damian's letters. As Blume notes, the identity of Leo in the letter is unclear, as Damian communicated with three different

monks by that name. Most likely this man was Leo of Sitria (see Blum 1989, Letter 28, 255–256n2).

[17] Reindel 1983–1993, Letter 28, 256, *sancta aecclesia et in omnibus sit una et in singulis tota, nimirum in pluribus per fidei unitatem simplex et in singulis per karitatis glutinum diversaque dona karismatum multiplex, quia enim ex uno omnes, omnes unum.*

[18] Reindel, 1983–1993, Letter 28, 256.

[19] *Augustini Confessiones* 4.4.7.

[20] For example: "Sancta namque aecclesia licet personarum sit multiplicitate diversa, in unum tamen est sancti Spiritus igne conflata atque idea etiam, si per corporalem situm partibus videatur dividi, unitatis tamen intimae sacramentum nullatenus a sua valet integritate corrumpi" (Reindel 1983–1993, Letter 28, 256).

[21] "Sacerdos ergo, ut hoc dominicum praeceptum non solum corde custodiat, sed etiam per exterioris speciem ritus ostendat, antequam Deo fundendae orationis offerat sacrificium, per mutuae salutationis indicium ostendit se in fraterna karitate unanimiter foederatum" (Reindel 1983–1993, Letter 28, 271).

[22] "O cella spititale prorsus habitaculum, quae de superbis humiles, de gulosis sobrios, de crudelibus pios, de iracundis mites, de odiosis reddis in fraterna karitate ferventes" (Reindel 1983–1993, Letter 28, 276).

[23] Jestice 1997, 222.

[24] Reindel 1983–1993, Letter 44, 7.

[25] Ibid., Letter 44, 8.

[26] *Regula Benedicti*, Ch. 7.

[27] Reindel 1983–1993, Letter 44, 11–12.

[28] Ibid., Letter 44, 31.

[29] Ibid., Letter 44, 31.

[30] Ibid., Letter 44, 31.

[31] Ibid., Letter 62, 220.

[32] For example, see Letter 57 (Reindel 1983–1993, Letter 57, 167).

[33] "Deus omnipotens,venerabilis frater, et ex impensae karitatis officio multiplex tibi praemium reddat . . ." (Reindel 1983–1993, Letter 63, 225).

[34] Messina 2011, 57. Augustine, *Enchiridion ad laurentium sive fide, spe, e caritate* CXXI.

[35] Ranft 2011, 8–11.

36 Ibid., 145. See Reindel 1983–1993, Letter 39, 378.

37 *Regula Benedicti*, ch. 24.

38 See Reindel 1983–1993, Letter 39, 378.

39 Ibid., Letter 39, 378.

40 Towards the end of his life Damian's tone and attitude lost the hopefulness of his earlier letters.

41 Although Peter Damian never referenced Plautus specifically when writing about false *caritas*, in his understanding of *caritas* we find echoes of what Renata Raccanelli has defined as a "theory of false friendship" in the plays of Plautus (see Raccanelli 1998, 78–81).

42 See Reindel 1983–1993, Letter 153, 65.

43 The community of Saint Gregory at Conca is excluded here, as it never observed the practices and ideals established by the congregation. See D'Acunto 2008, 119.

44 See the discussion on this approach to monastic life in Jasper 2012, 193–207

45 See Reindel 1983–1993, Letter 50, 98–99.

46 "Quod si aliquo t(em)pore vestros monachos ibidem ponere ad habitandum vel ad restaurandum, cum caritate accepimus" (Pierucci and Polverari 1972, doc. 18, 47).

47 "Hac eciam nostra precepcione decernimus ut monasterium et heremus hoc inter se invicem debeant quatinus, cum necessarium fuerit, et monasterium infirmos fratres heremi ad refocillandum et sustentandum usque ad sanitatem cum licencia prioris fraterna benignitate suscipiat et heremite fratres heremi monachus de monasterio venientes, cum licencia abbatis, libenter admittant" (Pierucci and Polverari 1972, doc. 15, p. 38).

48 "Quod si aliquo t(em)pore vestros monachos ibi ponere ad abitandum vel aliquid vestris usibus tollere cum caritate" (Pierucci and Polverari 1972, doc. 15, 27).

49 As discussed below, Damian ended the practice of shared goods between 1065 and 1071 (Reindel 1983–1993, Letter 134, 455–56).

50 Reindel 1983–1993, Letter 153, 51.

51 In practice, granting and exchanging favors in the Middle Ages became just as complicated as it had been in Cicero's and Seneca's day. On the historical and epistemological foundations of gift-giving in the Classical world see Wilcox 2012 and Carosso 2009, 47–95.

52 *Gratia* came to refer to Christian grace.

53 For example, see Reindel 1983–1993, Letter 97, 64–83.

54 "Respondi, ut quod suum erat tollens, amicitiam nostram non more saecularium mercede redimeret, sed quod inter fratres legitimum est, gratuito possideret" (Reindel 1983–1993, Letter 76, 382).

55 Reindel 1983–1993, Letter 101, 117.

56 Damian's interpretation turned Christological: Christ received new garments from an angel in exchange for his filthy ones (Zachariah, 3, 3–4). The angel stripped Jesus, here embodying the Church, of grief and sadness and clothed him in the glory of blessed immortality. According to Reindel, the letter dates to ca. 1063. "[E]t corpus Iesu, quod est aecclesia, omni luctus atque tristitiae squalore deposito beatae inmortalitatis Gloria vestietur . . ." (Reindel 1983–1993, Letter 101, 117).

57 [E]t extraneis atque longuinquis et heremis et monasteriis vestrum nomen adsciberem, fratrumque vos orationibus humili devotionis studio commendarem (Reindel 1983–1993, Letter 101, 117).

58 Reindel 1983–1993, Letter 146, 532–33.

59 Ibid., Letter 100, 103.

60 McGuire 1988, 134–179; McDonie 2010, 311–313.

61 See Cariboni 2008, 105–118.

62 Pierucci and Polverari, doc. 15, 36. The charter also required the hermits to receive willingly any monks who sought the eremitic life.

63 Reindel 1983–1993, Letter 134, 455–56.

64 I owe sincere thanks to the editors of this volume for their erudite suggestions on earlier versions. I am also profoundly grateful to my predecessor at Illinois State University, Professor Emeritus John B. Freed, for his time in reading multiple drafts and for his excellent comments.

The Ever-Ending Story: The Role of Ambiguity In Supplements to the *Aeneid*

Patrick M. Owens

A ncient epic poetry is set in a surreal and otherworldly landscape of gods and heroes which is populated by mysterious creatures, plays tricks with time and space, and blends the worlds of men and beasts, the living and the dead. The dreamlike quality that characterizes heroic myth allows—even compels—the audience to suspend disbelief, tolerate inconsistencies, and embrace the narrative ambiguities and alternative dimensions of myth. While this hypnogogic quality is often recognizable in those parts of the narrative that pertain to the supernatural,[1] it is particularly noticeable at the dénouement of the narrative. Ancient epics are characterized by vague and indefinite endings[2] that often leave readers uncertain about subsequent action.[3] This ambiguity permeates the whole range of Latin and Greek epic poetry, from the oral tradition before the ninth century BCE to the Vergilian continuators of the seventeenth century CE. As the genre of ancient epic developed, ambiguity became one of its defining features. While scholarship has already addressed the ambiguity of epic codas in classical literature, this chapter will examine the nature of such ambiguity in Renaissance supplements to the *Aeneid*.

The Greek tradition of oral composition is characterized by its multiformity (its intrinsic capacity for narrative variation) and by its undefined boundaries.[4] Both in theory and practice, the oral poet defies the notions of beginning and end, authorial identity and control, and exclusivity of narrative with which modern readers are familiar.[5] The open-ended conclusions of the oral tradition encouraged the growth of the mythic tradition surrounding notable characters and conflicts. The events that became the center of the *Iliad* and the *Odyssey* were thus already part of the legendary narrative that encircled them. At some point in the Late Bronze Age or Early Iron Age, the story of Achilles, the fall of Troy, and Odysseus' wanderings were precipitated from this fluid, rhapsodic narrative into canonical forms.[6] The *Iliad* and *Odyssey* thus represent the best-established episodes from a larger institution of rhapsodic creation and performance of heroic saga.[7] To the modern reader, the creation of the fixed texts of the *Iliad* and the *Odyssey* marks both the pinnacle and completion of the oral tradition. While both texts grew in canonical stature, the remainder of the oral tradition wilted into obscurity and oblivion.[8]

The historical facts surrounding the premature deaths of Vergil and other authors of Latin epics further complicate the completed status of their poems. Nearly half of the seven surviving epics of the Golden and Silver ages of Latin literature remained unfinished at the time of the author's death.[9] In addition, none of the pre-Vergilian Latin epics survive except in fragments.

Three Latin epics preceded Vergil's *Aeneid*. Livius Andronicus attempted to bring Homer's *Odyssey* to a Latin audience through translation.[10] Naevius and Ennius clearly established the mythical connection of Rome to Troy, presaging Vergil's plot and approach. Livius' contributions to the tradition were an interpretation of Homer and a suitably epic Latin diction. It is safe to assume that he preserved the ending (and therefore the openness) of the *Odyssey*. Naevius' *Bellum Punicum*, treating the First Punic War and Rome's victory therein, was most likely composed in or about 204 BCE, after the siege of Saguntum and the first phase of the Second Punic War, but before its conclusion. Ancient grammarians and commentators testify that

Ennius initially conceived his now-fragmentary *Annales* as a project of fifteen books, later adding three more[11]—thereby becoming his own continuator and demonstrating the elasticity and boundlessness of his own work.

Vergil was indebted to all these works, but the special ambiguities of the *Aeneid* set it apart, indeed above, the other works of Latin epic. When he left Italy in 19 BCE, conscious that his final work was incomplete, Vergil begged his friend Varius to destroy the manuscript should he die without finishing it. After his death, Varius and Tucca edited the manuscript only slightly, leaving the lacunae unfilled. The ring composition and proleptic references to Roman ascent in the *Aeneid* make it unlikely that Vergil intended much more than a polishing of the text and a completion of the lacunae, but this is far from certain. It is this uncertainty, born of literary artifice and historic infelicity, which invites the imaginative additions of later authors.

By death or by design, Vergil leaves conceptual gaps, inconsistencies, and evocative ambiguities which force the reader to adopt multiple hermeneutical keys simultaneously. The poetic artifice that perpetually defers and mediates any sense of closure beguiles the reader: the ambiguities create a kaleidoscope that shifts according to the applied interpretation. Although Vergil's death may have contributed to some of the unintentional contradictions in the *Aeneid,* the work is marked by many ambiguities which appear to be intentionally provocative. In book one Jupiter tells Venus that after a massive war in Italy, Aeneas will establish the customs and walls of a new city, rule it for three years, and leave Ascanius as his heir.[12] And yet in book six, Anchises prophesies that Aeneas will beget a son of mixed blood in his old age,[13] although Jupiter has earlier prophesied that Aeneas has only three more years to live. The question of Aeneas' heir at the end of the *Aeneid* is one of the most interesting ambiguities: who will initiate the line of the Alban Kings? Will it be Ascanius-Iulus or Silvius Postumus, the son of Aeneas and Lavinia? In book one,[14] Jupiter seems to prophesize that it will be Iulus, but in book six[15] it is certainly Silvius.

Several other parts of Jupiter's initial prophecy also are left ambiguous. In book twelve we find that the Italians whom Aeneas is destined to subdue and provide with new *mores* will actually keep their own customs.[16] Finally, at the end of book twelve, where Jupiter's prophecy in the first book leads the reader to expect that Aeneas will establish the walls and customs of a new city, marry Lavinia, and honor the fallen, he does none of these things, but instead slays his nemesis Turnus as he lies helpless.[17] Whether intended as ambiguity or an ironic irresolution, this dark and abrupt ending of the story has left readers dangling in anticipation since antiquity.[18]

After centuries of engagement with the epic tradition through prose adaptations, commentaries, and artistic representations, the Renaissance ushered in a return to direct imitation of the literary monuments of antiquity. Petrarch (1304–1374), the "Father of Humanism," led the way by writing what he hoped would be his primary legacy and claim to lasting fame: the *Africa,* a nine-book Latin hexameter epic on the Second Punic War, indebted for its diction and structure to Vergil and Lucan. Though the work earned Petrarch immense praise in his own day, it remained unfinished and unpublished at its author's death, like its principal stylistic model, the *Aeneid.*

Petrarch conceived his *Africa* as a classical Latin epic, quite different from the late-antique and medieval poetic tradition and entirely distinct from works in the vernacular. In scope and nature it is a response to the medieval commentators and medieval heroic poems. The *Africa* was designed to engage in a competitive confrontation with Dante's *Divina Commedia.* Petrarch's attempt to replace Dante's typological work with his own philological epic reflected his hope of initiating a literary revolution and a return to Classical models. But the work lacks more than polish. As many as three books are missing from the end, and book four is only partially written. Critics have often pointed out that the *Africa's* verses are generally stilted, and some lines are either incomplete or completely unmetrical. It was only upon his death that his friends and those devoted to Petrarch's fame collected and collated his drafts to publish the work in 1397.

If the reception by posterity is a measure, the *Africa* was itself a failure. Nevertheless, Petrarch's fame made it influential in its time, and it served to found the genre of classical Renaissance epic. Petrarch's return to ancient models electrified the *literati* and proclaimed the humanistic goal of living, remaining, and conversing with the greatest figures of antiquity. His noble attempt at a classical epic paved the way for future successful attempts, including the notable continuators of the *Aeneid*.

Petrus Candidus Decembrius, the first of our Renaissance continuators, was another prominent early Italian humanist. Best known to posterity for his Latin translations of Plato, he was secretary to the Duke of Milan, Filippo Maria Visconti, and served in the curia of two or three popes. Although only ninety lines of Decembrius' epic survive—perhaps he set the poem aside when he foresaw his friend Vergius' more monumental work—it demonstrates a deep appreciation of epic style and Vergilian diction. Decembrius begins at the moment *Aeneid* 12 leaves off:

> *Postquam magnanimus morientia sanguine fudit*
> *pectora et ingentes expirans luminis iras Daunius*
> *Iliacos satiavit vulnere manes, componit senior regni*
> *iam fracta Latinus culmina, disiectos urbis iubet aggere*
> *muros attolli, quibus aereas deducere turres cura sit, et*
> *summis Vulcanum pellere tectis imponit.* (Decembrii
> *Supplementum* 1–8)

> High-spirited, his chest soaked with his dying blood,
> preternatural anger streaming from his eyes, the son
> of Daunus appeased the ghosts of Troy with a wound.
> Afterwards now old Latinus rebuilds the shattered
> houses of his dominion. The walls of the city, which
> lie in scattered heaps, he commands to be set back in

place; he orders those charged with bringing down the bronze towers to extinguish the rooftop fires as well.

Being unfinished, Decembrius' text is obviously marked by the same openness and unfinished ending as its master text.

Maphaeus Vegius is certainly the most celebrated of the four authors under discussion, a member of the inner circle of Roman *literati*, serving alongside Poggio Bracciolini and Flavio Biondo in the curia of Pope Eugenius IV. His *Supplementum*, published in 1428, was so successful that for nearly three centuries it was frequently reprinted along with Vergil's twelve books, with little more than its title to differentiate it from them. It was translated into every major European language, and Badius Ascensius published a detailed commentary on the *Supplementum* in 1501. Vegius' work has received considerable modern attention, including a critical edition and more than a dozen scholarly articles.[19] This *Supplementum* declares its subject matter clearly in the first few lines:

> *Turnus ut extremo devictus Marte profudit effugientem animam medioque sub agmine victor magnanimus stetit Aeneas, Mavortius heros.* (Vegius, *Supplementum* 1–3)

> As Turnus, having been overcome in the final fight, poured forth his fleeing spirit, in middle of the crowd stood great-souled Aeneas, the warlike hero.

The rest of the book tells the story of Turnus' funeral, the destruction of Ardea, and the founding of Lavinium. At the outset of the action, Vegius echoes the opening lines of the master text in a speech by Aeneas, which creates a sense of self-authorization and a step towards closure:

nunc, Rutuli, hinc auferte ducem vestrum; arma virumque largior atque omnem deflendae mortis honorem. (Vegius, *Supplementum* 39–40)

Now, Rutulians, carry-off your leader; I grant the arms and the man and every honor of lamentable death.

Iohannes Foreestius (1586–1651) composed two supplementary books to the Aeneid in which he resolves both the Iliadic and Odyssean themes. Foreestius was a Dutch student of literature at the University of Leiden who had authored a celebrated volume of Greek epigrams and shorter epics.[20] His later works in Latin were not as widely published and have never been collected. Foreestius' book thirteen opens in the immediate aftermath of Turnus' death. An extensive ekphrasis of armor alludes to other well-known ekphrases in the epic tradition as well as to *Iliad* book twenty, where Demoleon, son of Antenor, is killed by Achilles.

sic ait atque illi demit Pallantis amici exuvias, misero monimentum triste parenti, et simul astanti servandas tradit Achati substituens insigne suum, quo Demoleonta exuit ad Troiam, non impar mole nec arte, in solido caelatum auro vetus argumentum. Infelix lacrimat virgo religata catenis e scopulo; iuxta squamisque et dentibus horret bellua terribilis visu, tremit illa pavore. Aligeroque in equo iuvenis super aequore pendet, certa ferae meditans falcato vulnera ferro. (Foreestius, *Supplementum* 13.47–57)

So he spoke, and took from him the spoils that Turnus had robbed from him—a sad remembrance for the unhappy father—and handed them over to Achates, who stood there; substituting his own baldric, which he had taken from Demoleon at Troy, equal in size and art, decorated with an old motif, worked in pure gold: an unhappy girl wept, tied to a cliff. There was a terrible monster with frightening scales and teeth, while the girl trembled with fear. But on a winged horse a young man was already hovering over the sea, wondering how, with his crooked sword, he would be able to deliver a certain blow to the beast with his curved blade.

Foreestius describes the destruction of the war through a number of speeches which draw heavily on parallels from elsewhere in Vergil, from Homeric speeches, and even from other Latin poets.[21] In Foreestius' version, Latinus returns the body of Turnus to the Rutulians, but on Mount Olympus, Pilumnus (Turnus' grandfather or ancestor) mourns over Turnus' body, a passage which evokes analogs with Iliadic scenes of grief.

In addition to these clear parallels to the *Iliad,* Foreestius also includes elements which address the Odyssean themes of loyalty, vengeance, and homecoming. Latinus takes Ascanius under his wing in such a paternal way as to secure himself as the adoptive ancestor of what is to come in Latium.[22] But the tutelary gods of the Rutulians incite a renewal of hostilities, which ultimately resolve to a *Pax Latina*, with all of Latium defeated or allied with the newcomers.[23] Back on Mount Olympus, Pilumnus is repentant before Jupiter, and the hostile parties, both in Latium and on Olympus, exchange olive branches.[24] The wedding between Aeneas and Lavinia is deferred to a later date when things have calmed down.[25] This *supplementum* ends when the king and our hero head back to their respective homes in the evening.[26]

The fourth and final continuation appeared in 1698. Simon Villanova served at the court of Duke Philippe of Orleans at the end of the 17th century and dedicated his 827-line *Supplementum ad Aeneida* to the Duke's son.[27] In Villanova's addition, the action begins as Aeneas is contemplating what to do with Turnus' body. After his flash of wrath and vengeance against Turnus has passed, Aeneas' piety is reconfirmed when Ascanius suggests to his father that it is right and just to return Turnus' corpse to his people.

> *Tunc sic affari Ascanius "Dux maxime Teucrum cui semper pietatis honos, cui sola deorum religio curae; prius umbris debita Turni solvantur, Rutulis placeat dimittere corpus. Hac pietate tua flectentur sanguine manes, hoc pietatis opus tollent ad sidera nati."*
> (Villanova, 13.9–14)

> Then Ascanius answered as follows: O great commander of the Teucrans, to whom there has always been the honor of piety, to whom the worship of the gods is dear to the heart: the obligation that is due to the spirit of Turnus should first be fulfilled, and then it seems right to return the corpse to the Rutulians. By such an action, you will appease the spirits of the dead with blood. Your descendants will lift this pious deed into the heavens.

This episode highlights Ascanius' prudence and maturity as Aeneas' son. Peace negotiations follow with King Latinus, who is happy to give Lavinia to Aeneas in a magnificent wedding celebration.[28] The book is replete with descriptions of rituals and revelry.[29] Latinus and Aeneas immediately enter a lasting peace, but Aeneas receives the epithet *anxius* when he gets too close to Lavinia. He is so struck with her beauty that he can hardly speak, and at the sight of her collar, he is overcome with desire for all her virtues, described as "*fas omne nefasque*" ("of every speakable and unspeakable kind").[30] Latinus is so impressed with Ascanius that he gives him a most precious gift: the sacred Annales of the Latins, which one day, the king says, will be sung by the greatest poets: Vergil and Villanova.[31] Juno is enraged at the death of Turnus and machinates another war for the Trojans.[32] Evander, an ally of the Trojans, is attacked by a new character, Lauzellus, stepson of Lausus. The bellicose scenes make up roughly a third of Villanova's book and read much like Vergilian battles punctuated with more Homeric descriptions of weapons and wounds. Finally, Lauzellus and his comrades are defeated.[33] As the Trojans begin to rebuild Laurentum and found Lavinium, an otherwise *pius* Aeneas taunts Minerva. Marveling at the newly built city, he exclaims to her *"naturam vicimus arte"* (We have conquered nature by skill).[34] Shortly thereafter he receives word that Anna, Dido's sister, has thrown herself into a nearby river. In fact, this is an ambush set by the last of Lauzellus' allies.[35] During the fight, Aeneas drowns in the river, and a formal apotheosis follows.[36]

> *potatam animam abstulit unda. exsurgit subito*
> *fragranti ventus odore; scintillam renitens inter sic*
> *fertur ab unda, sic fugat ille novum densissima nubila*
> *sidus, spectantumque oculos puro sic flamine stringit.*
> (Villanova, 13.809–13)

The water carried off his drowned breath. Suddenly a wind rose with a pleasant fragrance; shining back with a glimmer he was thus raised out of the water, then he became a new star and put the dense fog to flight and blinded the onlookers with a cleansing breeze.

> *Aeneae hinc sacros latices ripisque sub ipsis uxor*
> *constructum iussit de marmore templum; illius ad*
> *postes inscripto carmine nomen: "moribus Aeneam*
> *divi, pietate vel armis aequalem fecere sibi; gens omnia*
> *speret."* (Villanova, 13.823–7)

Then his wife ordered that a temple of marble be built on the shores of the sacred waters; his name was praised in an inscription above the entrance: "On account of his character, the immortal gods made

> Aeneas equal to themselves in piety and arms. His
> race should hope for all things."

After Aeneas' departure into the pantheon, Lavinia gives birth to Silvius Albus, thereby resolving some of the apparent contradictions about Aeneas' heir and offspring.[37] Villanova's *Supplementum* marries extremely novel material with the traditional mythology from Ovid, Silvius Italicus, and Servius. He introduces some elements of contemporary warfare in proper epic terms,[38] describes the royal couple's first embrace,[39] develops otherwise-obscure family trees with mythic backgrounds,[40] and ultimately resolves book twelve to the necessary apotheosis of Aeneas as predicted by the tradition.

Scholars have often dismissed the *supplementa* as thoughtless pastiches designed for a time or by versifiers who did not understand the nature of ancient epic and could not bear the *Aeneid*'s ambiguities. The view that the *supplementa* represent an attempt to simply "tie up loose ends" does not bear scrutiny as criticism. In fact, by deciding to write *supplementa* as opposed to commentaries to the *Aeneid*, the continuators chose to enter into direct dialogue with all aspects of the epic. Almost every line of the various *supplementa* resounds with Vergilian diction and character. For the most part, the continuators are unexpectedly conservative in regard to the plot content of their additions; with few exceptions, they do not wander far from the canonical material that is either explicitly or implicitly foretold in the *Aeneid* or in the "*Little Aeneid*" of Ovid's *Metamorphoses*.[41]

The continuators take the relationship between beginnings and endings from the master text. They do not begin *ab ovo* or require any preface; instead, they follow the epic pattern of plunging straight into the narrative, "hurrying to the action and snatching the listener into the middle of things," as Horace recommends.[42] This technique, along with the initial repetition of significant markers linking the supplements with the master text, has an "authorizing power"[43] which causes the reader to accept the supplements as an authentic part of the epic tradition and, therefore, to expect the works to follow epic characteristics, including the use of ambiguity.

The *supplementa* represent a new form of classical interpretation—a path blazed by Petrarch's *Africa*—which dares once again to conceive of the classical epic canon as elastic and imitable, in contrast to the ancient and medieval mode of engaging with epic texts mainly through commentaries and glosses.[44] This humanistic method represents a holistic comprehension and subjective approach to literature, emphasizing the experience of a literary work as a dialogue with the author rather than as a static text. Such an approach allows the continuators to pick up the story where Vergil left off and reanimate his characters.

In so doing, the continuators were engaging with the text more deeply than many of their contemporaries and perhaps more deeply than nearly all modern scholars, who tend to keep the objects of their study at a critical distance. They entered the inner sanctum of the Muses in the same way that the ancient authors of the lost *Aethiopis*, or *Lesches*, or *Kypria* did. While not surpassing the ancient master texts, they still participated in the epic tradition and helped shape its reception. The meta-narrative of the *Aeneid* is constantly being repeated and reworked without attaining completion. The ambiguity of its closure leaves open the possibility for continuing the epic in perpetuity. Villanova states quite plainly in his preface that he intends to add to the *Aeneid* those matters it left open and incomplete. He expresses his desire that his work be considered the fruit of erudition and a recreational delight.[45] The continuators thus stage a process of post-Vergilian reception, with an eye to the literary supplementation that Ovid has already exercised with the *Aeneid*. In this way, Renaissance and early modern *supplementa* become supplements of supplements and a part of a growing epic mythology.

Designed to evoke simultaneously the plot of the prior epics and the pathos of the Renaissance audience, the *supplementa* show how openness and ambiguity can be interpreted. For the humanists, Vergil is the supreme model of both artistic perfection and mimetic synthesis. A close look at the *supplementa* themselves shows that, however misplaced the intention to end the *Aeneid* might seem to a modern critic, the supplements are sophisticated critiques of his work which deal not only with the gap at the end but also with other open-ended dissatisfactions within the epic. In practice, the continuators engage the ambiguities of the *Aeneid* to varying degrees of resolution. The *supplementa* unanimously tell what happens to Turnus' corpse: it is returned to the Rutulians.[46] Two of the four *supplementa* narrate the wedding of Aeneas and Lavinia, while Foreestius' version of events affirms their future wedding but does not contain it.[47] In the three finished *supplementa*, the Trojans completely dominate their enemies and Latium.[48]

These are not, however, the burning questions at the end of the *Aeneid*. No careful reader is left at the end of book twelve wondering what Aeneas will do with Turnus' body or whether he will marry Lavinia and rule. (Two continuators have Aeneas become a god,[49] and only two describe his wedding to Lavinia.[50]) The continuators, therefore, leave the gritty questions largely unanswered or unresolved, and none of them adequately resolves the question of lineage.[51] These supplements do not provide the dénouement or satisfying full stop that most scholarship has suggested the continuators were offering. Replacing epic ambiguity with certitude and closure was not, in fact, the aim of the supplements. Instead, as humanists fully aware of the role of openness and uncertainty in the epic genre, the continuators consciously work within the ambiguities, resolving some questions while adding new uncertainties of their own.[52]

* * *

Quid retribuam Domino pro omnibus quae retribuit mihi? In paying public tribute to Reginald we are honoring one of the most influential Latinists of the last century. I am reminded of the immense excitement I felt when as a young man I received my multicolored letters of acceptance to his *schola aestiva*. Reginaldus changed my life by introducing me to a deep appreciation of Latin literature from all periods. To say that I am grateful to him is an understatement. I am indebted to him for all the joys of my intellectual life and for those still to come.

BIBLIOGRAPHY

Bettini, M. 2006. "Forging Identities: Trojans and Latins, Romans and Julians in the Aeneid." In *Herrschaft ohne Integration? Rom und Italien in republikanischer Zeit. Studien zur Alten Geschichte 4.* ed. M. Jehne and R. Pfeilschifter, 269–91. Frankfurt: Verlag.

Blandford, D. W. 1959. "Virgil and Vegio." *Vergilius* 5:29–30

Brinton, A. C. 1930. *Maphaeus Vegius and His Thirteenth Book of the Aeneid.* London: Bristol Press.

Buckley, E. 2006. "Ending the *Aeneid*? Closure and Continuation in Maffeo Vegio's *Supplementum*." *Vergilius* 52:108–137

Burkert, Walter. 1987. "The Making of Homer in the Sixth Century B.C.: Rhapsodes versus Stesichorus." In *Papers on the Amasis Painter and his World,* 43–62. Malibu: Getty Museum.

Foreestius, Joannes. 1605. *Idyllia sive Heroes, et alia poematia quaedam.* Antwerp: Plantin.

Hardie, Philip. 1997. "Closure in Latin Epic." In *Classical Closure: Reading the End in Greek and Latin Literature,* ed. D. H. Roberts et al., 139–62. Princeton: Princeton University Press.

Hijmans, B. L. 1971-2. "Aeneia Virtus: Vegio's Supplementum to the Aeneid." *CJ* 67.2:144–155

Holmberg, Ingrid. 1998. "The Creation of the Ancient Greek Epic Cycle." *Oral Tradition* 13/2:456–478.

Maguinness, W. S. 1968. "Maffeo Vegio Continuatore dell' *Eneide*." *Aevum* 42.5/6:478–485

McCahill, E. M. 2009. "Rewriting Vergil, Rereading Rome: Maffeo Vegius, Poggio

Bracciolini, Flavio Biondo, and Early Quattrocento Antiquarianism." *Memoirs of the American Academy in Rome* 54:165–199.

Nagy, Gregory. 2004. *Homer's Text and Language.* Urbana: University of Illinois.

Oertel, H-L. 2001. *Die Aeneissupplemente des Jan van Foreest und des C. Simonet de Villeneuve.* Hildesheim: Olms.

O'Hara, James. 2007. *Inconsistency in Roman Epic: Studies in Catullus, Lucretius, Vergil, Ovid and Lucan*. Cambridge: Cambridge University Press.

Pigman, G. W. 1980. "Versions of Imitation in the Renaissance." *RenQ* 33:1–32.

Reed, J. D. 2010. "Vergil's Roman." In *A Companion to Vergil's Aeneid and Its Tradition*, ed. J. Farrell and M. C. J. Putnam, 66–79. Oxford: Wiley-Blackwell.

Regn, G. 2009. "Petrarch's Rome: The History of the *Africa* and the Renaissance Project." *MLN* 124:86–102.

Scaife, Ross. 1995. "The Kypria and its Early Reception" *CA* 14:164–97.

Villanova, C. S. 1698. *Supplementum ad Aeneida*. Paris: Aubouyn.

Wilson-Okamura, D., ed. and trans. 1996. *Decembrio, Pier Candido: The Thirteenth Book of the Aeneid*. Internet. 23 November 2016. www.virgil.org/supplementa/decembrio.htm.

ENDNOTES

[1] E.g., divine genealogies, contradicted or unfulfilled prophecies.

[2] Cf. Hardie, 139

[3] E.g., when Aeneas stands over Turnus's corpse, it is ambiguous how Turnus's death will affect a lasting peace, what will precipitate the foundation of the city, and who is Aeneas' heir. In the *Odyssey*, peace may be restored to Ithaca in book twenty-four, but Tiresias's prophecy from book twenty-three (regarding Odysseus' necessary travels) remains unfulfilled and unresolved, leaving us to wonder whether he will stay at home with Penelope or must continue travelling. The trajectory of the plot may be clear (for instance, at the end of the *Aeneid*, Aeneas has certainly overcome the obstacles between the Trojans and their foundation of a new city), but the irresolution prevents clarity and creates ambiguity surrounding the epic's conclusion.

[4] Cf. Nagy, 25–39.

[5] Holmberg, 457.

[6] Ibid., 456–78.

7   The Homeric epics themselves testify, internally, to this ancient custom, even beyond the linguistic analyses that suggest their composition may have spanned several generations. In the *Odyssey*, the bard Demodocus provides a glimpse into the nature of the oral tradition (Od. 8.62–67; 256–366; 496–520). Furthermore, each of the epics has alternate endings which draw the reader into the next episode within the cycle. The various works in this group include introductions to the Homeric poems and episodic supplements thereto. Along with the *Iliad* and the *Odyssey*, these works complete a cycle of the legends connected with the siege of Troy and the events following the capture of the city. The Greek epic cycle provides the exemplar of a narrative tradition that attests to the expanding nature of the epic universe from which the *Iliad* and *Odyssey* are only the most prominent remains. It is this cycle which provided the foundations of Roman epic poetry, and at least two of its poems were probably extensive narratives approaching epic length or depth, the *Kypria* and the *Aethiopis* (cf. Scaife 1995 and Holmberg 1998). Though also very fragmented, the Stesichorean tradition (Stesichorus c. 630–555 BCE) included embellishment of characters from Greek epic and may preserve elements of the improvising and expansion dependent upon the *de facto* canonical Homeric epics. Ironically, this lyric tradition probably had a polarizing effect that precipitated a further canonization of the Homeric works, immortalizing the *Iliad* and the *Odyssey* as the epic master texts (cf. Burkert 1987). The various songs from the Epic Cycle serve as examples of how the boundless nature and ambiguous endings in the epic poems potentiate further narrative expansion and growth of the larger tradition.

8   After this development, any cohesive, mutually dependent, and singular narrative originating with the oral tradition nearly disappears from sight, rendering unattainable the vision of a unified and consonant text traversing the epic universe.

9   Vergil's *Aeneid*, Lucan's *Bellum Civile*, Statius' *Achilleid*. Cf. Hardie, 139.

10   Livius Andronicus (c. 284–c. 205 BCE). Though more original in his material, Gnaeus Naevius (c. 270–c. 201 BCE) similarly adapted many features of Greek literature to Latin when he composed the first native epic, the *Bellum Punicum*, about the First Punic War. The starting point of Naevius' work is Aeneas's flight from Troy, which functions as the background to the discussion of the Punic War. Only a few decades

later, Quintus Ennius (239–169 BCE) continued the tradition of tracing the founding of Rome to the Trojans. His *Annales* tells the history of Aeneas' travels to Carthage, Sicily, and Latium.

[11] Cf. Skutsch, 553, 563–5, as quoted by Hardie, 140.

[12] *Aen.* 1.261–8. For discussion of this and other inconsistencies in the work cf. O'Hara, 77–103.

[13] *Aen.* 6.763–5; 1.265.

[14] Ibid. 1.267–71

[15] Ibid. 6.760–6

[16] Ibid. 12.834–7

[17] Beyond the myriad inconsistencies that can creep into a massive work, there are the obviously calculated ambiguities. After Anchises narrates the future great men of Rome, he dispatches Aeneas from the underworld through the Gate of False Dreams. What is the reader to make of the glorious future and the prophecies of Father Anchises? The bid to exit through the Gate of False Dreams casts a cloak of ambiguity over the entire scene. For more on the ambiguities introduced by Jupiter's prophecy cf. Bettini 2006.

[18] The *Aeneid*'s ambiguities are not a mere by-product of poetic language: the *Aeneid* exploits the nature of poetic language to create a nuanced and versatile boundlessness; its abrupt end draws the reader into the story to extrapolate from elements within the text and discover what happens next. The gaps, inconsistences, opacities, and ambiguous ending function to frustrate, but they also captivate the imagination and propel the next episode. Vergil leaves open the opportunity to resolve narrative ambiguities and to supplement the *Aeneid*, just as other writers in the epic tradition had done. Within thirty years of the publication of the *Aeneid*, Ovid developed further details of Aeneas' journey from Troy and eventual apotheosis in books thirteen and fourteen of the *Metamorphoses*. In paying homage to the *Aeneid* by expatiating upon its aftermath, Ovid further accentuated the fluidity and openness of the epic narrative.

[19] Blandford 1959; Brinton 1930; Hijmans 1972; Buckley 2006; Maguiness 1968.

[20] Cf. Foreestius, *Idyllia sive Heroes, et alia poematia quaedam.*

[21] For example, he includes two carefully placed and obvious allusions to Catullus 101, at 13.322–45 and 14.139–48.

[22] Foreestius 14.495

23 Foreestius 13.153–75; 14.363–5

24 Foreestius 14.467–82

25 *Connubii ritus et sacra gaudia festi / deferri placuit dum laetior aethere Titan / fulserit.* (They decided to defer the festive rights and sacred joys of marriage until a happier day shown in the sky.) Foreestius 14.558–560.

26 *His ita compositis rex urbem, Troius heros / castra petunt, iunctis in pacis pignora dextris.* (When these things were so arranged and after their right hands were joined in the promise of peace, the King make for his city and the Trojan Hero his barracks.) Foreestius 14.477.

27 Oertel, 117–125.

28 Villanova 13.104–150.

29 Ibid., 13.239–317.

30 Ibid., 13.180.

31 Ibid., 13.194–216.

32 Ibid., 13.345–370.

33 Ibid., 13.371–484.

34 Ibid., 13.689.

35 Ibid., 13.490–577.

36 Ibid., 13. 621–776; the apotheosis is contained in 804–25.

37 Ibid., 13.820–2.

38 *Dextera parte leo frendens ruit, illius ore / aera per medium tormenta, feruntur et ignes. / Laeva parte draco centum capita, oraque centum: / mille vomit, revomitque nitrato pulvere culmos.* (On the right side a growling lion casts out of his mouth a shot, and flames are carried forth. On the left stands a hundred-headed dragon with a hundred mouths: he spews forth and spews out again a thousand stalks.) Villanova 13.246–249

39 *Impatiens Veneris, thalamo se immittit uterque; / coniugis hic miratus, eburno in corpore, formam. / Incensusque novo, omnia vota reduxit ad unum.* (Impatient for loving-making, both hurl themselves onto the marriage bed. Aeneas, marveling at his wife's beauty and ivory body, burns with a new desire, resolves all his vows to this.) Villanova 13.315–317.

40 Primarily that of Lausus, Mezentius, and Lauzellus. Villanova 13.370–3. *Nepotis Mezenti: Intellige Lauzellum ... Hic Lauzellus quem nepotem Mezentii descripsi, privignus fingitur Lauzi.* (Of the grandson of Mezentius: Understand this to be Lauzellus ... This Lauzellus whom

I described as the grandson of Mezentius is conceived of as the stepson of Lausus.) Villanova, n. in 370, p. 29.

41 Ov. *Met.* 14.573–608. McCahill, 170.

42 *Nec gemino bellum Trojanum orditur ab ovo; / semper ad eventum festinat et in medias res / non secus ac notas auditorem rapit.* Hor. *Ars* 147–9.

43 Buckley, 112.

44 The classical commentary on the *Aeneid* is best represented by Servius; medieval examples are Bernardus Silvestris and Fulgentius.

45 *Si vero altera facie, id est carmen epicum scribendum Lector attenderit; ne temeritatis et audaciae obiuratum ipse, et rei litterariae periti me velint, quin hoc supplemento addito de se bene meritum me iterata evolutione comprobabunt: enim vero cum poema epicum definiatur imitatio actionis unius illustris completae et cet. aliquid ad perfectionem Aeneidos desiderari videtur: cum ex omni parte non fit completa.* Villanova, p. xi.

46 Cf. Decembrius 13.20–27, Vegius 13.36–43, 185–201, Foreestius 13.243–59, Villanova 13.9–16.

47 Cf. Vegius 13.440–77, Foreestius 13.388–9, Villanova 13.430–586.

48 Cf. Vegius 13.331–73, 517–528, Foreestius 14.363–482, Villanova 13.430–586.

49 The apotheoses are at Vegius 13.577–82 and Villanova 13.804–25.

50 Vegius 13.440–77 and Villanova 13.133–98

51 Villanova mentions a posthumous Silvius Albus, but he does not explain which one will rule in Lavinium or how this residual uncertainty will be resolved.

52 I would like to thank the editors of this volume for their helpful feedback on my chapter.

Ambiguity in Erasmus' *Echo*

Michael Sloan

This paper examines Erasmus' dialogue *Echo*, found in his collection of *Colloquies*. Specifically, I identify how ambiguity, perhaps more than any other device, helps Erasmus achieve the literary and didactic aims of *Echo*. Ambiguity weighs heavily on the movement of topics, supports the ethical advice offered by the respondent, and generates literary interest in the work beyond its efficacy as a pedagogical text for the study of Latin.

1. Introduction to *Colloquies*

Written and compiled for his students twenty years before their first publication in 1518, the *Colloquies* modeled "polite conversation and good writing in Latin" (Thompson, *CWE*, 39.xx). The following year, Erasmus authorized Dirk Marten to publish an edition. Over the next fifteen years, Erasmus revised old dialogues and wrote new ones. An uncountable number of editions, reprints, and versions appeared before the final authorized edition of 1533, containing sixty-one dialogues. No longer mere examples of polite conversation, the revised and expanded dialogues contributed to the *Colloquies'* reception as a rounded work of fiction. Dynamic characters and cultural, literary, and religious themes populate the work, yet the added dialogues consistently retain the original colloquies' thrust as pedagogical exercises.

The years in which Erasmus composed his *Colloquies* provided plenty of fodder for discussion. Reports of the New World were filtering into Europe, and Leonardo Da Vinci was advancing the disciplines of art and science. The *Colloquies* reference the Reformation, the printing press, and the development of national monarchies, among many other current issues. The ongoing upheaval in Christianity made religion their most common theme. Yet Erasmus responds the turmoil of his age with surprising whimsy, and relies on his vast classical learning for continuity in its flux. The *Colloquies* are not only a reservoir of pedagogical exercises in Latin, but also commendable literature and a Vanity Fair of those turbulent years in Europe.

2. Introduction to Erasmus' *Echo*

As a dialogue, *Echo* takes a somewhat peculiar form: a character repeats the last word, words, or syllables of her interlocutor's previous speech. This form alludes to an ancient tradition represented by Euripides' *Andromeda* and Aristophanes' *Thesmorphoriazusae*. In Erasmus' dialogue, a Youth seeks advice from the mythical character Echo, a nymph whose tale is most famously recorded with Narcissus' in Ovid's *Metamorphoses* 3.339–510. The brief dialogue consists of only fifty-three exchanges; the Youth speaks entirely in Latin, but seventeen of Echo's responses are in Greek. Margolin (1988, 78) notes Erasmus' departure from the Ovidian legend of Echo, a myth for which Erasmus had little use, and then suggests that Erasmus otherwise takes advantage of the famous trait of the character—the inability to say anything except as an echo—to employ clear prose and models of Ciceronian imitation. The dialogue begins with some polite, playful exchanges, but turns to academics and religion after Echo's third response, before lamenting the lack of virtue among students and offering marriage advice. After a swift transition, the conversation explores various vocations and returns to the pursuit of literature, particularly the question of whether or not the Youth ought to become a Ciceronian.

3. Ambiguity in *Echo*

Erasmus' use of ambiguity promotes *Echo* as good fiction and as a practical pedagogical exercise for teaching both Latin and ethics. Below I have identified nine examples of ambiguity within *Echo* to demonstrate the importance of this tool as it aids the objectives of the dialogue: to train the reader in Latin and to infuse the dialogue with pastoral advice, both of which endeavors are undertaken with humor allowed by this versatile tool, ambiguity. I have classified the nine examples into two sub-categories. The first classification reveals syntactic, lexical, and grammatical concerns through four examples of ambiguity. The second classification contains five examples of ambiguity that reveal more complex interpretive and ethical concerns of issues and vocations that Erasmus treats elsewhere: marriage, monarchs, military life, and tradespeople.

The first example of ambiguity occurs in the second exchange, in a word that yields multiple meanings beyond the one suggested by context.

IUVENIS	*et si venio tibi gratus iuvenis.*
ECHO	*venis.*

This exchange humorously reinforces the personal endings of the first and second person active address. Echo, who can only speak when spoken to, follows the conventional practice in Latin of affirming a statement by repeating its most salient element (normally the verb), or in this case the pragmatic focus. Yet *venis* could also represent the dative or ablative plural of *vena, -ae* ("blood vessel, vein; cavity"). This ambiguous word may ironically recall the physical nature of Echo, whose essence dissipated and thus became a hollow being with no veins or blood vessels. As a point of emphasis in reference to the Youth coming in (or with) veins, Erasmus' potential ambiguity in this instance offers a subtle joke in a context that allows only one suitable rendering of *venis*. By employing a modest instance of ambiguity infused with humor, the first and second personal endings of an

269

active verb are illustrated, and the reader is forced to recognize the similarity, often confusing to elementary students, between a second person singular active ending of a verb and the dative and ablative plural endings of first- and second-declension nouns.

The next example of ambiguity involves two words also often confused by elementary students of Latin: *novus, -a, -um* and *nosco, noscere, novi, notum*.

IUVENIS	*et Graece nosti? quid istuc novi?*
ECHO	*novi.*

The Youth invites the ambiguous response of Echo by using two different words which share similar forms. The syncopated form of *novo* brings the idea of "knowing" into the conversation, while the idiomatic phrase *quid istuc novi* anticipates the ambiguity of Echo's response. As a verb form, Echo's *nōvi* (long *o*: "I know") answers the first question, "And do you know Greek?" However, as an echo of the Youth's last word, Echo's response *nŏvi* (short *o*) answers the second question, "What is new?" However, the length is not marked in the text, and as an exercise in silent reading, the ambiguity remains until or unless the oral quality of the vowel is realized. This literary pun engages the discerning abilities of readers, challenging their knowledge of pronunciation in order to disambiguate Echo's response. Additionally, like the previous example, it requires the reader to identify and distinguish between common noun and verb endings.

For the more advanced reader, or one with a knowledge of Ovid, the ambiguity of *novi* as "I knew" and "new" engages the theme of "knowing," which is crucial to Ovid's and Erasmus' dialogues that involve Echo. In the previous exchange of Erasmus' dialogue, the Youth asked Echo if she was able to speak about his future, or in other words, help him to know new things about himself. This theme develops throughout *Echo*, influenced by Ovid's tale of Echo and Narcissus. For Ovid, "knowing thyself" is the surprisingly fatal condition of Narcissus' transformation:

de quo consultus, an esset tempora maturae visurus
longa senectae fatidicus vates "si se non noverit" inquit.
vana diu visa est vox auguris: exitus illam resque probat
letique genus novitasque furoris. (Ov. *Met.* 3.346-50)

Tiresias the prophet, asked whether Narcissus would see a long life of a ripe old age, said, "if he will never know himself." For a long time, the words of the prophet seemed empty: but as it turned out the event, the kind of death, and the newness (strangeness) of his madness proved the veracity of his prediction.

Ovid here plays verbally with notions of seeing, newness, and knowing in connection with the cause and eventuality of Narcissus' transformation. The lexical wordplay demonstrated in these lines, along with their implications, may have inspired Erasmus' own pun.

For Erasmus, the entire dialogue is an exercise in "knowing thyself" and pursuing *studia* which complement that theme. Further still, the tension between "knowing" and "new" is a polemical concern of Erasmus throughout his treatises on education, in which he advocates the reading of ancient Greek and Latin authors to properly form and humanize youth amidst the vastly and quickly changing new world. By using the ambiguous *novi*, Erasmus gives a practical lesson in Latin morphology and vocabulary, while also encouraging reflection on the humanistic importance of studying Greek and Latin literature.

My third example of ambiguity is a variation on Echo's repetition of the Youth's last word. Previously, *venis* followed *venio* and *novi* followed *novi*. The ambiguity of these terms is only realized through exploring their possible multiple meanings. The following example exploits the ambiguity of the Latin form *suis*.

IUVENIS	*quam igitur mentem habent isti, qui haec studia linguis traducunt suis?*
ECHO	*suis.*

271

Morphologically, *suis* could be one of three possible words: "you are stitching," the dative or ablative plural of "their own," or the genitive singular for "pig." The question wants a genitive to qualify what kind of mind these people have. The context easily clarifies the function of *suis*, but the elementary student of Latin also learns some other things. This example, like *novi* above, offers a grammatical lesson related to the sound of Latin: *suis* as a dative or ablative plural has a long *i*, whereas the genitive singular has a short *i*. Furthermore, by recognizing a different word that shares the *form* (though not sound) of the reflexive adjective, the student is reminded of the latter's function, which is tied to the relative clause—and thereby gets a lesson in the role of relative pronouns as well.

Next comes another exchange in which the syntax of the Youth's question dictates the likely form of Echo's response, which is otherwise ambiguous.

IUVENIS	*quid facere censes eos, qui terunt aetatem in sophistico doctrinae genere?*
ECHO	*nere.*
IUVENIS	*fortassis telas aranearum?*
ECHO	*harum.*
IUVENIS	*at Penelopes telas texunt ac retexunt.*
ECHO	*texunt.*

Nere boasts many possibilities of form, but the ensuing context suggests a particular meaning. The syntactical construction of the question posed to Echo, an indirect statement, clarifies any abstract morphological ambiguity contained in *nere*. The reader learns two grammatical lessons: the components of an indirect statement and the importance of tenses. Because the question occurs in indirect discourse, one may anticipate an infinitive in response. Yet a third plural indicative (a syncopated form of the perfect tense) is also possible, in response to the Youth's *eos* ("them"), in his question "What do you think they are doing?" But because the Youth uses a present infinitive, *facere*, and not the perfect active infinitive *fecisse*, a present infinitive is more fitting than a perfect indicative in Echo's answer. Here Erasmus requires his readers to know Latin syntax and morphology to arrive at the proper reading, which takes the infinitive *nere* as the verb in an implied indirect statement.

After the discussion of weavers, related to sophistic persons and education, the Youth begins a line of inquiry that covers an assortment of weightier issues and the value of certain professional pursuits. Many are topics Erasmus takes up elsewhere, both in other writings and as focused subjects within individual *Colloquies*. In a way, Erasmus allows the character of Echo to echo his teachings found in these other writings. Furthermore, he exploits ambiguity to expand the topics for consideration and reflection by the reader without adding discursive teachings tangential to the central issue. This practice not only creates a succinct dialogue, but also allows a more natural rhetorical flow of subjects between the interlocutors. The result is concise responses, merely alluding to teachings elsewhere, that infuse the dialogue with humor and ethics.

Immediately after asking, *cui suades, ut me dem vitae instituto* ("What custom of life do you suggest I pursue?"), the Youth asks Echo if he should marry. The response is ambiguous, and this time neither the morphology nor the syntax clarifies the issue. Here and in the ensuing examples, we may note an increasing emphasis on ethics in the ambiguous answers.

IUVENIS	*quid si mihi veniat usu, quod his, qui incident in uxores parum pudicas, parumque frugiferas?*
ECHO	*feras.*
IUVENIS	*atqui cum talibus morte durior est vita.*
ECHO	*vita.*

Feras could mean "you must bear it" and/or "wild beasts." "You must bear it" makes more sense in the present context, and the Youth apparently understands the reply as such. One clue within the sentence for the reader is the dative *mihi*, which suggests an answer may be directed to him, but *feras* as an accusative plural meaning "beasts" echoes the feminine plural adjectives of the question, and the conventions of the dialogue allow accusative responses. In an unambiguous response a few lines later, Erasmus uses the accusative singular *unam* to echo and refer to *fortunam*. Also, understanding *feras* as "beasts" echoes other writings from Erasmus. Marriage and related subjects such as celibacy, divorce, and adultery were especially contentious in the age of Erasmus (Leushuis 1284–1286). He discusses them in other *Colloquies*, in one of which we find spouses described as beastly. In Erasmus' dialogue on marriage, *Coniugium*, he writes: *Nulla est fera tam immanis, quin officiis cicuretur; ne desperes in homine* ("No beast is so savage as to be incapable of taming; do not lose hope in the person"). In that dialogue, two married women discuss unfaithful and violent husbands, whose loose living is characterized as beastly, and Erasmus may be making a similar comment in *Echo*. Ultimately, *Echo* continues to assume a rendering of "you must bear it," but Erasmus' ambiguous *feras* allows a suggestive characterization of unchaste behavior, which underscores both the pedagogical and morally didactic function of this dialogue. Thus the play on words that *feras* introduces adds literary and ethical texture, and the ambiguity is part of the dialogue's success.

The exchange following Echo's *feras* contains another ambiguous response. Echo's *vita*, when read and not spoken, could be either the nominative singular for "life" or the second singular imperative for "avoid." The *CWE* offers the following translation: "IU: But life with such women would be a fatal mistake. EC: Take no part in it." If one agrees with the translator, Erasmus violates the rules of pronunciation in a pure echo by lengthening the final vowel. He clearly allows himself liberties with pronunciation elsewhere in the dialogue: Echo responds to the last word *ocio* with *scio* and *opifex* with *faex*. But there is no evident ambiguity in these examples, and the responses are self-explanatory in their context. The immediate context of *vita* does not clarify the matter. The Youth's statement allows both renderings, each of which follows teachings Erasmus espoused elsewhere: that one ought to avoid marrying such women and that life poses difficulties.

Both answers carry a humorous and didactic message for a youth. On one hand, it is important to avoid pitfalls through wisdom in choosing a spouse, and on the other, forbearance is a virtue. Perhaps Erasmus intends the suggestions that both renderings offer. As many Latin teachers may testify, forms of the verb *vito* are often confused with the noun *vita*. By positioning this word in a context that allows either translation, Erasmus may be reminding us that the forms are similar, that context is important, and that life requires wisdom and forbearance.

In the discussion of various vocations, the Youth questions Echo about entering into the monarchical courts. Echo's response may be obscure to the unaware reader, as it is a loaded comment that alludes to Erasmus' political views expressed in other works. To fully appreciate the ambiguity of *fici*, the larger context within the dialogue is necessary.

IUVENIS	*quid fructus erit, si me conferam in aulam eorum, qui praecellunt monarchica dignitate.*
ECHO	*ate.*
IUVENIS	*at non paucos video, qui solent illinc sibi praeclaram felicitatem ariolari.*
ECHO	*λάροι.*
IUVENIS	*at interim dum incedunt holosericati, vulgo videntur homines magnifici.*
ECHO	*fici.*
IUVENIS	*foris igitur aureos, intus ficulneos homines dicis, si quis inspiciat cominus?*
ECHO	*minus.*

The lexical definitions for *fici* are either "figs" or "hemorrhoids." Most translators render the word as "figs," which suits the Youth's earlier question about fruit, but "hemorrhoids" humorously answers that question too. Erasmus elsewhere records an old expression, traced by Metzger from Menander to Martial to Erasmus, that depends on the ambiguity of *ficus*. To call a fig a fig was the equivalent of our "to call a spade a spade," that is, "to be outspoken, not choosing dainty words to express coarse ideas" (Metzger 1938, 230). Erasmus records a version of it in two different dialogues. In *Pseudochei et Philetymi*, the latter claims: *at istam artem nos crassiores solemus vocare furtum, qui ficum vocamus ficum, et scapham scapham* ("But we who are coarser and call a hemorrhoid a hemorrhoid and a skiff a skiff are accustomed to call that art theft"). And in *Diliculum* (*Early to Rise*), Erasmus writes: *nec dicam ficum aliud quam ficum* ("I won't call a hemorrhoid anything but a hemorrhoid"). Thus, when Erasmus refers to the monarchial crowd as *fici*, he is likely recalling its double meaning as figs *and* hemorrhoids.

Erasmus employs *fici*, rather unusually, in another context related to monarchy. In his *Adagia* (LB. 653 f.), he translates a line from Aristophanes as: *ut fici oculis incumbunt* ("As sties press upon the eyes"). Erasmus applies the image to his begrudging acceptance of monarchs in politics, lest anarchy replace tyranny. Erasmus may not have expected all of his readers to note the intersections of *ficus* with hemorrhoids and princes, but his ambiguous employment of *fici* in *Echo* suggests he was intending something more than mere "figs." The ensuing sentence indicates that the Youth understood *fici* as the fruit, since he calls courtiers *ficulneos*, yet Erasmus points the reader back to the meaning of *fici* as "hemorrhoids" when he answers the Youth with *minus* ("not quite"). Overall, the ambiguity of the word *fici* allows a crass assessment of monarchs, depending upon the reader's wider awareness of literary precedents and Erasmus' treatment of the subject in other works.

The next example of ambiguity plays on the ontological state of Echo, but the syntax clarifies the meaning.

IUVENIS   *nec militare genus magno aestimabis fortasse.*
ECHO   *asse.*

Asse can be a form either of the adjective *assus*, ranging in meaning from "dry" to "(musically) unaccompanied," or of the noun *as*, "copper coin." As the former, it could refer to the dry, shallow existence of a mercenary, as outlined in Erasmus' dialogue *Militis et Cartusiani* (The Soldier and Carthusian), but accepting that meaning would make Echo's response a vocative. The verb used by the Youth, *aestimabis*, typically employs a genitive or ablative of price, hence *magno* in the ablative. Thus, *asse* as an ablative singular for "penny" answers the question in the expected form. It also points to predominance of mercenaries, with which Erasmus took great exception, in the armies of his time. By using a word with ambiguous meanings and multiple intersections with modern practice, Erasmus places a premium on morphological and syntactical awareness.

Another ambiguity in *Echo* occurs near the end of the dialogue.

IUVENIS   *itane nihil praeterea adferunt artes boni aut mali?*

ECHO   *ali.*

Ali could be translated as either the noun for "garlic" or the passive infinitive for "to be supported" or more idiomatically as "a maintenance." The CWE translates it the latter. Garlic may not be as nonsensical as it first seems. Erasmus frequently discusses garlic in his other dialogues. For example, in *Diversoria* ("The Inns") boorish characters belch and reek of garlic, and in *Synodus grammaticorum* ("Assembly of Grammarians") a tribe characterized as barbarian, the Peligni, serve a dish comprised of tree bark and garlic. Thus in the *Colloquies*, garlic is described as having a pungent and lasting effect, and is associated with craftsmen and other marginalized, coarse persons. In this example in *Echo*, *ali* may suggest that the craftsmen of good and bad wares are like garlic, or perhaps that their trade does not afford them anything except (a bit of) garlic. Their profession is base, malodorous, and productive of little gain. Furthermore, *ali* as garlic plays off the verb *alo* ("nourish"). The ambiguous meanings deliver a humorous and memorable admonishment to avoid the pursuit of handiwork and instead to pursue the life of the mind.

4. Conclusion

Erasmus employs ambiguity throughout *Echo* to enforce rudimentary Latin morphology and syntax, to entertain and instruct the student on preferable vocations and professions, and to evoke irony and (for the more sophisticated reader) thoughtful literary reflection on previous texts of his own and of classical writers. The device of Echo in particular allows Erasmus to express multiple views and sentiments in ambiguous, one-word replies.

BIBLIOGRAPHY

Hardin, Richard F. 1982. "The Literary Conventions of Erasmus' Education of a Christian Prince: Advice and Aphorism." *Renaissance Quarterly* 35.2:151–163.

Leushuis, Reinier. 2004. "The Mimesis of Marriage: Dialogue and Intimacy in Erasmus's Matrimonial Writings." *Renaissance Quarterly* 57.4:1278–1307.

Margolin, J. C. 1988. "Culture, rhétorique, et satire dans l'Echo d'Erasme." In *Dix conférences sur Erasme*, ed. Claude Blum, 49–78. Paris: Champion; Geneva: Slatkine.

Metzger, Bruce M. 1938. "'To Call a Spade a Spade' in Greek and Latin." *CJ* 33.4:229-231.

Thompson, Craig R., tr. 1997. *Collected Works of Erasmus: Colloquies*, vols. 39–40. University of Toronto Press.